Construction Patterns

BUILDER (159) Move the construction logic for an object outside the class to instantiate, typically to allow piecemeal construction or to simplify the object.

FACTORY METHOD (167) Define the interface for creating an object while retaining control of which class to instantiate.

ABSTRACT FACTORY (175) Provide for the creation of a family of related or dependent objects.

PROTOTYPE (187) Provide new objects by copying an example.

MEMENTO (193) Provide for the storage and restoration of an object's state.

Operation Patterns

TEMPLATE METHOD (217) Implement an algorithm in a method, deferring the definition of some steps of the algorithm so that other classes can supply them.

STATE (229) Distribute state-specific logic across classes that represent an object's state.

STRATEGY (241) Encapsulate alternative strategies, or approaches, in separate classes that each implement a common operation.

COMMAND (251) Encapsulate a request as an object, so that you can parameterize clients with different requests; queue, time, or log requests; and allow a client to prepare a special context in which to invoke the request.

INTERPRETER (261) Let developers compose executable objects according to a set of composition rules that you define.

Extension Patterns

DECORATOR (287) Let developers compose an object's behavior dynamically.

ITERATOR (305) Provide a way to access the elements of a collection sequentially.

VISITOR (325) Let developers define a new operation for a hierarchy without changing the hierarchy classes.

DESIGN PATTERNS IN JAVA™

The Software Patterns Series

Series Editor: John M. Vlissides

The Software Patterns Series (SPS) comprises pattern literature of lasting significance to software developers. Software patterns document general solutions to recurring problems in all software-related spheres, from the technology itself, to the organizations that develop and distribute it, to the people who use it. Books in the series distill experience from one or more of these areas into a form that software professionals can apply immediately.

Relevance and *impact* are the tenets of the SPS. Relevance means each book presents patterns that solve real problems. Patterns worthy of the name are intrinsically relevant; they are borne of practitioners' experiences, not theory or speculation. Patterns have impact when they change how people work for the better. A book becomes a part of the series not just because it embraces these tenets, but because it has demonstrated it fulfills them for its audience.

Titles in the series:

Data Access Patterns: Database Interactions in Object-Oriented Applications; Clifton Nock

Design Patterns Explained, Second Edition: A New Perspective on Object-Oriented Design; Alan Shalloway and James Trott

Design Patterns in C#; Steven John Metsker

Design Patterns in Java™; Steven John Metsker and William C. Wake

Design Patterns Java™ Workbook; Steven John Metsker

.NET Patterns: Architecture, Design, and Process; Christian Thilmany

Pattern Hatching: Design Patterns Applied; John M. Vlissides

Pattern Languages of Program Design; James O. Coplien and Douglas C. Schmidt

Pattern Languages of Program Design 2; John M. Vlissides, James O. Coplien, and Norman L. Kerth

Pattern Languages of Program Design 3; Robert C. Martin, Dirk Riehle, and Frank Buschmann

Pattern Languages of Program Design 5; Dragos Manolescu, Markus Voelter, and James Noble

Patterns for Parallel Programming; Timothy G. Mattson, Beverly A. Sanders, and Berna L. Massingill

Software Configuration Management Patterns: Effective Teamwork, Practical Integration; Stephen P. Berczuk and Brad Appleton

The Design Patterns Smalltalk Companion; Sherman Alpert, Kyle Brown, and Bobby Woolf

Use Cases: Patterns and Blueprints; Gunnar Övergaard and Karin Palmkvist

For more information, check out the series web site at www.awprofessional.com/series/swpatterns

DESIGN PATTERNS
IN JAVA™

Steven John Metsker
William C. Wake

♦♦ Addison-Wesley

Upper Saddle River, NJ • Boston • Indianapolis • San Francisco
New York • Toronto • Montreal • London • Munich • Paris • Madrid
Capetown • Sydney • Tokyo • Singapore • Mexico City

Many of the designations used by manufacturers and sellers to distinguish their products are claimed as trademarks. Where those designations appear in this book, and the publisher was aware of a trademark claim, the designations have been printed with initial capital letters or in all capitals.

The authors and publisher have taken care in the preparation of this book, but make no expressed or implied warranty of any kind and assume no responsibility for errors or omissions. No liability is assumed for incidental or consequential damages in connection with or arising out of the use of the information or programs contained herein.

The publisher offers excellent discounts on this book when ordered in quantity for bulk purchases or special sales, which may include electronic versions and/or custom covers and content particular to your business, training goals, marketing focus, and branding interests. For more information, please contact:

U.S. Corporate and Government Sales
(800) 382-3419
corpsales@pearsontechgroup.com

For sales outside the United States, please contact:

International Sales
international@pearsoned.com

Visit us on the Web: www.awprofessional.com

Library of Congress Cataloging-in-Publication Data

Metsker, Steven John.
   Design patterns in Java / Steven John Metsker, William C. Wake.
         p.   cm.
   Includes bibliographical references and index.
   ISBN 0-321-33302-0 (hardback : alk. paper)
   1. Java (Computer program language)   2. Software patterns.   I. Wake, William C., 1960–
II. Title.

   QA76.73.J38M482 2006
   005.13'3—dc22   2006003471

ISBN 0-321-33302-0
Text printed in the United States on recycled paper at Courier in Westford, Massachusetts.
First printing, April 2006

CONTENTS

PREFACE

DESIGN PATTERNS ARE class- and method-level solutions to common problems in object-oriented design. If you're an intermediate-level Java programmer who wants to become advanced or an advanced-level Java programmer who hasn't yet studied design patterns, this book is for you.

Design Patterns in Java™ takes a workbook approach. Each chapter focuses on a particular pattern. In addition to explaining the pattern, the chapter includes a number of challenges, each asking you to explain something or to develop code that solves a problem.

We strongly urge you to stop and work through the challenges rather than try to read this book straight through. You'll learn more by putting in the work to do the challenges, even if it's only a chapter or two a week.

An Update

This book merges and updates two previous books: *Design Patterns Java Workbook™* and *Design Patterns in C#.* This book combines the Java orientation of the former with the more stand-alone approach of the latter. If you've already worked through the previous books, you won't need this one.

Coding Conventions

The code for this book is available online. See Appendix C: Oozinoz Source on page 427 for details on how to obtain it.

We've used a style generally consistent with Sun's coding conventions. Braces are omitted where possible. We have had to make a couple of compromises to fit the book format. To fit the narrow columns, variable names are sometimes shorter than we'd really use. And to avoid the complications of source control, we name multiple versions of a file with a digit appended to the name (e.g., `ShowBallistics2`). In real life, you'd use source control and work only with the latest version of a class.

Acknowledgments

A book is a challenging undertaking. Along the way, a number of reviewers have provided us with valuable advice: Daryl Richter, Adewale Oshineye, Steven M. Luplow, Tom Kubit, Rex Jaeschke, Jim Fox, and David E. DeLano. Each one made suggestions that improved the end result. Readers and reviewers of the earlier books have contributed as well.

Thanks also to the editorial staff at Addison-Wesley, especially Chris Guzikowski, Jessica D'Amico, and Tyrrell Albaugh. Other editors helped along the way, including Mary O'Brien and John Wait.

We'd like to thank the late John Vlissides for his encouragement and advice on this and other books. John was the editor of the Software Patterns Series, coauthor of the original *Design Patterns* book, a friend, and an inspiration.

In addition to relying heavily on *Design Patterns*, we have benefited from many other books: See the Bibliography on page 447. In particular, *The Unified Modeling Language User Guide* [Booch, Rambaugh, and Jacobsen 1999] provided clear explanations of UML, and *Java™ in a Nutshell* [Flanagan 2005] provided concise and accurate help on Java topics. *The Chemistry of Fireworks* [Russell 2000] has been the source for information on realistic fireworks examples.

Finally, we're grateful to everyone on the production staff for their hard work and dedication. They're the ones who turn the bytes into printed words.

Steve Metsker (Steve.Metsker@acm.org)
Bill Wake (William.Wake@acm.org)

1

INTRODUCTION

THIS BOOK COVERS the same set of techniques as the classic book *Design Patterns*, written by Erich Gamma, Richard Helm, Ralph Johnson, and John Vlissides [Gamma et al. 1995] and provides examples in a Java setting. This book also includes many "challenges"—exercises designed to help you strengthen your ability to apply design patterns in your own programs.

This book is for developers who know Java and who want to improve their skills as designers.

Why Patterns?

A **pattern** is a way of doing something: a way of pursuing an intent, a technique. The idea of capturing effective techniques applies to many endeavors: making food, fireworks, software, and other crafts. In any new craft that is starting to mature, the people working on it will begin to find common, effective methods for achieving their aims and solving problems in various contexts. The community of people who practice a craft usually invent jargon that helps them talk about their craft. Some of this jargon will refer to patterns, or established techniques for achieving certain aims. As a craft and its jargon grows, writers begin to play an important role. Writers document a craft's patterns, helping to standardize the jargon and to publicize effective techniques.

Christopher Alexander was one of the first writers to encapsulate a craft's best practices by documenting its patterns. His work relates to architecture—of buildings, not software. In *A Pattern Language: Towns, Buildings Construction* (Alexander, Ishikouwa, and Silverstein 1977), Alexander provides patterns for architecting successful buildings and towns. His writing is powerful and has influenced the software community, partially because of the way he looks at intent.

You might think that the intent of architectural patterns would be something like "to design buildings." But Alexander makes it clear that the intent of architectural patterns is to serve and inspire the people who will occupy buildings and towns. Alexander's work showed that patterns are an excellent way to capture and convey the wisdom of a craft. He also established that properly perceiving and documenting the intent of a craft is a critical, philosophical, and elusive challenge.

The software community has resonated with the patterns approach and has created many books that document patterns of software development. These books record best practices for software process, software analysis, high-level architecture, and class-level design. New pattern books appear every year. If you are choosing a book to read about patterns, you should spend some time reading reviews of available books and try to select the book that will help you the most.

Why Design Patterns?

A **design pattern** is a pattern—a way to pursue an intent—that uses classes and their methods in an object-oriented language. Developers often start thinking about design after learning a programming language and writing code for a while. You might notice that someone else's code seems simpler and works better than yours does, and you might wonder how that developer achieves such simplicity. Design patterns are a level up from code and typically show how to achieve a goal using a few classes. A pattern represents an idea, not a particular implementation.

Other people have discovered how to program effectively in object-oriented languages. If you want to become a powerful Java programmer, you should study design patterns, especially those in this book—the same patterns that *Design Patterns* explains.

Design Patterns describes 23 design patterns. Many other books on design patterns have followed, so there are at least 100 design patterns worth knowing. The 23 design patterns that Gamma, Helm, Johnson, and Vlissides placed in *Design Patterns* are probably not absolutely the most useful 23 design patterns to know. On the other hand, these patterns *are* near the top of the list. The authors of *Design*

Patterns chose well, and the patterns they document are certainly worth learning. These patterns can serve as a foundation as you branch out and begin learning patterns from other sources.

GoF

You may have noted the potential confusion between "design patterns" the topic and *Design Patterns* the book. Because the topic and the book title *sound* alike, many speakers and some writers distinguish them by referring to the book as the "Gang of Four," or the "GoF," book, referring to the number of its authors. In print, it is not so confusing that *Design Patterns* refers to the book and "design patterns" refers to the topic. Accordingly, this book avoids using the term "GoF."

Why Java?

This book gives its examples in Java, the object-oriented (OO) language developed at Sun. Java, its libraries, and associated tools form a suite of products for developing and managing systems with multi-tiered, object-oriented architectures.

One reason Java is important is that it is a **consolidation language**, designed to absorb the strengths of earlier languages. This consolidation has fueled the popularity of Java and helps ensure that future languages may well evolve from this language rather than depart radically from it. Your investment in Java will almost surely yield value in any language that supplants Java.

The patterns in *Design Patterns* apply to Java because, like Smalltalk, C++, and C#, Java follows a class/instance paradigm. Java is much more similar to Smalltalk and C++ than it is to, say, Prolog or Self. Although competing paradigms are important, the class/instance paradigm is a practical step forward in applied computing. This book uses Java because of its popularity and because Java appears to lie along the evolutionary path of languages that we will use for years to come.

UML

Where this book's challenges (exercises) have solutions in code, this book uses Java. But many of the challenges ask you to draw a diagram of how classes, packages, and other elements relate. You can use any notation you like, but this book uses **Unified Modeling Language** (UML) notation. Even if you are familiar with UML, it is a good idea to have a reference handy. Two good choices are *The Unified Modeling Language User Guide* [Booch, Rumbaugh, and Jacobsen 1999], and *UML Distilled* [Fowler with Scott 2003]. The bare minimum of UML knowledge that you need for this book is provided in "Appendix D: UML at a Glance" on page 431.

Challenges

No matter how much you read about doing something, you won't feel as though you know it until you do it. This is true partially because until you exercise the knowledge you gain from a book, you won't encounter subtleties, and you won't grapple with alternative approaches. You won't feel confident about design patterns until you apply them to some real challenges.

The problem with learning through experience is that you can do damage as you learn. You can't apply patterns in production code before you are confident in your own skills. But you need to start applying patterns to gain confidence. What a conundrum! The solution is to practice on example problems, where mistakes are valuable but painless.

Each chapter in this book begins with a short introduction and then sets up a series of challenges for you to solve. After you come up with a solution, you can compare your solution with one given in Solutions, page 347. The solution in the book may take a different slant from your solution or may provide you with some other insight.

You probably can't go overboard in how hard you work to come up with answers to the challenges in this book. If you consult other books, work with a colleague, and write sample code to check out your solution, terrific! You will not regret investing your time and energy in learning how to apply design patterns.

A danger lurks in the solutions that this book provides. If you flip to the solution immediately after reading a challenge, you will not gain much from this book. The solutions in this book won't do you any good if you don't first create your own solutions.

The Organization of This Book

There are many ways to organize and categorize patterns. You might organize them according to similarities in structure, or you might follow the order in *Design Patterns*. But the most important aspect of any pattern is its intent, that is, the potential value of applying the pattern. This book organizes the 23 patterns of *Design Patterns* according to their intent.

Having decided to organize patterns by intent raises the question of how to categorize intent. This book adopts the notion that the intent of a design pattern is usually easily expressed as the need to go beyond the ordinary facilities that are built into Java. For example, Java has plentiful support for defining the interfaces that a class implements. But if you have a class with the "wrong" interface and need to somehow make it meet the needs of a client, you may decide to apply the ADAPTER pattern. The intent of the ADAPTER pattern is to help you go beyond the interface facilities built into Java.

This book places design pattern intent in five categories, as follows:

1. Interfaces
2. Responsibility
3. Construction
4. Operations
5. Extensions

These five categories account for the five parts of this book. Each part begins with a chapter that discusses and presents challenges related to features built into Java. For example, Part I begins with a chapter on ordinary Java interfaces. This chapter will challenge your understanding of the Java interface construct, especially in comparison to abstract classes. The remaining chapters of Part I address patterns whose primary intent involves the definition of an interface, the set of methods that a client can call from a service provider. Each of these patterns addresses a need that cannot be addressed solely with Java interfaces.

Categorizing patterns by intent does not result in each pattern supporting only one type of intent. When it supports more than one type of intent, a pattern appears as a full chapter in the first part to which it applies and gets a brief mention in subsequent parts. Table 1.1 shows the categorization behind the organization of this book.

TABLE 1.1   A Categorization of Patterns by Intent

Intent	Patterns
Interfaces	ADAPTER, FACADE, COMPOSITE, BRIDGE
Responsibility	SINGLETON, OBSERVER, MEDIATOR, PROXY, CHAIN OF RESPONSIBILITY, FLYWEIGHT
Construction	BUILDER, FACTORY METHOD, ABSTRACT FACTORY, PROTOTYPE, MEMENTO
Operations	TEMPLATE METHOD, STATE, STRATEGY, COMMAND, INTERPRETER
Extensions	DECORATOR, ITERATOR, VISITOR

We hope that you will question the categorization in Table 1.1. Do you agree that SINGLETON is about responsibility, not construction? Is COMPOSITE an interface pattern? Categorizing patterns is subjective. But we hope that you will agree that thinking about the intent behind patterns and thinking about how you will apply patterns are very useful exercises.

Welcome to Oozinoz!

The challenges in this book all cite examples from Oozinoz Fireworks, a fictional company that manufactures and sells fireworks and puts on fireworks displays. (**Oozinoz** takes its name from the sounds heard at Oozinoz exhibitions.) You can acquire the code from www.oozinoz.com. For more information about building and testing the source code, see Appendix C: Oozinoz Source, page 427.

Summary

Patterns are distillations of accumulated wisdom that provide a standard jargon, naming the concepts that experienced practitioners apply. The patterns in the classic book *Design Patterns* are among the most useful class-level patterns and are certainly worth learning. This book explains the same patterns as those documented in *Design Patterns* but uses Java and its libraries for its examples and challenges. By working through the challenges in this book, you will learn to recognize and apply an important part of the accumulated wisdom of the software community.

PART I

INTERFACE PATTERNS

2

INTRODUCING INTERFACES

A CLASS'S **interface**, speaking abstractly, is the collection of methods and fields that the class permits objects of other classes to access. This interface usually represents a commitment that the methods will perform the operation implied by their names and as specified by code comments, tests, and other documentation. A class's **implementation** is the code that lies within its methods.

Java elevates the notion of interface to be a separate construct, expressly separating interface—what an object must do—from implementation—how an object fulfills this commitment. Java interfaces allow several classes to provide the same functionality, and they open the possibility that a class can implement more than one interface.

Several design patterns use the features that Java builds in. For example, you might use an interface to adapt a class's interface to meet a client's needs by applying the ADAPTER pattern. But before going beyond the basics built into Java, it's worthwhile ensuring that you are comfortable with how Java features work, starting with interfaces.

Interfaces and Abstract Classes

The original book *Design Patterns* [Gamma et al. 1995] frequently mentions the use of abstract classes but does not describe the use of interfaces at all. This is because the C++ and Smalltalk languages, which *Design Patterns* uses for its examples, do not have an interface construct. This has a minor impact on the utility of that book for Java developers, because Java interfaces are quite similar to abstract classes.

CHALLENGE 2.1

Write down three differences between abstract classes and interfaces in Java.

A solution appears on page 347.

If you had to live without interfaces, you could get by using abstract classes, as C++ does. Interfaces, however, play a critical role in *n*-tier development and certainly warrant first-class status as a separate construct.

Consider the definition of an interface that rocket-simulation classes must implement. Engineers design many different rockets, including solid- and liquid-fueled rockets, with completely different ballistics. Regardless of how a rocket is composed, a simulation for the rocket must provide figures for the rocket's expected thrust and mass. Here is the code that Oozinoz uses to define the rocket-simulation interface:

```
package com.oozinoz.simulation;

public interface RocketSim {
    abstract double getMass();
    public double getThrust();
    void setSimTime(double t);
}
```

CHALLENGE 2.2

Which of the following statements are true?

A. All three methods of the RocketSim interface are abstract, although only getMass() declares this explicitly.

B. All three methods of the interface are public, although only getThrust() declares this explicitly.

C. The interface is declared "public interface", but it would be public even if the public keyword were omitted.

D. It is possible to create another interface, say, RocketSimSolid, that extends RocketSim.

E. Every interface must have at least one method.

F. An interface can declare instance fields that an implementing class must also declare.

G. Although you can't instantiate an interface, an interface definition can declare constructor methods that require an implementing class to provide constructors with given signatures.

Solutions appear on page 347.

Interfaces and Obligations

An essential benefit of Java interfaces is that they limit the interaction between objects. This limitation turns out to be a liberation. A class that implements an interface can undergo dramatic change in how it fulfills an interface, even though its clients remain unaffected.

A developer who creates a class that implements RocketSim is responsible for writing getMass() and getThrust() methods that return measures of a rocket's performance. In other words, the developer must fulfill the contracts for these methods.

Sometimes, the methods that an interface designates do not carry any obligation to perform a service for the caller. In some cases, the implementing class can even ignore the call, implementing a method with an empty body.

CHALLENGE 2.3

Give an example of an interface with methods that do not imply responsibility on the part of the implementing class to return a value or even to take any action on behalf of the caller at all.

A solution appears on page 348.

If you create an interface that specifies a collection of notification methods, you may consider also supplying a **stub**—a class that implements the interface with methods that do nothing. Developers can subclass the stub, overriding only those methods in the interface that are important to their application. The WindowAdapter class in java.awt.event is an example of such a class, as Figure 2.1 shows. (For a whirlwind introduction to UML, see Appendix D: UML at a Glance on page 431.) The WindowAdapter class implements all the methods in the WindowListener interface, but the implementations are all empty; the methods contain no statements.

In addition to declaring methods, an interface can declare constants. In the following example, ClassificationConstants declares two constants that classes implementing this interface will have access to.

```
public interface ClassificationConstants {
    static final int CONSUMER = 1;
    static final int DISPLAY = 2;
}
```

Interfaces have one other key way in which they differ from abstract classes. Although it may declare that it extends one other class, a class may declare that it implements any number of interfaces.

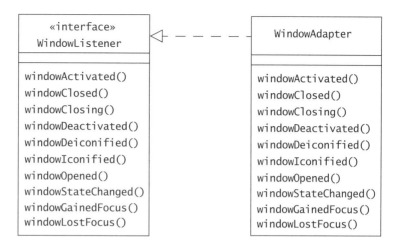

FIGURE 2.1 The WindowAdapter class makes it easy to register for window events while ignoring any events you are not interested in.

Summary

The power of interfaces is that they delineate what is and isn't expected in how classes collaborate. Interfaces are similar to purely abstract classes, defining expectations but not implementing them.

Mastering both the concepts and the details of applying Java interfaces is well worth the investment of your time. This powerful construct is at the heart of many strong designs and several design patterns.

Beyond Ordinary Interfaces

You can simplify and strengthen your designs with appropriate application of Java interfaces. Sometimes, though, the design of an interface has to go beyond the ordinary definition and use of an interface.

If you intend to	Apply the pattern
• Adapt a class's interface to match the interface a client expects	ADAPTER
• Provide a simple interface into a collection of classes	FACADE
• Define an interface that applies to both individual objects and groups of objects	COMPOSITE
• Decouple an abstraction from its implementation so that the two can vary independently	BRIDGE

The intent of each design pattern is to solve a problem in a context. Interface-oriented patterns address contexts in which you need to define or redefine access to the methods of a class or group of classes. For example, when you have a class that performs a service you need but with method names that do not match a client's expectations, you can apply the ADAPTER pattern.

3

ADAPTER

AN OBJECT IS A **client** if it needs to call your code. In some cases, client code will be written after your code exists and the developer can mold the client to use the interfaces of the objects that you provide. In other cases, clients may be developed independently of your code. For example, a rocket-simulation program might be designed to use rocket information that you supply, but such a simulation will have its own definition of how a rocket should behave. In such circumstances, you may find that an existing class performs the services that a client needs but has different method names. In this situation, you can apply the ADAPTER pattern.

The intent of ADAPTER **is to provide the interface that a client expects while using the services of a class with a different interface.**

Adapting to an Interface

When you need to adapt your code, you may find that the client developer planned well for such circumstances. This is evident when the developer provides an interface that defines the services that the client code needs, as the example in Figure 3.1 shows. A client class makes calls to a `requiredMethod()` method that is declared in an interface. You may have found an existing class with a method with a name such as `usefulMethod()` that can fulfill the client's needs. You can adapt the existing class to meet the client's needs by writing a class that extends `ExistingClass`, implements `RequiredInterface`, and overrides `requiredMethod()` so that it delegates its requests to `usefulMethod()`.

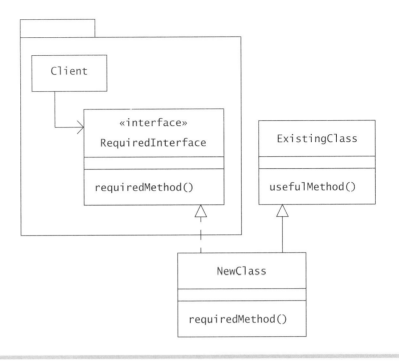

FIGURE 3.1 When a developer of client code thoughtfully defines the client's needs, you may be able to fulfill the interface by adapting existing code.

The NewClass class in Figure 3.1 is an example of ADAPTER. An instance of this class is an instance of RequiredInterface. In other words, the NewClass class meets the needs of the client.

For a more concrete example, suppose that you are working with a package that simulates the flight and timing of rockets such as those you manufacture at Oozinoz. The simulation package includes an event simulator that explores the effects of launching several rockets, along with an interface that specifies a rocket's behavior. Figure 3.2 shows this package.

Suppose that at Oozinoz, you have a PhysicalRocket class that you want to plug into the simulation. This class has methods that supply, approximately, the behavior that the simulator needs. In this situation, you can apply ADAPTER, creating a subclass of PhysicalRocket that implements the RocketSim interface. Figure 3.3 partially shows this design.

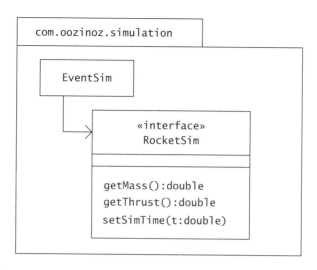

FIGURE 3.2 The Simulation package clearly defines its requirements for simulating the flight of a rocket.

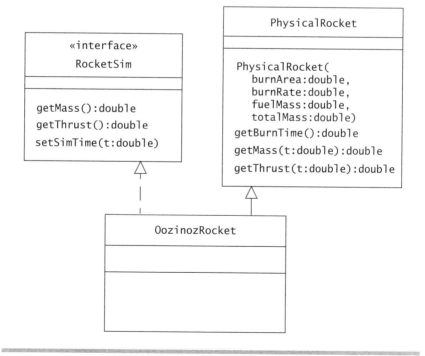

FIGURE 3.3 When completed, this diagram will show the design of a class that adapts the Rocket class to meet the needs of the RocketSim interface.

The PhysicalRocket class has the information that the simulator
needs, but its methods do not exactly match those that the simulation declares in the RocketSim interface. Most of the differences occur
because the simulator keeps an internal clock and occasionally
updates simulated objects by calling a setSimTime() method. To
adapt the PhysicalRocket class to meet the simulator's needs, an
OozinozRocket object can maintain a time instance variable that it
can pass to the methods of the PhysicalRocket class as needed.

CHALLENGE 3.1

Complete the class diagram in Figure 3.3 to show the design of an
OozinozRocket class that lets a PhysicalRocket object participate in
a simulation as a RocketSim object. Assume that you can't alter
either RocketSim or PhysicalRocket.

A solution appears on page 348.

The code for PhysicalRocket is somewhat complex, as it embodies
the physics that Oozinoz uses to model a rocket. However, that is
exactly the logic that we want to reuse. The OozinozRocket adapter
class simply translates calls to use its superclass's methods. The code
for this new subclass will look something like this:

```
package com.oozinoz.firework;
import com.oozinoz.simulation.*;

public class OozinozRocket
        extends PhysicalRocket implements RocketSim {
    private double time;

    public OozinozRocket(
            double burnArea, double burnRate,
            double fuelMass, double totalMass) {
        super(burnArea, burnRate, fuelMass, totalMass);
    }

    public double getMass() {
        // Challenge!
    }
```

```
        public double getThrust() {
            // Challenge!
        }

        public void setSimTime(double time) {
            this.time = time;
        }
    }
```

CHALLENGE 3.2

Complete the code for the OozinozRocket class, including methods getMass() and getThrust().

A solution appears on page 349.

When a client defines its expectations in an interface, you can apply ADAPTER by supplying a class that implements that interface and that subclasses an existing class. You may also be able to apply ADAPTER even if no interface exists to define a client's expectations. In this situation, you must use an "object adapter."

Class and Object Adapters

The designs in Figures 3.1 and 3.3 are *class adapters* that adapt through subclassing. In a class adapter design, the new adapter class implements the desired interface and subclasses an existing class. This approach will not always work, notably when the set of methods that you need to adapt is not specified in an interface. In such a case, you can create an **object adapter**—an adapter that uses delegation rather than subclassing. Figure 3.4 shows this design. (Compare this to the earlier diagrams.)

The NewClass class in Figure 3.4 is an example of ADAPTER. An instance of this class is an instance of the RequiredClass class. In other words, the NewClass class meets the needs of the client. The NewClass class can adapt the ExistingClass class to meet the client's needs by using an instance of ExistingClass.

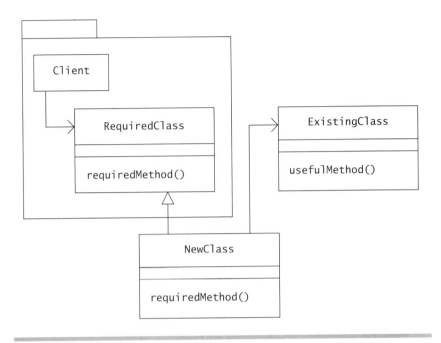

FIGURE 3.4 You can create an object adapter by subclassing the class that you need, fulfilling the required methods by relying on an object of an existing class.

For a more concrete example, suppose that the simulation package worked directly with a Skyrocket class, without specifying an interface to define the behaviors that the simulation needs. Figure 3.5 shows this class.

The Skyrocket class uses a fairly primitive model of the physics of a rocket. For example, the class assumes that the rocket is entirely consumed as its fuel burns. Suppose that you want to apply the more sophisticated physical model that the Oozinoz PhysicalRocket class uses. To adapt the logic in the PhysicalRocket class to the needs of the simulation, you can create an OozinozSkyrocket class as an object adapter that subclasses Skyrocket and that uses a Physical-Rocket object, as Figure 3.6 shows.

As an object adapter, the OozinozSkyrocket class subclasses from Skyrocket, not PhysicalRocket. This will allow an OozinozSkyrocket object to serve as a substitute wherever the simulation client needs a Skyrocket object. The Skyrocket class supports subclassing by making its simTime variable protected.

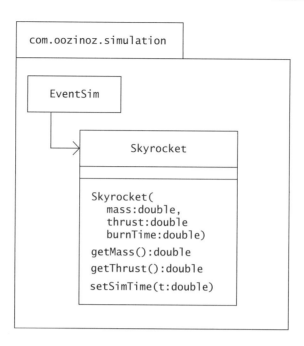

FIGURE 3.5 In this alternative design, the `com.oozinoz.simulation` package does not specify the interface it needs for modeling a rocket.

CHALLENGE 3.3

Complete the class diagram in Figure 3.6 to show a design that allows OozinozRocket objects to serve as Skyrocket objects.

A solution appears on page 350.

The code for the OozinozSkyrocket class might be as follows:

```
package com.oozinoz.firework;
import com.oozinoz.simulation.*;

public class OozinozSkyrocket extends Skyrocket {
    private PhysicalRocket rocket;
```

```
public OozinozSkyrocket(PhysicalRocket r) {
    super(
        r.getMass(0),
        r.getThrust(0),
        r.getBurnTime());
    rocket = r;
}

public double getMass() {
    return rocket.getMass(simTime);
}

public double getThrust() {
    return rocket.getThrust(simTime);
}
}
```

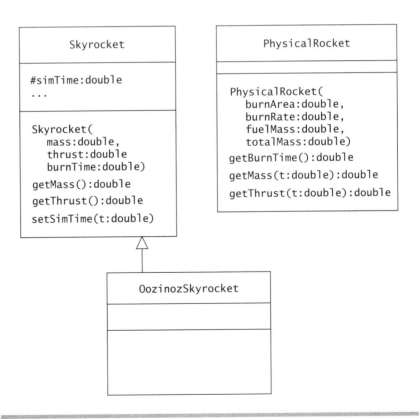

FIGURE 3.6 When completed, this diagram will show an object adapter design that uses information from an existing class to meet the needs that a client has of a Skyrocket object.

The OozinozSkyrocket class lets you supply an OozinozSkyrocket object anywhere that the simulation package requires a Skyrocket object. In general, object adapters partially overcome the problem of adapting an object to an interface that is not expressly defined.

CHALLENGE 3.4

Name one reason why the object adapter design that OozinozSkyrocket class uses may be more fragile than a class adapter approach.

Solutions appear on page 350.

The object adapter for the Skyrocket class is a riskier design than the class adapter that implements the RocketSim interface. But we should not complain too much. At least no methods were marked final, which would have prevented us from overriding them.

Adapting Data for a JTable

A common example of an object adapter comes when you want to display data in a table. Swing provides the JTable widget to display tables. Obviously, the designers of this widget didn't know what data you would want to display. Rather than hard-code some data structure into the widget, they provided an interface, TableModel. JTable does its work in terms of this interface. You then provide an adapter that makes your data conform to the TableModel. See Figure 3.7.

Many of the methods in TableModel suggest the possibility of a default implementation. Fortunately, the **Java Development Kit** (JDK) supplies an abstract class that provides default implementations of all but the most domain-specific methods in TableModel. Figure 3.8 shows this class.

Suppose that you want to show a few rockets in a table, using a Swing user interface. As Figure 3.9 shows, you can create a RocketTableModel class that adapts an array of rockets to the interface that TableModel expects.

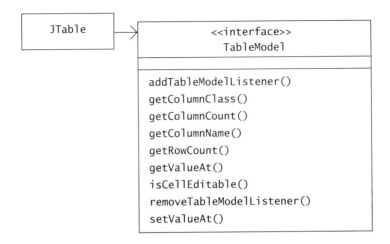

FIGURE 3.7 The JTable class is a Swing component that displays data from an implementation of TableModel into a GUI table.

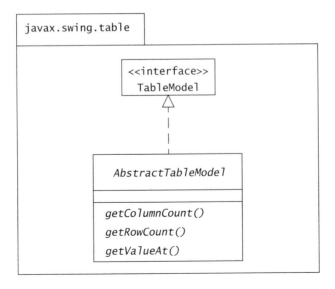

FIGURE 3.8 The AbstractTableModel class provides defaults for all but a few of the methods in TableModel.

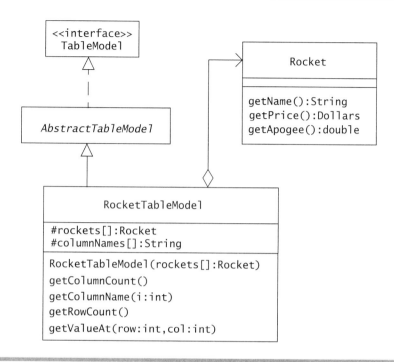

FIGURE 3.9 The RocketTableModel class adapts the TableModel interface to the Rocket class from the Oozinoz domain.

The RocketTableModel class has to subclass AbstractTableModel because AbstractTableModel is a class, not an interface. Whenever the interface you are adapting to is supported with an abstract class that you want to use, you must use an object adapter. In this instance, a second reason you do not want to use a class adapter is that a RocketTableModel is not a kind or a subtype of Rocket. When an adapter class must draw on information from more than one object, you will usually implement it as an object adapter.

Note the difference: A class adapter subclasses an existing class and implements a target interface; an object adapter subclasses a target class and delegates to an existing class.

Once you create the RocketTableModel class, you can easily display information about rockets in a Swing JTable object, as Figure 3.10 shows.

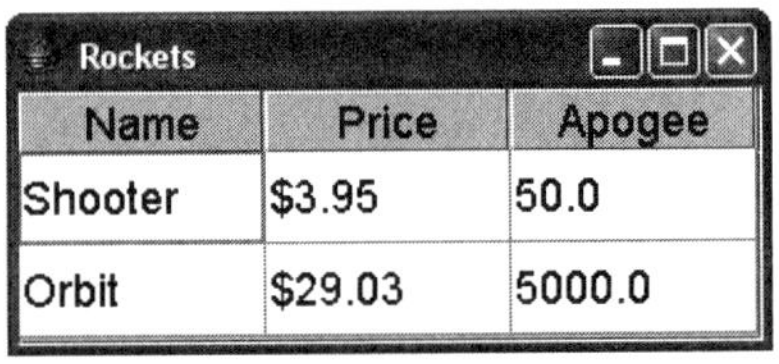

FIGURE 3.10 An instance of JTable fueled with rocket data

```
package app.adapter;
import javax.swing.table.*;
import com.oozinoz.firework.Rocket;

public class RocketTableModel extends AbstractTableModel {
    protected Rocket[] rockets;
    protected String[] columnNames =
        new String[] { "Name", "Price", "Apogee" };

    public RocketTableModel(Rocket[] rockets) {
        this.rockets = rockets;
    }

    public int getColumnCount() {
        // Challenge!
    }

    public String getColumnName(int i) {
        // Challenge!
    }

    public int getRowCount() {
        // Challenge!
    }

    public Object getValueAt(int row, int col) {
        // Challenge!
    }
}
```

CHALLENGE 3.5

Fill in the code for the RocketTableModel methods that adapt an array of Rocket objects to serve as a TableModel.

A solution appears on page 352.

To launch the display that Figure 3.10 shows, you can create a couple of example rocket objects, place them in an array, construct an instance of RocketTableModel from the array, and use Swing classes to display the table. The ShowRocketTable class provides an example:

```java
package app.adapter;

import java.awt.Component;
import java.awt.Font;

import javax.swing.*;

import com.oozinoz.firework.Rocket;
import com.oozinoz.utility.Dollars;

public class ShowRocketTable {
    public static void main(String[] args) {
        setFonts();
        JTable table = new JTable(getRocketTable());
        table.setRowHeight(36);
        JScrollPane pane = new JScrollPane(table);
        pane.setPreferredSize(
            new java.awt.Dimension(300, 100));
        display(pane, " Rockets");
    }

    public static void display(Component c, String title) {
        JFrame frame = new JFrame(title);
        frame.getContentPane().add(c);
        frame.setDefaultCloseOperation(
            JFrame.EXIT_ON_CLOSE);
        frame.pack();
        frame.setVisible(true);
    }
```

```
        private static RocketTableModel getRocketTable() {
            Rocket r1 = new Rocket(
                "Shooter", 1.0, new Dollars(3.95), 50.0, 4.5);
            Rocket r2 = new Rocket(
                "Orbit", 2.0, new Dollars(29.03), 5000, 3.2);
            return new RocketTableModel(new Rocket[] { r1, r2 });
        }

        private static void setFonts() {
            Font font = new Font("Dialog", Font.PLAIN, 18);
            UIManager.put("Table.font", font);
            UIManager.put("TableHeader.font", font);
        }
    }
```

With fewer than 20 statements of its own, the ShowRocketTable class sits above thousands of statements that collaborate to produce a table component within a **graphical user interface** (GUI) framework. The JTable class can handle nearly every aspect of displaying a table but can't know in advance what data you will want to present. To let you supply the data it needs, the JTable class sets you up to apply ADAPTER. To use JTable, you implement the TableModel interface that JTable expects, along with a class that provides the data you want to display.

Identifying Adapters

In Chapter 2, you explained the value of the WindowAdapter class. The MouseAdapter class, as Figure 3.11 shows, is another example of a class that stubs out the methods required by an interface.

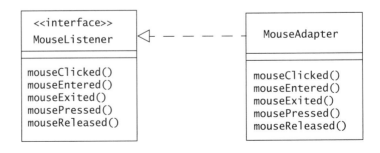

FIGURE 3.11 The MouseAdapter class stubs out the requirements of the MouseListener interface.

CHALLENGE 3.6

Are you applying the ADAPTER pattern when you use the
MouseAdapter class? Explain how (or why not).

A solution appears on page 353.

Summary

The ADAPTER pattern lets you use an existing class to meet a client
class's needs. When a client specifies its requirements in an interface,
you can usually create a new class that implements the interface and
subclasses an existing class. This approach creates a **class adapter** that
translates a client's calls into calls to the existing class's methods.

When a client does not specify the interface it requires, you may still
be able to apply ADAPTER, creating a new client subclass that uses an
instance of the existing class. This approach creates an *object adapter*
that forwards a client's calls to an instance of the existing class. This
approach can be dangerous, especially if you don't (or perhaps can't)
override all the methods that the client might call.

The JTable component in Swing is a good example of a class whose
developers applied the ADAPTER pattern. A JTable component sets
itself up as a client that needs table information as defined by the
TableModel interface. This makes it easy for you to write an adapter
that feeds the table data from domain objects, such as instances of the
Rocket class.

To use JTable, you frequently write an object adapter that delegates
calls to instances of an existing class. Two aspects of JTable make it
less likely that you'll use a class adapter. First, you will usually create
your table adapter as a subclass of AbstractTableModel, so you can't
also subclass your existing class. Second, the JTable class requires a
collection of objects, and an object adapter is best suited to adapt
information from more than one object.

When you design your own systems, consider the power and flexibility that you and other developers can derive from an architecture that
uses ADAPTER to advantage.

4

FACADE

A GREAT ADVANTAGE OF OO programming is that it helps keep applications from becoming monolithic programs with hopelessly tangled pieces. In an OO system, an **application** is, ideally, a minimal class that knits together the behaviors from reusable toolkits of other classes. A toolkit or subsystem developer often creates packages of well-designed classes without providing any applications that tie these classes together. The packages in Java's class libraries are generally like this; they are toolkits from which you can weave an endless variety of domain-specific applications.

The reusability of toolkits comes with a problem: The diverse applicability of classes in an OO subsystem may offer an oppressive variety of options. A developer who wants to use the toolkit may not know where to begin. An **integrated development environment** (IDE), such as Eclipse, can isolate a developer from some of a toolkit's complexity, but IDEs sometimes create large amounts of code that a developer may not want to manage.

Another approach to simplifying the use of a toolkit is to supply a facade—a small amount of code that provides a typical, no-frills usage of the classes in a class library. A facade is a class with a level of functionality that lies between a toolkit and a complete application, offering a simplified usage of the classes in a package or subsystem.

The intent of the FACADE pattern is to provide an interface that makes a subsystem easy to use.

Facades, Utilities, and Demos

A facade class may have all static methods, in which case it is called a **utility** in UML [Booch, Rumbaugh, and Jacobsen 1999]. Later, we'll introduce a UI (user interface) class, which could have been given all static methods, although doing so would prevent overriding these methods in future subclasses.

A **demo** is an example that shows how to use a class or subsystem. As such, demos provide much of the same value as facades.

CHALLENGE 4.1

Write down two differences between a demo and a facade.

A solution appears on page 353.

The javax.swing package contains JOptionPane, a class that makes it easy to pop up a standard dialog box. For example, the following code displays and redisplays a dialog until the user clicks the Yes button, as Figure 4.1 shows.

```
package app.facade;

import javax.swing.*;
import java.awt.Font;

public class ShowOptionPane {
    public static void main(String[] args) {
        Font font = new Font("Dialog", Font.PLAIN, 18);
        UIManager.put("Button.font", font);
        UIManager.put("Label.font", font);

        int option;
        do {
            option = JOptionPane.showConfirmDialog(
                    null,
                    "Had enough?",
                    "A Stubborn Dialog",
                    JOptionPane.YES_NO_OPTION);
        } while (option == JOptionPane.NO_OPTION);
    }
}
```

FIGURE 4.1 The JOptionPane class makes it easy to display dialogs such as this one.

CHALLENGE 4.2

The JOptionPane class makes it easy to display a dialog. Say whether this class is a facade, a utility, or a demo, and justify your answer.

A solution appears on page 353.

CHALLENGE 4.3

Few facades appear in the Java class libraries. Why is that?

A solution appears on page 354.

Refactoring to FACADE

Facades often arise out of normal application development. As you separate your code's concerns into different classes, you may **refactor** (restructure) the system by extracting a class whose primary job is to provide simplified access to a subsystem. Consider an example from the early days at Oozinoz, when there were not yet standards for GUI development. Suppose that you come across an application that a developer has created to show the flight path of an unexploded shell. Figure 4.2 shows this class.

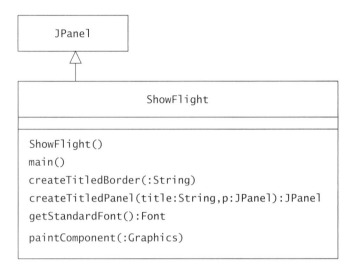

FIGURE 4.2 The ShowFlight class displays the flight path of an unexploded shell.

Aerial shells are designed to explode high in the sky with spectacular results. But occasionally, a shell does not explode at all (it is a **dud**). If a shell does not explode, its return to Earth becomes interesting. Unlike a rocket, a shell is unpowered, so if you ignore the effects of wind and air resistance, the flight path of a dud is a simple parabola. Figure 4.3 shows a screen shot of the window that appears when you execute ShowFlight.main().

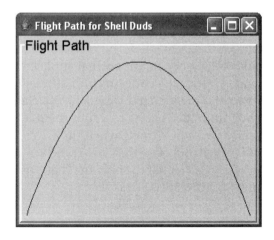

FIGURE 4.3 The ShowFlight application shows where a dud may land.

There is a problem with the ShowFlight class: It intermingles three purposes. Its primary purpose is to act as a panel that displays a flight path. Another purpose is to act as a complete application, wrapping the flight path panel in a titled border and displaying it. A final purpose of this class is to calculate a parabolic flight path. The Show-Flight class currently performs this calculation in its paintComponent() code:

```
protected void paintComponent(Graphics g) {
    super.paintComponent(g); // paint the background
    int nPoint = 101;
    double w = getWidth() - 1;
    double h = getHeight() - 1;
    int[] x = new int[nPoint];
    int[] y = new int[nPoint];
    for (int i = 0; i < nPoint; i++) {
        // t goes 0 to 1
        double t = ((double) i) / (nPoint - 1);
        // x goes 0 to w
        x[i] = (int) (t * w);
        // y is h at t = 0 and t = 1, and y is 0 at t = .5
        y[i] = (int) (4 * h * (t - .5) * (t - .5));
    }
    g.drawPolyline(x, y, nPoint);
}
```

See the sidebar Parametric Equations on page 39 for an explanation of how this code establishes the x and y values of the dud's path.

There's no need for a class constructor. There are static utility methods to wrap a title around the panel and define a standard font.

```
public static TitledBorder createTitledBorder(String title){
    TitledBorder tb = BorderFactory.createTitledBorder(
        BorderFactory.createBevelBorder(BevelBorder.RAISED),
        title,
        TitledBorder.LEFT,
        TitledBorder.TOP);
    tb.setTitleColor(Color.black);
    tb.setTitleFont(getStandardFont());
    return tb;
}
```

```
public static JPanel createTitledPanel(
      String title, JPanel in) {
    JPanel out = new JPanel();
    out.add(in);
    out.setBorder(createTitledBorder(title));
    return out;
}

public static Font getStandardFont() {
    return new Font("Dialog", Font.PLAIN, 18);
}
```

Note that the `createTitledPanel()` method tucks the provided control inside a bevel border to provide a little padding, to keep the flight path curve from touching the sides of the panel. The `main()` method also adds padding to the form object that it uses to contain the application's controls:

```
public static void main(String[] args) {
    ShowFlight flight = new ShowFlight();
    flight.setPreferredSize(new Dimension(300, 200));
    JPanel panel = createTitledPanel("Flight Path", flight);

    JFrame frame = new JFrame("Flight Path for Shell Duds");
    frame.setDefaultCloseOperation(JFrame.EXIT_ON_CLOSE);
    frame.getContentPane().add(panel);

    frame.pack();
    frame.setVisible(true);
}
```

Executing this program produces the display shown in Figure 4.3.

Parametric Equations

When you need to plot a curve, it can be difficult to describe the y values as functions of x values. **Parametric equations** let you define both x and y in terms of a third parameter that you introduce. Specifically, you can define that time t goes from 0 to 1 as the curve is drawn and define x and y as functions of the parameter t.

For example, suppose that you want the parabolic flight of a nonexploding shell to stretch across the width w of a `Graphics` object. Then a parametric equation for x is easy:

```
x = w * t
```

Note that as t goes from 0 to 1, x goes from 0 to w.

The y values for a parabola must vary with the square of the value of t, and y values increase going down the screen. For a parabolic flight, y should be 0 at time t = .5, so we can write an initial equation as follows:

```
y = k * (t - .5) * (t - .5)
```

Here, k represents a constant that we still need to determine. The equation provides for y to be 0 at t = .5 and provides for y to have the same value at t = 0 and t = 1. At those two times, y should be h, the height of the display area. With a little algebraic manipulation, you can find the complete equation for y, as follows:

```
y = 4 * h * (t - .5) * (t - .5)
```

Figure 4.3 shows the equations for a parabola in action.

Another advantage of parametric equations is that with them, there is no problem drawing curves that have more than one y value for a given x value. Consider drawing a circle. The equation for a circle with a radius of 1 is:

```
x² + y² = r²
```

or

```
y = +- sqrt (r²- x²)
```

Handling the fact that two **y** values emerge for every **x** value is complicated. It's also difficult to adjust these values to plot correctly within a **Graphics** object's height and width. Polar coordinates make the function for a circle simpler:

```
x = r * cos(theta)
y = r * sin(theta)
```

These formulas are parametric equations that show **x** and **y** as functions of a new parameter **theta**. The variable **theta** represents the sweep of an arc that varies from 0 to **2*pi** as a circle is drawn. You can set the radius of a circle so that it will fit within the height **h** and width **w** of a **Graphics** object. A handful of parametric equations suffice to plot a circle within the bounds of a **Graphics** object, as follows:

```
theta = 2 * pi * t
r = min(w, h)/2
x = w/2 + r * cos(theta)
y = h/2 - r * sin(theta)
```

Translating these equations into code produces the circle that Figure 4.4 shows. (The code that produced this display is in the **ShowCircle** application in the code from **oozinoz.com**.)

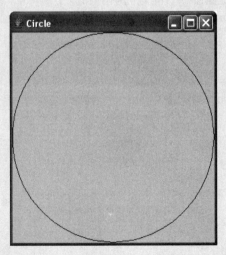

FIGURE 4.4 Parametric equations simplify the modeling of curves where y is not a single-valued function of x.

The code that draws a circle is a fairly direct translation of the mathematical formulas. One subtlety is that the code reduces the height and width of the Graphics object because the pixels are numbered from 0 to height - 1 and from 0 to width - 1:

```java
package app.facade;

import javax.swing.*;
import java.awt.*;

import com.oozinoz.ui.SwingFacade;

public class ShowCircle extends JPanel {
    public static void main(String[] args) {
        ShowCircle sc = new ShowCircle();
        sc.setPreferredSize(new Dimension(300, 300));
        SwingFacade.launch(sc, "Circle");
    }
    protected void paintComponent(Graphics g) {
        super.paintComponent(g);
        int nPoint = 101;
        double w = getWidth() - 1;
        double h = getHeight() - 1;
        double r = Math.min(w, h) / 2.0;
        int[] x = new int[nPoint];
        int[] y = new int[nPoint];
        for (int i = 0; i < nPoint; i++) {
            double t = ((double) i) / (nPoint - 1);
            double theta = Math.PI * 2.0 * t;
            x[i] = (int) (w / 2 + r * Math.cos(theta));
            y[i] = (int) (h / 2 - r * Math.sin(theta));
        }
        g.drawPolyline(x, y, nPoint);
    }
}
```

Defining x and y functions in terms of t lets you divide the tasks of determining x values and y values. This is often simpler than defining y in terms of x and often facilitates the mapping of x and y onto a Graphics object's coordinates. Parametric equations also simplify the plotting of curves where y is not a single-valued function of x.

The code in the ShowFlight class works, but you can make it more maintainable and more reusable by refactoring it into classes that have separate concerns. Suppose that you hold a design review and decide to make the following changes.

- Introduce a Function class with a method f() that accepts a double (the value of time) and returns a double (the function's value).

- Move the plotting code of the ShowFlight class into a PlotPanel class but adjust it to use Function objects for x and y values. Define the PlotPanel constructor to accept two Function instances and the number of points to plot.

- Move the createTitledPanel() method to the existing UI utility class to manufacture a panel with a title, as the ShowFlight class does currently.

CHALLENGE 4.4

Complete the diagram in Figure 4.5 to show the code for ShowFlight refactored into three types: a Function class, a PlotPanel class that plots two parametric functions, and a UI facade class. In your redesign, make the ShowFlight2 class create a Function for y values, and have a main() method that launches the application.

A solution appears on page 354.

After refactoring, the Function class defines how a parametric equation looks. Suppose that you create a com.oozinoz.function package to contain the Function class and other types. Then the heart of Function.java might be:

```
public abstract double f(double t);
```

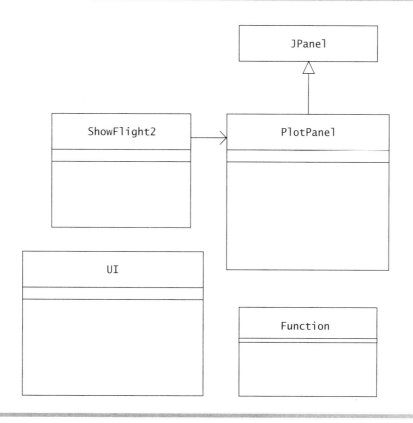

FIGURE 4.5 The flight path application refactored into classes that each have one job

The PlotPanel class emerges from the refactoring as a class that has just one job: displaying a pair of parametric equations:

```
package com.oozinoz.ui;

import java.awt.Color;
import java.awt.Graphics;

import javax.swing.JPanel;
import com.oozinoz.function.Function;

public class PlotPanel extends JPanel {
    private int points;
```

```
private int[] xPoints;
private int[] yPoints;

private Function xFunction;
private Function yFunction;

public PlotPanel(
        int nPoint, Function xFunc, Function yFunc) {
    points = nPoint;
    xPoints = new int[points];
    yPoints = new int[points];
    xFunction = xFunc;
    yFunction = yFunc;
    setBackground(Color.WHITE);
}

protected void paintComponent(Graphics graphics) {
    double w = getWidth() - 1;
    double h = getHeight() - 1;

    for (int i = 0; i < points; i++) {
        double t = ((double) i) / (points - 1);
        xPoints[i] = (int) (xFunction.f(t) * w);
        yPoints[i] = (int) (h * (1 - yFunction.f(t)));
    }

    graphics.drawPolyline(xPoints, yPoints, points);
}
}
```

Note that the PlotPanel class is now part of the com.oozinoz.ui package, the same one in which the UI class resides. After refactoring the ShowFlight class, the UI class also has createTitledPanel() and createTitledBorder() methods. The UI class is growing into a facade that makes it easy to use Java controls.

An application that uses these controls may be a small class whose only job is to lay out the controls and display them. For example, the code for the ShowFlight2 class is as follows:

```
package app.facade;

import java.awt.Dimension;
import javax.swing.JFrame;
import com.oozinoz.function.Function;
import com.oozinoz.function.T;
import com.oozinoz.ui.PlotPanel;
import com.oozinoz.ui.UI;

public class ShowFlight2 {
    public static void main(String[] args) {
        PlotPanel p = new PlotPanel(
            101,
            new T(),
            new ShowFlight2().new YFunction());
        p.setPreferredSize(new Dimension(300, 200));

        JFrame frame = new JFrame(
            "Flight Path for Shell Duds");
        frame.setDefaultCloseOperation(
            JFrame.EXIT_ON_CLOSE);
        frame.getContentPane().add(
            UI.NORMAL.createTitledPanel("Flight Path", p));

        frame.pack();
        frame.setVisible(true);
    }


    private class YFunction extends Function {
        public YFunction() {
            super(new Function[] {});
        }

        public double f(double t) {
            // y is 0 at t = 0, 1; y is 1 at t = .5
            return 4 * t * (1 - t);
        }
    }
}
```

The ShowFlight2 class provides the YFunction class for the flight path of a dud. The main() method lays out the user interface and displays it. Running this class produces the same results as running the original ShowFlight class. But now you have a reusable facade that simplifies the creation of a graphical user interface in Java applications.

Summary

Ordinarily, you should refactor the classes in a subsystem until each class has a well-defined purpose. This will make your code easier to maintain, but it can also make it difficult for a user of your subsystem to know where to begin. To help the developer who is using your code, you can supply demos or facades that go with your subsystem. A demo is usually a stand-alone, nonreusable application that shows one way to apply a subsystem. A facade is a configurable, reusable class with a higher-level interface that makes the subsystem easier to use.

5
COMPOSITE

A **COMPOSITE** IS A group of objects in which some objects may contain others, so that some objects represent groups and others represent individual items, or **leaves**. When you model a composite, two powerful concepts emerge. One important idea is to design groups so that they can contain either individual items or other groups. (A common error is to define groups so that they can contain only leaves.) A second powerful concept is to define behaviors common to both individual objects and compositions. You can bring these ideas together by defining a common type for groups and items and modeling groups as containing a collection of objects of this type.

The intent of the COMPOSITE **pattern is to let clients treat individual objects and compositions of objects uniformly.**

An Ordinary Composite

Figure 5.1 shows a typical composite structure. The Leaf and Composite classes share a common interface that Component abstracts, and a Composite object retains a collection of other Composite and Leaf objects.

Note that the Component class in Figure 5.1 is an abstract class with no concrete operations, so you could define it as an interface that Leaf and Composite implement.

CHALLENGE 5.1

Why does the Composite class in Figure 5.1 maintain a collection of Component objects instead of simply a collection of leaves?

A solution appears on page 356.

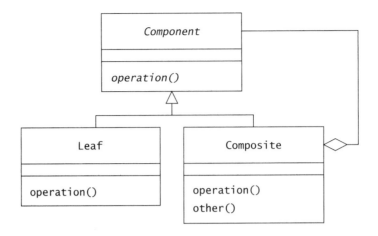

FIGURE 5.1 The key ideas of COMPOSITE are that composites can contain other composites (not just leaves) and that composite and leaf nodes share a common interface.

Recursive Behavior in Composites

Engineers at Oozinoz perceive a natural composition in the processing machines that they use to produce fireworks. The factory is composed of bays; each bay has one or more manufacturing lines; a line is a collection of machines that collaboratively produce material to meet a schedule. The developers at Oozinoz have modeled this domain by treating factories, bays, and lines as composite "machines," using the class structure shown in Figure 5.2.

As the figure shows, one behavior that applies to both individual machines and collections of machines is getMachineCount(), which returns the number of machines in any given component.

CHALLENGE 5.2

Write the code for the getMachineCount() methods implemented by Machine and by MachineComposite.

Example solutions appear on page 357.

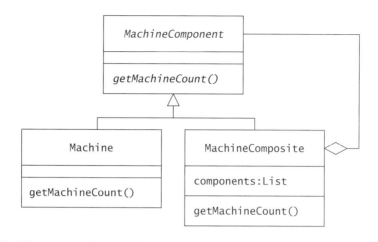

FIGURE 5.2 The getMachineCount() method is an appropriate behavior for both individual machines and composites.

Suppose that we're considering adding the following methods to MachineComponent:

Method	Behavior
isCompletelyUp()	Says whether all the machines in a component are in an "up" state
stopAll()	Directs all the machines in a component to stop processing
getOwners()	Returns a set of process engineers responsible for the machines in a component
getMaterial()	Returns all the in-process material in a machine component

The definition and operation of each method in MachineComponent is recursive. For example, the count of machines in a composite is the sum of the counts of machines in its components.

CHALLENGE 5.3

For each method declared by MachineComponent, give recursive definitions for MachineComposite and nonrecursive definitions for Machine.

Method	Class	Definition
getMachineCount()	MachineComposite	Return the sum of the counts for each component in components.
	Machine	Return 1.
isCompletelyUp()	MachineComposite	??
	Machine	??
stopAll()	MachineComposite	??
	Machine	??
getOwners()	MachineComposite	??
	Machine	??
getMaterial()	MachineComposite	??
	Machine	??

A solution appears on page 358.

Composites, Trees, and Cycles

In a composite structure, we can say that a node is a tree if it holds references to other nodes. However, this definition is too loose. To be more precise, we can apply a few terms from graph theory to object modeling. We can start by drawing an object model as a **graph**—a collection of nodes and edges—with objects as nodes and object references as edges.

Consider an object model of an **assay**, or analysis, of a batch of a chemical. The Assay class has a batch attribute of type Batch, and the Batch class has a chemical attribute of type Chemical. Suppose that there is a particular Assay object a whose batch attribute refers to a Batch object b. Suppose too that the chemical attribute of the Batch object b refers to a Chemical c. Figure 5.3 shows two alternative diagrams for this object model. (For information on how to depict object models using UML, see Appendix D: UML at a Glance, page 431.)

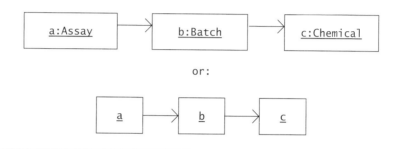

FIGURE 5.3 The two UML diagrams here show alternative representations of the same information: Object a refers to object b, and object b refers to object c.

There is a **path**, a series of object references, from a to c because a refers to b and b refers to c. A **cycle** is a path in which a particular node appears twice. There would be a cycle of references in this object model if the c Chemical object referred back to the a Assay object.

Object models are **directed graphs**, as each object reference has a direction. **Graph theory** usually applies the term **tree** to refer to certain undirected graphs. However, a directed graph may be called a tree if

- It has a **root** node that has no references to it.

- Each other node has exactly one **parent**, the node that refers to it.

Why worry about this graph notion of trees? Because COMPOSITE fits especially well with structures that fit this form. (As we'll see, you can still make COMPOSITE work with directed acyclic graphs or even with cyclic graphs, but it takes extra work and extra care.)

The object model that Figure 5.3 depicts is a trivial tree. For larger object models, it can be difficult to tell whether the model is a tree. Figure 5.4 shows the object model of a factory, called plant, that is a MachineComposite object. This plant contains a bay that has three machines: mixer, press, and assembler. The object model also shows that the plant object's list of machine components contains a direct reference to the mixer.

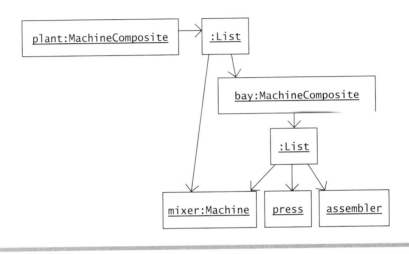

FIGURE 5.4 An object model that forms a graph that is neither cyclic nor a tree

The object graph in Figure 5.4 does not contain a cycle, but it is not a tree because two objects refer to the same mixer object. If we remove or disregard the plant object and its list, the bay object *is* the root of a tree.

Methods that work on composites may have defects if they assume that all composites are trees and if your system allows composites that are not trees. Challenge 5.2 asked for a definition of a getMachine-Count() operation. The Machine class implementation of this operation as given in the solution to this challenge is arguably correct:

```
public int getMachineCount() {
    return 1;
}
```

The MachineComposite class also correctly implements getMachine-Count(), returning the sum of the counts for each of a composite's components:

```
public int getMachineCount() {
    int count = 0;
    Iterator i = components.iterator();
    while (i.hasNext()) {
        MachineComponent mc = (MachineComponent) i.next();
        count += mc.getMachineCount();
    }
    return count;
}
```

These methods are correct so long as MachineComponent objects are trees. It can happen, though, that a composite that you suppose is a tree suddenly becomes not a tree. This is especially likely to occur when users can edit the composition. Consider an example that might occur at Oozinoz.

The fireworks engineers at Oozinoz use a GUI application to record and update the composition of machinery in the factory. One day, they report a defect regarding the number of machines that are reported to exist in the factory. You can reproduce their object model with the plant() method of the OozinozFactory class:

```
public static MachineComposite plant() {
    MachineComposite plant = new MachineComposite(100);
    MachineComposite bay = new MachineComposite(101);
    Machine mixer = new Mixer(102);
    Machine press = new StarPress(103);
    Machine assembler = new ShellAssembler(104);
    bay.add(mixer);
    bay.add(press);
    bay.add(assembler);
    plant.add(mixer);
    plant.add(bay);
    return plant;
}
```

This code produces the plant object that Figure 5.4 shows.

CHALLENGE 5.4

What does the following program print out?

```
package app.composite;
import com.oozinoz.machine.*;

public class ShowPlant {
    public static void main(String[] args) {
        MachineComponent c = OozinozFactory.plant();
        System.out.println(
            "Number of machines: " + c.getMachineCount());
    }
}
```

A solution appears on page 358.

The GUI application that Oozinoz uses to let engineers build object
models of a factory's machinery should check whether a node already
exists in a component tree before adding it a second time. A simple
way to do this is to maintain a set of existing nodes. You may not,
however, always have control over how a composite is formed. In this
case, you can write an isTree() method to check whether a composite is a tree.

We'll regard an object model as a tree if an algorithm can traverse its
references without encountering the same node twice. You can implement an isTree() method on the abstract class MachineComponent so
that it delegates to an isTree() method that maintains a collection
of visited nodes. The MachineComponent class can leave the implementation of the parameterized isTree(set:Set) method abstract.
Figure 5.5 shows the placement of the isTree() methods.

The MachineComponent code delegates an isTree() call to its abstract
isTree(s:Set) method:

```
public boolean isTree() {
    return isTree(new HashSet());
}
protected abstract boolean isTree(Set s);
```

These methods use the Set class from the Java class library.

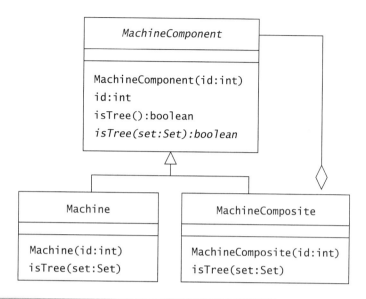

FIGURE 5.5 An isTree() method can detect whether a composite is in fact a tree.

The Machine and MachineComposite classes must implement the abstract isTree(s:Set) method. The implementation of isTree() for Machine is simple, reflecting the fact that individual machines are always trees:

```
protected boolean isTree(Set visited) {
    visited.add(this);
    return true;
}
```

The MachineComposite implementation of isTree() must add the receiving object to the visited collection and then iterate over the composite's components. The method can return false if any component has been previously visited or if any component is not itself a tree. Otherwise, the method can return true.

CHALLENGE 5.5

Write the code for MachineComposite.isTree(Set visited).

A solution appears on page 359.

With some care, you can guarantee that an object model is a tree by refusing changes that would make `isTree()` false. On the other hand, you may decide to allow composites that are not trees, particularly when the problem domain that you are modeling contains cycles.

Composites with Cycles

The nontree composite that Challenge 5.4 refers to was an accident that stemmed from a user's marking a machine as part of both a plant and a bay. For physical objects, you may want to disallow the notion that an object is contained by more than one other object. However, a problem domain can have nonphysical elements for which cycles of containment make sense. This occurs frequently when modeling process flows.

Consider the construction of aerial shells, such as the one that Figure 5.6 depicts. We launch a shell from a **mortar**, or tube, by igniting the lifting charge of black powder that is seated beneath the core charge. The secondary fuses burn while the shell is in the air, eventually reaching the core. When the shell core explodes, its **stars** ignite, creating the visual effects of aerial fireworks.

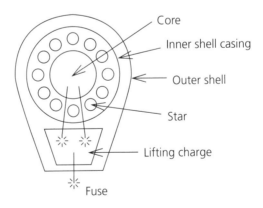

FIGURE 5.6 An aerial shell uses two charges: one for initial lift and one to expel explosive stars when the shell is at its peak.

The process flow for making an **aerial shell** consists of building an inner shell, having it inspected, and then either reworking it or finishing its assembly.

To make the inner shell, an operator uses a shell assembler that places stars in a hemispherical casing, inserts a black powder core, attaches more stars on top of the core, and seals this subassembly with another hemispherical casing.

An inspector verifies that the inner shell meets safety and quality standards. If it doesn't, the operator disassembles the inner shell and makes it again, grumbling. When an inner shell passes inspection, the operator finishes the shell, using a fuser that connects a lifting charge to the inner shell with fusing. Finally, the operator manually wraps the complete aerial shell.

As with machine composites, Oozinoz engineers have a GUI that lets them describe the composition of a process. Figure 5.7 shows the class structure that supports process modeling.

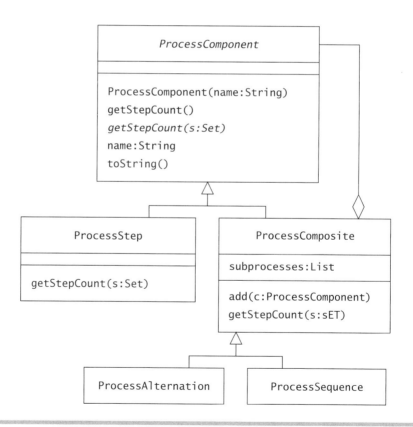

FIGURE 5.7 The process for manufacturing fireworks includes some steps that are alternations or sequences of other steps.

Figure 5.8 shows the objects that represent the process flow for making an aerial shell. The `make` process is a sequence of the `buildInner` step, the `inspect` step, and the `reworkOrFinish` subprocess. The `reworkOrFinish` subprocess takes one of two alternative paths. It may require a `disassemble` step followed by the `make` process, or it may require only `finish` step.

CHALLENGE 5.6

Figure 5.8 shows the objects in a model of the shell assembly process. A complete object diagram would show links between any objects that refer to each other. For example, the diagram shows the references that the `make` object retains. Your challenge is to fill in the missing links in the diagram.

A solution appears on page 359.

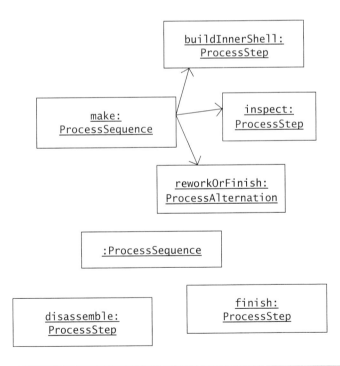

FIGURE 5.8 This diagram, when completed, will show an object model of the Oozinoz process for making aerial shells.

The getStepCount() operation in the ProcessComponent hierarchy counts the number of individual processing steps in a process flow. Note that this count is not the length of the process but rather the number of leaf node processing steps in the process's object graph. The getStepCount() method has to be careful to count each step only once and to not enter an infinite loop when a process contains a cycle. The ProcessComponent class implements the getStepCount() method so that it relies on a companion method that passes along a set of visited nodes:

```
public int getStepCount() {
    return getStepCount(new HashSet());
}
public abstract int getStepCount(Set visited);
```

The ProcessComposite class takes care in its implementation of the getStepCount() method not to visit a previously visited node:

```
public int getStepCount(Set visited) {
    visited.add(getName());
    int count = 0;
    for (int i = 0; i < subprocesses.size(); i++) {
        ProcessComponent pc =
            (ProcessComponent) subprocesses.get(i);
        if (!visited.contains(pc.getName()))
            count += pc.getStepCount(visited);
    }
    return count;
}
```

The ProcessStep class implementation of getStepCount() is simple:

```
public int getStepCount(Set visited) {
    visited.add(name);
    return 1;
}
```

The Oozinoz com.oozinoz.process package contains a ShellProcess class that has a make() method that returns the make object that Figure 5.8 depicts. The com.oozinoz.testing package has a ProcessTest class that provides automated tests of various types of process graphs. For example, the ProcessTest class includes a method that tests that the getStepCount() operation correctly counts the number of steps in the cyclic make process:

```
public void testShell() {
    assertEquals(4, ShellProcess.make().getStepCount());
}
```

This test runs and passes within the **JUnit** testing framework. See www.junit.org for more information about JUnit.

Consequences of Cycles

Many operations on a composite, such as counting its number of leaf nodes, make sense even if the composite is not a tree. Usually, the only difference that nontree composites introduce is that you have to be careful not to operate on a given node twice. However, some operations become meaningless if the composite contains a cycle. For example, we can't algorithmically determine the maximum number of steps that might be required to make an aerial shell at Oozinoz, because the rework step may be repeated an arbitrarily large number of times. Any operation that depends on the length of a path in a composite won't make sense if the composite contains a cycle. So, although we can talk about the height of a tree—the longest path from the root to a leaf—there is no maximum-length path in a cyclic graph.

Another result of allowing composites that are not trees is that you lose the ability to assume that each node has a single parent. If a composite is not a tree, a node may have more than one parent. For example, the process that Figure 5.8 models might have several composite steps that use the inspect step, giving the inspect object multiple parents. There is no inherent problem in a node's having multiple parents, but your model and code must then take that into account.

Summary

COMPOSITE contains two powerful, related concepts. One concept is that a group can contain either individual items or other groups. Related to this concept is the idea that groups and individual items share a common interface. These ideas come together in object modeling, whereby you can create an abstract class or a Java interface that defines the behaviors that are common to groups and to individual objects.

Modeling composites often leads to recursive definition of methods on composite nodes. When recursion is present, there is a danger of writing code that produces an infinite loop. To avoid such problems, you can take steps to guarantee that your composites are always trees. Alternatively, you can allow cycles to occur in a composite, but you have to modify your algorithms to watch for infinite recursion.

6

BRIDGE

THE BRIDGE, OR Driver, pattern focuses on the design of an abstraction. The word **abstraction** refers to a class that relies on a set of abstract operations, where several implementations of the set of abstract operations are possible.

The ordinary way to implement an abstraction is to create a class hierarchy, with an abstract class that defines the abstract operations at the top; each subclass in the hierarchy provides a different implementation of the set of abstract operations. This approach becomes insufficient when you need to subclass the hierarchy for some other reason.

You can create a BRIDGE by moving the set of abstract operations to an interface, so that an abstraction will depend on an implementation of the interface.

The intent of the BRIDGE pattern is to decouple an abstraction from the implementation of its abstract operations, so that the abstraction and its implementation can vary independently.

An Ordinary Abstraction: On the Way to BRIDGE

Nearly every class is an abstraction, in the sense that each class is an approximation, an idealization, or a simplification of the class of real objects that it models. When discussing BRIDGE, though, we specifically use the word *abstraction* to mean a class that relies on a set of abstract operations.

Suppose that you have machine control classes that interact with some of the physical machines that produce fireworks at Oozinoz. The classes reflect differences in how the machines operate. However, you might want to create some abstract operations that would achieve the same result on any machine. Figure 6.1 shows the current control classes from package `com.oozinoz.controller`.

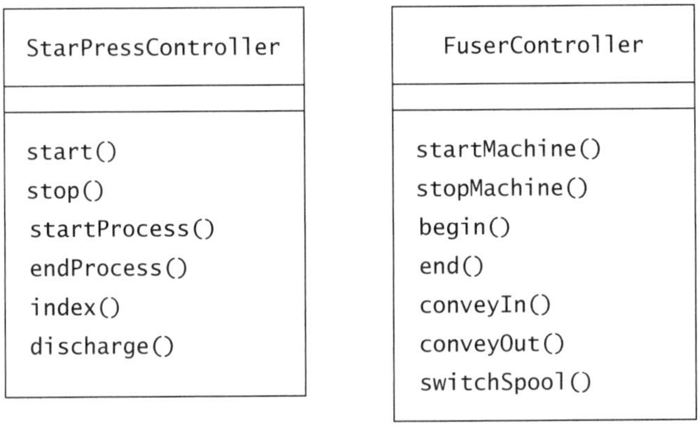

StarPressController	FuserController
start()	startMachine()
stop()	stopMachine()
startProcess()	begin()
endProcess()	end()
index()	conveyIn()
discharge()	conveyOut()
	switchSpool()

FIGURE 6.1 The two classes shown have similar methods that you might abstract into a common model for driving machines.

Both controller classes in Figure 6.1 have methods to start and stop the machines they control, although the StarPressController class names these methods start() and stop(), whereas the FuserController class names them startMachine() and stopMachine(). Both controllers also have methods for moving a bin into the processing area (index() and conveyIn()), for beginning and ending processing of a bin, and for removing a bin (discharge() and conveyOut()). The FuserController class also has a method that can switch in a backup spool of fuse.

Now suppose that you want to create a shutdown() method that ensures an orderly shutdown, performing the same steps on both machines. To simplify the writing of a shutdown() method, you would like to standardize the names for common operations, such as startMachine(), stopMachine(), startProcess(), stopProcess(), conveyIn(), and conveyOut(). But it turns out that you can't change the controller classes, because one of them comes from the machine supplier.

CHALLENGE 6.1

State how you could apply a design pattern to allow controlling various machines with a common interface.

A solution appears on page 360.

Figure 6.2 shows the introduction of an abstract MachineManager class with subclasses that forward machine control calls, adapting them into methods that FuserController and StarPressController support.

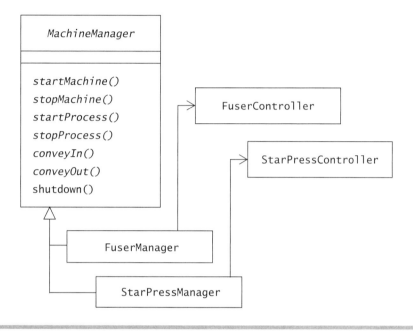

FIGURE 6.2 The FuserManager and StarPressManager classes implement the abstract methods of MachineManager by passing through the calls to corresponding methods of FuserController and StarPressController objects.

There is no problem if a machine controller has some operations that are unique to a particular machine type. For example, although Figure 6.2 doesn't show it, the FuserManager class also has a switchSpool() method that forwards to the switchSpool() method of a FuserController object.

CHALLENGE 6.2

Write a shutdown() method that will stop processing for the MachineManager class, discharge the bin that was in process, and stop the machine.

A solution appears on page 360.

The MachineManager class's shutdown() method is concrete, not abstract. However, we can say it is an *abstraction* because the method universalizes, or *abstracts*, the definition of what steps are taken to shut down a piece of equipment.

From Abstraction to BRIDGE

The MachineManager hierarchy is factored along the lines of different equipment, so that each machine type requires a different subclass of the MachineManager class. What happens if you need to organize the hierarchy along another line? For example, suppose that you work on the machines themselves so that they provide acknowledgment of the steps they complete. Correspondingly, you want to create a hand-shaking MachineManager subclass with methods that let you parameterize the interaction with the machine, such as setting a time-out value. However, you still need different machine managers for star presses and fusers. If you don't reorganize the MachineManager hierarchy first, your new hierarchy might look like Figure 6.3.

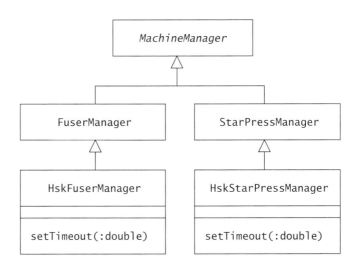

FIGURE 6.3 The handshaking (Hsk) subclasses add parameterization of how long to wait for acknowledgment from a real machine.

The hierarchy in Figure 6.3 factors classes along two lines: according to machine type and according to whether handshaking is supported. This dual principle for factoring creates problems. In particular, a method such as `setTimeout()` may contain identical code in two places, but we cannot factor it up in the hierarchy, because the super-classes do not support the handshaking idea.

In general, there is no way for the handshaking classes to share code, as there is no handshaking superclass. As we add more classes to the hierarchy, the problem gets worse. If we eventually have controllers for five machines and then decide to change the `setTimeout()` method, we may have to change code in five places.

In this situation, we can apply Bridge. We can decouple the Machine-Manager abstraction from the implementation of its abstract operations by moving its abstract methods to a separate hierarchy. The Machine-Manager class remains an abstraction; the effect of calling its methods will depend on whether we are controlling a star press or a fuser.

Separating the abstraction from the implementation of its abstract methods lets the two hierarchies vary independently. We can add support for new machines without affecting the MachineManager hierarchy. We can also extend the MachineManager hierarchy without changing any of the machine controllers. Figure 6.4 suggests the desired separation.

The goal of the new design is to separate the MachineManager hierarchy from the implementation of the hierarchy's abstract operations.

CHALLENGE 6.3

Figure 6.4 shows the MachineManager hierarchy refactored into a bridge. Fill in the missing labels.

A solution appears on page 360.

Note in Figure 6.4 that the MachineManager2 class becomes concrete, although it is still an abstraction. The abstract methods that Machine-Manager depends on now reside in the MachineDriver interface. The

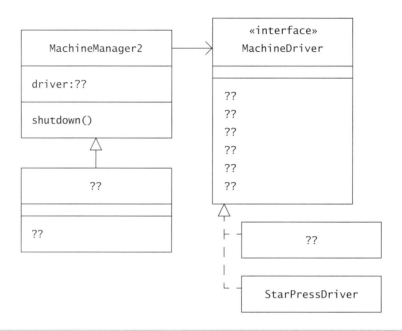

FIGURE 6.4 When completed, this diagram will show a separation of the Machine-Manager abstraction from the implementation of its abstract operations.

name of this interface suggests that the classes that adapt Machine-Manager requests to specific machines have become drivers. A **driver** is an object that operates a computer system or an external device according to a well-specified interface. Drivers provide the most common example of the BRIDGE pattern in practice.

Drivers as BRIDGES

Drivers are abstractions. The effect of running the application depends on which driver is in place. Each driver is an instance of the ADAPTER pattern, providing the interface a client expects by using the services of a class with a different interface. An overall design that uses drivers is an instance of BRIDGE. The design separates application development from the development of the drivers that implement the abstract operations on which the applications rely.

A driver-based design forces you to create a common, abstract model of the machine or system that will be driven. This has the advantage of letting code on the abstraction side apply to any of the drivers that it might execute against. Defining a common set of methods for the drivers may also incur the disadvantage of eliminating behavior that one driven entity might support. Recall from Figure 6.1 that a fuser controller has a `switchSpool()` method. Looking at the revised design in Figure 6.4, where did this method go? The answer is that we abstracted it out. You can include the `switchSpool()` method in the new `Fuser-Driver` class. However, this can lead to code on the abstraction side that must check to see whether its driver is a `FuserDriver` instance.

To avoid losing the `switchSpool()` method, we could have required every driver to implement this method, understanding that some drivers will simply ignore the call. When choosing an abstract model of the operations that a driver will support, you will often face this kind of choice. You can include methods that some drivers cannot support, or you can exclude methods that will either reduce what abstractions can do with the driver or that force the abstractions to include special-case code.

Database Drivers

An everyday example of applications using drivers appears in database access. Database connectivity in Java relies on **JDBC**. A good resource that explains how to apply JDBC is *JDBC™ API Tutorial and Reference (2/e)* [White et al. 1999]. In short, JDBC is an **application programming interface** (API) for executing **Structured Query Language** (SQL) statements. Classes that implement the interface are JDBC drivers, and applications that rely on these drivers are abstractions that can work with any database for which a JDBC driver exists. The JDBC architecture decouples an abstraction from its implementation so that the two can vary independently: an excellent example of BRIDGE.

To use a JDBC driver, you load it, connect to a database, and create a `Statement` object:

```
Class.forName(driverName);
Connection c = DriverManager.getConnection(url, user, pwd);
Statement stmt = c.createStatement();
```

A discussion of how the `DriverManager` class works is outside the scope of our discussion here. But at this point, `stmt` is a `Statement` object, capable of issuing SQL queries that return result sets:

```
ResultSet result = stmt.executeQuery(
            "SELECT name, apogee FROM firework");
while (result.next()) {
    String name = result.getString("name");
    int apogee = result.getInt("apogee");
    System.out.println(name + ", " + apogee);
}
```

CHALLENGE 6.4

Figure 6.5 shows a UML sequence diagram that illustrates the message flow in a typical JDBC application. Fill in the missing type names and the missing message name in this illustration.

A solution appears on page 361.

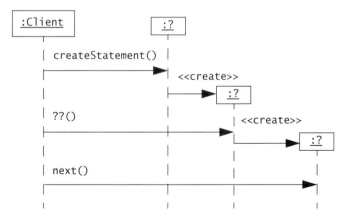

FIGURE 6.5 This diagram shows most of the typical message flow in a JDBC application.

CHALLENGE 6.5

Suppose that at Oozinoz, we currently have only SQL Server databases. Provide an argument that we should use readers and adapters that are specific to SQL Server. Provide another argument that we should *not* do this.

A solution appears on page 361.

The JDBC architecture clearly divides the roles of the driver writer and the application writer. In some cases, this division will not exist in advance, even if you are using drivers. You may be able to set up drivers as subclasses of an abstract superclass, with each subclass driving a different subsystem. In such a case, you may be pushed to set up a BRIDGE when you need more flexibility.

Summary

An abstraction is a class that depends on abstract methods. The simplest example of an abstraction is an abstract hierarchy, where concrete methods in the superclass depend on other abstract methods. You may be forced to move these abstract methods to another hierarchy if you want to factor the original hierarchy along another line. In this case, you are applying BRIDGE, separating an abstraction from the implementation of its abstract methods.

The most common example of BRIDGE occurs in drivers, such as database drivers. Database drivers provide good examples of the trade-offs that are inherent in a BRIDGE structure. A driver may require methods that an implementer cannot support. On the other hand, a driver may neglect useful methods that would apply to a particular database. This can push you back into writing code that is specific to an implementation instead of being abstract. It is not always clear whether you should value abstraction over specificity, but it is important to make these decisions consciously.

PART II

RESPONSIBILITY PATTERNS

7

INTRODUCING RESPONSIBILITY

THE RESPONSIBILITY OF an object is comparable to that of a representative in the Oozinoz call center. When you order fireworks from Oozinoz, the person you speak to is a representative—a proxy—for the company. He or she performs foreseeable tasks, usually by delegating them to other systems and people. Sometimes, the representative will delegate a request to a single, central authority who will mediate the situation or escalate problems up a chain of responsibility.

Like call center representatives, ordinary objects have the information and methods they need to operate independently. There are times, though, when you need to centralize responsibility, diverging from the normal independent operation of objects. Several design patterns address this need. There are also patterns that let objects escalate requests and that isolate an object from other objects that depend on it. Responsibility-oriented patterns provide techniques for centralizing, escalating, and limiting ordinary object responsibility.

Ordinary Responsibility

You probably have a strong sense of how attributes and responsibilities should come together in a well-formed class, although it can be challenging to explain your views.

CHALLENGE 7.1

The class structure shown in Figure 7.1 has at least ten questionable assignments of responsibility. Circle as many problems as you can find; then write a statement about what is wrong for four of these points.

Solutions appear on page 362.

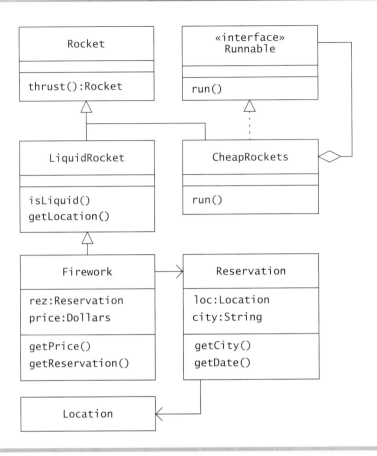

FIGURE 7.1 What's wrong with this picture?

Looking at all the oddities in Figure 7.1 may loosen up your thinking about appropriate object modeling. This is a good frame of mind to be in when you set out to define terms, such as a *class*. The value of defining terms increases as it helps people communicate and decreases as it becomes a goal in itself and a source of conflict. In this spirit, take the following difficult challenge.

CHALLENGE 7.2

Define the qualities of an effective, useful class.

Points to consider appear on page 363.

One feature that makes a class easier to use is that its method names suggest, accurately, what the methods do. There are times, though, when a method's name does not contain enough information for you to predict the exact effects of calling it.

CHALLENGE 7.3

Give an example where, for good reason, the effect of calling a method cannot be predicted from the method's name.

Some solutions appear on page 363.

Establishing principles for the proper assignment of responsibility in object-oriented systems seems to be an area ripe for progress in computer science. A system in which every class and method clearly defines its responsibilities and bears them correctly is a strong system, stronger than most systems we encounter today.

Controlling Responsibility with Visibility

It is common to speak of classes and methods bearing various responsibilities. In practice, this usually means that *you* bear responsibility for the solid design and proper functioning of your code. Fortunately, Java offers some relief. You can limit the visibility of your classes, fields, and methods and thereby limit your responsibility to developers who use your code. The visibility can be a sign to the reader of how exposed a part of a class should be. Table 7.1 gives informal definitions of the effects of access modifiers.

Several subtleties arise in practice that may require you to consider the formal definition rather than an intuitive definition of these modifiers. One area of subtlety to consider is whether visibility affects objects or classes.

TABLE 7.1 Informal Definitions of the Effects of Access Modifiers

Access	Informal Definition
public	Access not limited
(none)	Access limited to this package
protected	Access limited to the containing class, or types derived from the containing class
private	Access limited to the containing type

CHALLENGE 7.4

Can an object refer to a private member of another instance of the same class? Specifically, will the following code compile?

```
public class Firework {
    private double weight = 0;
    /// ...
    private double compare(Firework f) {
        return weight - f.weight;
    }
}
```

A solution appears on page 364.

Visibility modifiers help you limit your responsibility by limiting the services that you provide to other developers. For example, if you don't want other developers to be able to manipulate one of your class's fields, you can mark the field private. On the other hand, you will provide future developers with more flexibility if you mark your fields protected, though this bears the risk of coupling subclasses too tightly to the parent class. You should make a conscious decision, and perhaps establish a group policy, about how you want to limit access to restrict your current responsibilities while permitting future extensions.

Summary

As a Java developer, you take on responsibility for creating classes that form a logical collection of attributes and associated behaviors. Composing a good class is an art, but we can establish certain characteristics of well-designed classes. In the classes you write, you are also responsible for ensuring that your methods perform the services implied by their names. You can limit this responsibility with the proper use of visibility modifiers, but you should consider trade-offs between security and flexibility in the visibility of your code.

Beyond Ordinary Responsibility

Regardless of how a class limits access to its members, OO development normally distributes responsibility to individual objects. In other words, OO development promotes **encapsulation**, the idea that an object works on its own data.

Distributed responsibility is the norm, but several design patterns oppose this norm and move responsibility to an intermediary or central object. For example, the SINGLETON pattern concentrates responsibility into a single object and provides global access to this object. One way to remember the intent of SINGLETON and several other patterns is as exceptions to the ordinary rule of distributed responsibility.

If you intend to	Apply the pattern
• Centralize responsibility in a single instance of a class	SINGLETON
• Decouple an object from awareness of which other objects depend on it	OBSERVER
• Centralize responsibility in a class that oversees how a set of other objects interact	MEDIATOR
• Let an object act on behalf of another object	PROXY

If you intend to	Apply the pattern
• Allow a request to escalate up a chain of objects until one handles it	CHAIN OF RESPONSIBILITY
• Centralize responsibility in shared, fine-grained objects	FLYWEIGHT

The intent of each design pattern is to solve a problem in a context. Responsibility-oriented patterns address contexts in which you need to deviate from the normal rule that responsibility should be distributed as far as possible.

8

SINGLETON

OBJECTS CAN USUALLY act responsibly simply by performing their own work on their own attributes, without incurring obligations beyond self-consistency. Some objects, though, take on further responsibilities, such as modeling real-world entities, coordinating work, or modeling the overall state of a system. When a particular object in a system bears a responsibility on which other objects rely, you need some way of finding the responsible object. For example, you might need to find an object that represents a particular machine, a customer object that can construct itself from data in a database, or an object that initiates system memory recovery.

In some cases, when you need to find a responsible object, the object that you need will be the only instance of its class. For example, a fireworks factory might need exactly one `Factory` object. In this case, you can use SINGLETON.

The intent of the SINGLETON **pattern is to ensure that a class has only one instance and to provide a global point of access to it.**

SINGLETON Mechanics

The mechanics of SINGLETON are more memorable than its intent. It is easier to explain *how* to ensure that a class has only one instance than it is to say *why* you might want this restriction. You might categorize SINGLETON as a "creational" pattern, as *Design Patterns* does. You should, of course, think of patterns in whatever way helps you remember, recognize, and apply them. But the *intent* of the SINGLETON pattern implies that a specific object bears a responsibility on which other objects rely.

You have some options regarding how you create an object that takes on a unique role. But regardless of how you create a singleton, you have to ensure that other developers don't create new instances of the class you intend to limit.

CHALLENGE 8.1

How can you prevent other developers from constructing new instances of your class?

A solution appears on page 364.

When you design a singleton class, you need to decide when to instantiate the single object that will represent the class. One choice is to create this instance as a static field in the class. For example, a SystemStartup class might include the line:

```
private static Factory factory = new Factory();
```

This class could make its unique instance available through a public, static getFactory() method.

Rather than creating a singleton instance ahead of time, you might wait until the instance is first needed, then **lazy-initialize** it. For example, the SystemStartup class might make its single instance available with

```
public static Factory getFactory() {
    if (factory == null)
        factory = new Factory();
    // ...
    return factory;
}
```

CHALLENGE 8.2

Why might you decide to lazy-initialize a singleton instance rather than to initialize it in its field declaration?

A solution appears on page 365.

In either case, the SINGLETON pattern suggests that you provide a public, static method that gives access to the SINGLETON object. If this method creates the object, the method is responsible for ensuring that only one instance can be created.

Singletons and Threads

If you want to lazy-initialize a singleton in a multithreaded environment, you have to take care to prevent multiple threads from initializing the singleton. In a multithreaded environment, there is no guarantee that a method will run to completion before a method in another thread starts running. This opens the possibility, for example, that two threads will try to initialize a singleton at roughly the same time. Suppose that a method finds that a singleton is null. If another thread begins executing at that moment, it will also find that the singleton is null. Then both methods will proceed to initialize the singleton. To prevent this sort of contention, you need a locking facility to help coordinate methods running in different threads.

Java includes support for multithreaded development. In particular, Java supplies every object with a **lock**, an exclusive resource that represents possession of the object by a thread. To ensure that only one thread initializes a singleton, you can synchronize the initialization on the lock of a suitable object. Other methods that require exclusive access to the singleton can synchronize on the same lock. For advice on concurrent object-oriented programming, *Concurrent Programming in Java™* [Lea 2000] is an excellent resource. That book suggests synchronizing on the lock that belongs to the class itself, as in the following code:

```
package com.oozinoz.businessCore;
import java.util.*;

public class Factory {
    private static Factory factory;
    private static Object classLock = Factory.class;

    private long wipMoves;

    private Factory() {
        wipMoves = 0;
    }
```

```
public static Factory getFactory() {
    synchronized (classLock) {
        if (factory == null)
            factory = new Factory();

        return factory;
    }
}

public void recordWipMove() {
        // Challenge!
    }
}
```

The getFactory() code ensures that if a second thread begins to lazy-initialize the singleton after another thread has begun the same initialization, the second thread will wait to obtain the classLock object's lock. When it obtains the lock, the second thread will find that the singleton is no longer null. (Because there can only be one instance of the class, we can use the single, static lock.)

The wipMoves variable records the number of times that **work in process** (WIP) advances. Every time a bin moves onto a new machine, the subsystem that causes or records the move must call the factory singleton's recordWipMove() method.

CHALLENGE 8.3

Write the code for the recordWipMove() method of the Factory class.

A solution appears on page 365.

Recognizing SINGLETON

Unique objects are not uncommon. In fact, most objects in an application bear a unique responsibility: Why would you create two objects with identical responsibilities? Similarly, nearly every class has a unique role. Why would you develop the same class twice? On the other hand, singleton classes—classes that allow only a single instance—are relatively rare. The fact that an object or a class is unique does not imply that the SINGLETON pattern is at work. Consider the classes in Figure 8.1.

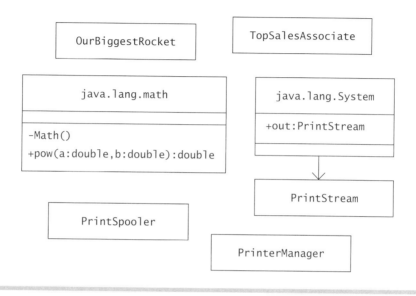

FIGURE 8.1 Which classes appear to apply SINGLETON?

CHALLENGE 8.4

For each class in Figure 8.1, say whether it appears to be a singleton class, and why.

Solutions appear on page 365.

SINGLETON is probably the best-known pattern, but it should be deep in your bag of tricks, as it's very easy to misuse. Don't let SINGLETONS become a fancy way to create global variables. The coupling that SINGLETON introduces isn't any better just because you've used a pattern. Minimize the number of classes that know they're working with a SINGLETON; it's better for classes to simply know that they have an object to work with, not the restrictions on its creation. Pay attention to the uses you want to make: If you need subclasses or different versions for testing, SINGLETON is probably not appropriate, as there isn't exactly one instance.

Summary

Code that supports SINGLETON ensures that a class has only one instance and provides a global point of access to it. A common way to achieve this is through lazy-initialization of a singleton object, instantiating it only when the singleton is first needed. In a multi-threaded environment, you must take care to manage the collaboration of threads that may access a singleton's methods and data at approximately the same time.

The fact that an object is unique does not necessarily mean that the SINGLETON pattern is in use. The SINGLETON pattern centralizes authority in a single instance of a class by hiding the constructor and providing a single point of access to object creation.

9

OBSERVER

CLIENTS ORDINARILY gather information from an interesting object by calling its methods. But when an interesting object changes, a problem arises: How do clients that depend on the object's information find out that the information has changed?

You may encounter designs that make an object responsible for informing clients when there is an interesting change in some aspect of that object. The problem with this is that the knowledge of which attributes about an object are interesting lies with the client. The interesting object shouldn't accept responsibility for updating the client. One solution is to arrange for clients to be informed when the object changes and leave it to the clients to follow up with interrogations about the object's new state.

The intent of the OBSERVER **pattern is to define a one-to-many dependency between objects so that when one object changes state, all its dependents are notified so that they can react to the change.**

A Classic Example: OBSERVER in GUIs

The OBSERVER pattern lets an object ask to be notified when another object changes. The most common example of OBSERVER occurs in graphical user interfaces. Whenever a user clicks a button or adjusts a slider, many objects in the application may need to react to the change. Java's designers have anticipated that you will be interested to know when a user changes a GUI component, and the OBSERVER pattern is evident throughout Swing. Swing refers to interested clients as "listeners" and lets you register as many listeners as you like to be notified of a component's events.

Consider a typical Oozinoz GUI application, such as the one that Figure 9.1 shows. This application lets a fireworks engineer experiment

visually with parameters that determine the relationship between a
rocket's thrust and the burn rate and surface area of its fuel.

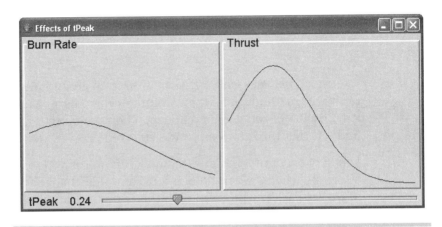

FIGURE 9.1 The curves shown change in real time as the user adjusts the **tPeak** variable with the slider.

When a solid rocket engine ignites, the part of its fuel that is exposed
to air burns, producing thrust. From ignition to maximum burn rate,
the burn area increases from the initial ignition area to the full surface area of the fuel. This maximum burn rate occurs at time t_{peak}. As
fuel burns off, the surface area reduces again until the fuel is consumed. The ballistics application normalizes time so that time is 0 at
ignition and 1 when the burning stops, so t_{peak} is a number between 0
and 1.

Oozinoz uses one set of burn rate and thrust equations:

$$rate = 25^{-(t - t_{peak})^2}$$

$$thrust = 1.7 \cdot \left(\frac{rate}{0.6}\right)^{1/0.3}$$

The application in Figure 9.1 shows how t_{peak} affects the burn rate
and thrust of a rocket. As a user moves the slider, the value of t_{peak}
changes, and the curves take on new shapes. Figure 9.2 shows the primary classes that make up the application.

The ShowBallistics class and the BallisticsPanel class are members of the app.observer.ballistics package. The BallisticsFunction interface is a member of the com.oozinoz.ballistics package. That package also contains a Ballistics utility class that provides the instances of BallisticsFunction that define the burn rate and thrust curves.

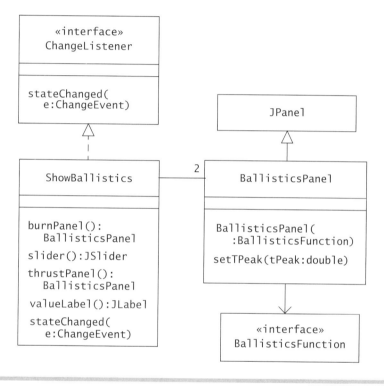

FIGURE 9.2 The ballistics application registers itself to receive slider events.

When the ballistics application initializes the slider, the application registers itself to receive slider events. When the slider changes, the application updates the panels that show the curves and updates the label that shows the value of t_{peak}.

CHALLENGE 9.1

Complete the `slider()` and `stateChanged()` methods for
ShowBallistics so that the ballistics panels and the t_{peak} label
reflect the slider's value.

```
public JSlider slider() {
    if (slider == null) {
        slider = new JSlider();
        sliderMax = slider.getMaximum();
        sliderMin = slider.getMinimum();
        slider.addChangeListener( ?? );
        slider.setValue(slider.getMinimum());
    }
    return slider;
}

public void stateChanged(ChangeEvent e) {
    double val = slider.getValue();
    double tp = (val - sliderMin) / (sliderMax - sliderMin);
    burnPanel(). ?? ( ?? );
    thrustPanel(). ?? ( ?? );
    valueLabel(). ?? ( ?? );
}
```

A solution appears on page 366.

The ShowBallistics class updates the burn panel, thrust panel, and
value label objects that depend on the slider's value. This is not
uncommon and not necessarily bad, but note that it completely
undoes the intent of OBSERVER. Swing applies OBSERVER so that the
slider is not responsible for knowing which clients are interested in it.
But the ShowBallistics application puts us back in the situation we
had hoped to avoid: A single object—the application—knows which
objects to update and takes responsibility for doling out the appropriate invocations instead of letting each dependent object register itself.

To create a more fine-grained OBSERVER, you can make a few changes
in the code to let each interested component register itself to receive
the slider's change events.

CHALLENGE 9.2

Provide a new class diagram showing a design that lets each
interested object register for slider events. Be sure to account for the
label that shows the slider's value.

A solution appears on page 367.

In this design, you can move the calls to addChangeListener() out of
the slider() method and into the constructors of the dependent
components:

```
public BallisticsPanel2(
        BallisticsFunction func,
        JSlider slider) {
    this.func = func;
    this.slider = slider;
    slider.addChangeListener(this);
}
```

When the slider changes, the BallisticsPanel2 object is notified.
The label recalculates its tPeak value and repaints itself:

```
public void stateChanged(ChangeEvent e) {
    double val = slider.getValue();
    double max = slider.getMaximum();
    double min = slider.getMinimum();
    tPeak = (val - min) / (max - min);
    repaint();
}
```

A new problem emerges in this refactoring. The design adjusts
responsibilities so that each interested object registers for and reacts
to changes in the slider. The distribution of responsibility is good,
but now each component that listens to the slider needs to recalcu-
late the value of tPeak. In particular, if you use a BallisticsLabel2
class—as the solution to Challenge 9.2 does—its stateChanged()
method will be nearly identical to the stateChanged() method of
BallisticsPanel2. To consolidate this duplicated code, we can
refactor again, extracting an underlying domain object from the
current design.

We can simplify the system by introducing a Tpeak class to contain the critical peak time value. We will let the application listen to the slider and update a Tpeak object and have all other interested components listen to the value of this object. This approach becomes a **Model/View/Controller** (MVC) design. (See [Buschmann et al. 1996] for a deeper discussion of the MVC approach.)

Model/View/Controller

As applications and systems grow, it is important to divide and redivide responsibility so that classes and packages stay small enough to maintain. The phrase *Model/View/Controller* refers to separating an interesting object—the model—from GUI elements that portray and manipulate it—the view and controller. Java can support this separation with listeners, but as the previous section shows, not all designs that use listeners are MVC designs.

The initial versions of the ShowBallistics application combine intelligence about an application GUI with information about ballistics. You can refactor this code, following MVC to divide this application's responsibilities. In this refactoring, the revised ShowBallistics class should retain the views and controllers in its GUI elements.

The creators of MVC envisioned that the look of a component (its *view*) might be separable from its feel (its *controller*). In practice, the appearance of a GUI component and its support for user interaction are tightly coupled, and typical use of Swing does not divide views from controllers. (If you delve more into the internals of Swing look-and-feel, you may see this division emerge.) The value of MVC is to push the *model* out of an application into its own domain.

The *model* in the ShowBallistics application is the tPeak value. To refactor to MVC, we might introduce a Tpeak class that would hold a peak time value and would allow interested listeners to register for change events. Such a class might look as follows:

```
package app.observer.ballistics3;
import java.util.Observable;

public class Tpeak extends Observable {
    protected double value;
```

```
        public Tpeak(double value) {
            this.value = value;
        }

        public double getValue() {
            return value;
        }

        public void setValue(double value) {
            this.value = value;
            setChanged();
            notifyObservers();
        }
    }
}
```

If you were to review this code at an Oozinoz code review, a key point would likely arise: Almost none of this code relates to the time at which a rocket engine's fuel burn rate peaks. In fact, this code looks like a fairly generic utility for holding a value and for alerting listeners when the value changes. We can refactor the code to mine out that genericity, but first, it is worth looking at a revised design that uses the Tpeak class.

Now we can create a design in which the application watches the slider, and everything else watches a Tpeak object. When the slider moves, the application sets a new value in the Tpeak object. The panels and the text box listen to the Tpeak object and update themselves when the value changes. The BurnRate and Thrust classes use the Tpeak object to calculate their functions, but they don't need to listen to—that is, register for—events.

CHALLENGE 9.3

Create a class diagram that shows the application depending on the slider and the text box and plotting panels depending on a Tpeak object.

A solution appears on page 368.

This design allows for the work of translating the slider's value into peak time value to be done once. The application updates a single Tpeak object, and all GUI objects that listen for change can query the Tpeak object for its new value.

However, the Tpeak class does little more than hold a value, so we want to try factoring out a value-holder class. In addition, it is likely that an observed number, such as peak time, is not a stand-alone value but rather is the attribute of a domain object. For example, peak time is an attribute of a rocket engine. We might want to improve our design to separate our classes, with a value-holding class that lets GUI objects observe domain objects.

When you divide GUI objects from domain objects, or **business objects**, you can create layers of code. A **layer** is a group of classes with similar responsibilities, often collected in a single Java package. Higher layers, such as a GUI layer, usually depend only on classes in equal or lower layers. Layering usually includes a clear definition of the interfaces between layers, such as a GUI and the business objects it represents. You can reorganize the responsibilities of the Show-Ballistics code, achieving a layered system, as Figure 9.3 shows.

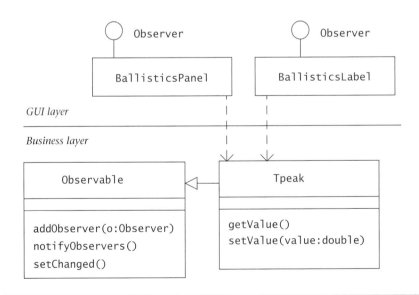

FIGURE 9.3 By creating an observable Tpeak class, you can separate a business logic layer from a GUI layer.

The design that Figure 9.3 illustrates creates a Tpeak class to model the t_{peak} value that is the critical value in the ballistics equations that the application displays. The BallisticsPanel and BallisticsLabel classes *depend* on Tpeak. Rather than making a Tpeak object responsible for updating GUI elements, the design applies OBSERVER so that interested objects can register for notification when Tpeak changes. The Java class libraries support this, providing an Observable class and an Observer interface in the java.util package. The Tpeak class can subclass Observable and can update its observers when its value changes:

```
public void setValue(double value) {
    this.value = value;
    setChanged();
    notifyObservers();
}
```

Note that you have to call setChanged() so that the notify-Observers() method, inherited from Observable, will broadcast the change.

The notifyObservers() method calls the update() method of each registered observer. The update() method is a requirement for implementers of the Observer interface, as Figure 9.4 shows.

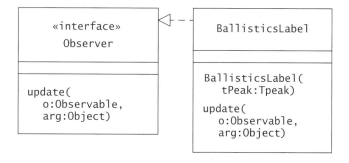

FIGURE 9.4 A BallisticsLabel is an Observer; it can register its interest in an Observable object so that the label's update() method is called when the Observable object changes.

A `BallisticsLabel` object need not retain a reference to the `Tpeak` object it observes. Rather, the `BallisticsLabel` constructor can register for updates when the `Tpeak` object changes. The label's `update()` method will receive the `Tpeak` object as its `Observable` argument. The method can cast the argument to `Tpeak`, extract the new value, change the label's text, and repaint.

CHALLENGE 9.4

Write the complete code for `BallisticsLabel.java`.

A solution appears on page 369.

The new design of the ballistics application separates a business object from the GUI elements that represent it. This design has two requirements to work.

1. Implementations of `Observer` must register their interest and must update themselves appropriately, often including repainting themselves.

2. Subclasses of `Observable` must remember to notify observers when their values change.

These two steps set up most of the wiring you need across layers in the ballistics application. You also need to arrange for a `Tpeak` object to change when the application's slider changes. You can achieve this by instantiating an anonymous subclass of `ChangeListener`.

CHALLENGE 9.5

Suppose that tPeak is an instance of Tpeak and an attribute of the ShowBallistics3 class. Complete the code for ShowBallistics3. slider() so that the slider's changes update tPeak:

```
public JSlider slider() {
    if (slider == null) {
        slider = new JSlider();
        sliderMax = slider.getMaximum();
        sliderMin = slider.getMinimum();
        slider.addChangeListener
            (
                new ChangeListener()
                {

                    // Challenge!

                }
            );
        slider.setValue(slider.getMinimum());
    }
    return slider;
}
```

A solution appears on page 369.

When you apply MVC, the flow of events may seem indirect. Slider movement in the ballistics application causes a ChangeListener to update a Tpeak object. In turn, a change in the Tpeak object notifies the application's label and panels, and these objects repaint themselves. Change propagates from the GUI layer to the business layer and back up to the GUI layer.

CHALLENGE 9.6

Fill in the messages in Figure 9.5.

A solution appears on page 370.

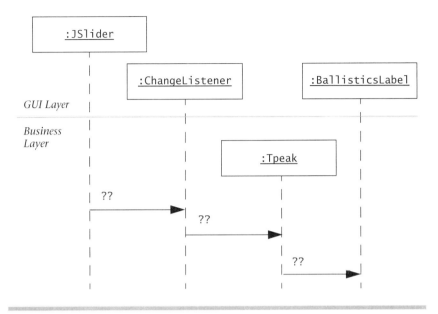

FIGURE 9.5 MVC causes calls to pass from a GUI layer into a business layer and back into the GUI layer.

The payback for a layered design is in the value of the interface and in the independence that you get between the layers. The layering of code is a layering of responsibility, which makes the code easier to maintain. For example, in the ballistics example, you can add a second GUI, perhaps for a handheld device, without having to change classes in the business object layer. In the business object layer, you might add a new source of change that updates a Tpeak object. In this case, the OBSERVER mechanics you have in place will automatically update objects in the GUI layer.

Layering also opens the possibility of arranging for different layers to execute on different computers. A layer or set of layers executing on a computer is a **tier** in an *n*-tier system. An *n*-tier design can reduce the amount of code that must execute on a user's desktop. It also lets you make changes in business classes without updating software on user machines, greatly simplifying deployment. However, sending messages between computers is not free, and you must make a move to an *n*-tier deployment judiciously. For example, you probably could not afford for users to wait as scroll events travel back and forth between a user's desktop and a server. In such a case, you would probably have to let scrolling occur on the user's machine, with a decision to commit to a new peak-time value left as a separate user action.

In short, OBSERVER supports MVC, which also encourages layering of software, which brings many practical advantages to software development and deployment.

Maintaining an Observable Object

You may not always be able to make the class you want to observe a subclass of Observable. In particular, your class may already be a subclass of something other than Object. In that case, you can provide your class with an Observable object and have your class forward key method calls to it. The Component class in java.awt uses this approach but uses a PropertyChangeSupport object instead of an Observable object.

The PropertyChangeSupport class is quite similar to the Observable class but is part of the java.beans package. The JavaBeans API exists to support the creation of reusable components. This API has found its greatest applicability to GUI components, but you can certainly apply it elsewhere. The Component class uses a PropertyChangeSupport object to let interested observers register for notification of changes in the properties of labels, panels, and other GUI components. Figure 9.6 shows the relationship between the Component class from java.awt and the PropertyChangeSupport class.

PropertyChangeSupport demonstrates an issue you will have to address in your use of OBSERVER: How much detail does the observed class go into explaining what changed? This class uses a *push* approach, whereby the model gives details of what happened. (In Property-ChangeSupport, the notification says that a property changed from this old value to that new value.) An alternative is the *pull* approach, where the model tells observers it changed, but they have to query the model to figure out how. Either choice can be appropriate. The push approach can be more work to develop and couples observers to the observed but offers the chance of better performance.

The Component class duplicates part of the interface of the PropertyChangeSupport class. These methods in Component each forward the message call to an instance of the PropertyChange-Support class.

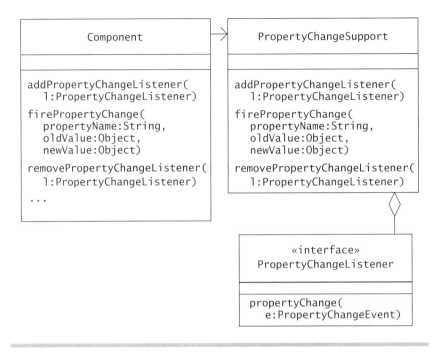

FIGURE 9.6 A Component object maintains a PropertyChangeSupport object that maintains a collection of listeners.

CHALLENGE 9.7

Complete the class diagram in Figure 9.7 to show Tpeak using a PropertyChangeSupport object to manage listeners.

A solution appears on page 371.

Whether you use Observer, PropertyChangeSupport, or another class to establish the OBSERVER pattern, the point is to define a one-to-many dependency between objects. When one object changes state, all its dependents are notified and updated automatically. This limits the responsibility and eases the maintenance of both interesting objects and their interested observers.

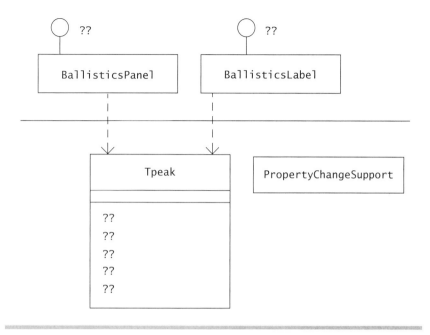

FIGURE 9.7 A Tpeak business object can delegate calls that affect listeners to a PropertyChangeSupport object.

Summary

The OBSERVER pattern appears frequently in GUI applications and is a fundamental pattern in Java's GUI libraries. With these components, you never have to change or subclass a component class simply to communicate its events to an interested object. For small applications, a common practice is to register a single object—the application—to receive all the events in a GUI. There is no inherent problem with this, but you should recognize that it reverses the distribution of responsibility that OBSERVER intends. For a large GUI, consider moving to an MVC design, letting each interested object register for events rather than introducing a mediating central object. MVC also lets you create loosely coupled layers that can change independently and that may execute on different machines.

10

MEDIATOR

ORDINARY OBJECT-ORIENTED development distributes responsibility as far as it will go, with each object doing its own work independently. For example, the OBSERVER pattern supports this distribution by minimizing the responsibility of an object that other objects find interesting. The SINGLETON pattern resists the distribution of responsibility and lets you centralize responsibility in particular objects that clients locate and reuse. Like SINGLETON, the MEDIATOR pattern centralizes responsibility, but for a particular set of objects rather than for all the clients in a system.

When the interactions between the objects gravitate toward the complex condition whereby every object in a group is aware of every other object in that group, it is useful to provide a central authority. Centralization of responsibility is also useful when the logic surrounding the interactions of the related objects is independent from the other behavior of the objects.

The intent of the MEDIATOR pattern is to define an object that encapsulates how a set of objects interact; this promotes loose coupling, keeping the objects from referring to one another explicitly, and lets you vary their interaction independently.

A Classic Example: GUI Mediators

You will probably encounter the MEDIATOR pattern most often when you develop an application with a GUI. Such applications tend to become *thick*, gathering code that you can refactor into other classes. The ShowFlight class in Chapter 4, FACADE, initially performed three roles. Before you refactored it, this class acted as a display panel, a complete GUI application, and a flight path calculator. After refactoring, the application that launches the flight panel display became

simple, containing only a few lines of code. Large applications, however, can remain complex after this type of refactoring, even when
they contain only the logic that creates components and that
arranges for the components' interaction. Consider the application in
Figure 10.1.

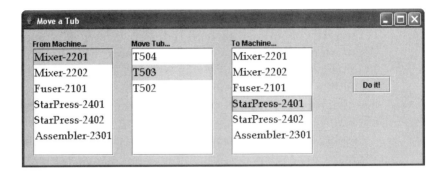

FIGURE 10.1 This application lets its user manually update the location of a tub of
chemicals.

Oozinoz stores chemical batches in rubber tubs. Machines at Oozinoz
read bar codes on the tubs to keep track of where tubs are in the factory. Sometimes, a manual override is necessary, particularly when
humans move a tub instead of waiting for a robot to transfer it.
Figure 10.1 shows a new, partially developed application that lets a
user specify the machine at which a tub is located.

In the MoveATub application—in package app.mediator.moveATub—
when the user selects one of the machines in the left-hand list, the list
of tubs changes to show the tubs at that machine. The user can then
select one of these tubs, select a target machine, and click the Do it!
button to update the location of the tub. Figure 10.2 shows some of
the application class.

The developer working on this application created it initially with a
wizard and has begun refactoring it. About half of the methods in

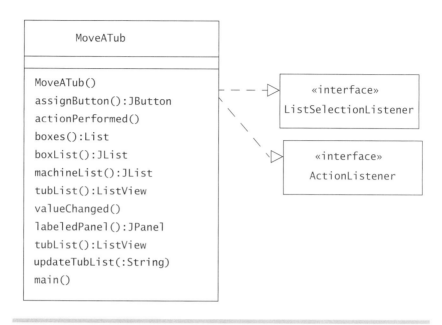

FIGURE 10.2 The MoveATub class has a mix of component-building, event-handling, and mock database methods.

MoveATub exist to lazy-initialize variables that contain the application's GUI components. The assignButton() method is typical:

```
private JButton assignButton() {
    if (assignButton == null) {
        assignButton = new JButton("Do it!");
        assignButton.setEnabled(false);
        assignButton.addActionListener(this);
    }
    return assignButton;
}
```

The programmer has already eliminated the hard-coded numbers that the wizard generated to specify the button's location and size. But the immediate problem is that the MoveATub class has a large number of methods mixing several purposes.

Most of the static methods provide a mock database of tub names and machine names. The developer will eventually drop this approach of working with only names and upgrade the application to work with Tub objects and Machine objects. Most of the remaining methods in the application contain logic that handles the application's events. For example, the valueChanged() method manages whether the assign button is enabled:

```
public void valueChanged(ListSelectionEvent e) {
    // ...
    assignButton().setEnabled(
            ! tubList().isSelectionEmpty()
        && ! machineList().isSelectionEmpty());
}
```

We might consider moving valueChanged() and the other event-handling methods into a separate mediator class. We should first note that the MEDIATOR pattern is already at work in this class: Components do not update one another directly. For example, neither the machine nor the list components update the assign button directly. Rather, the MoveATub application registers for the lists' selection events and then updates the button, based on whether items from both lists are selected. In the tub-moving application, a MoveATub object acts as a mediator, receiving events and dispatching corresponding actions.

The mechanics of the Java class libraries nudge you into using a mediator, although nothing in the JCL requires that an application must be its own mediator. Instead of mingling component-creation methods with event-handling methods and with mock database methods all in one class, you can move an application's methods into classes with separate specializations.

CHALLENGE 10.1

Complete the diagram in Figure 10.3 to show a refactoring of MoveATub, introducing a separate mock database class and a mediator class to receive the events of the MoveATub GUI.

A solution appears on page 372.

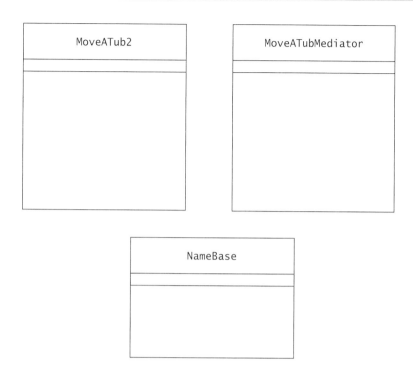

FIGURE 10.3 Separate the component-building, event-handling, and mock database parts of the application.

The refactoring consolidates the mediator into a separate class, letting you develop it and focus on it separately. Now when the MoveATub application runs, components pass events to a MoveATubMediator object. The mediator may take action on non-GUI objects: for example, to update the database when an assignment is made. The mediator object may also call back components in the GUI: for example, to disable the button after the assignment is made.

CHALLENGE 10.2

Draw a diagram that shows what happens when the user clicks the Do it! button. Show whichever objects you think are most important, and show the messages that pass between these objects.

A solution appears on page 373.

GUI components may apply the MEDIATOR pattern as a matter of course, notifying a mediator when events occur rather than taking responsibility for updating other components directly. GUI applications give rise to perhaps the most common application of the MEDIATOR pattern, but there are other cases in which you may want to introduce a mediator.

Whenever the interaction of a set of objects is complex, you can centralize the responsibility for this interaction in a mediator object that stands outside the interacting group. This promotes **loose coupling**—a reduction in the responsibility that the interacting objects bear to one another. Managing the interaction of objects in an independent class also has the advantage of simplifying and standardizing the interaction rules. One example of the value of a mediator occurs when you need to manage relational integrity.

Mediators of Relational Integrity

Part of the strength of the object-oriented paradigm is that it lets you easily map connections between Java objects and objects in the real world. However, a Java object model's ability to reflect the real world has at least two fundamental deficits. First, objects in the real world vary with time, but Java has no built-in support for this. For example, assignment statements obliterate any previous value instead of remembering it, as a human might. Second, in the real world, relations are as important as objects, but relations receive little support in today's object-oriented languages, including Java. For example, there is no built-in support for the fact that if Star Press 2402 is in Bay 1, Bay 1 must contain Star Press 2402. In fact, it is quite possible for such relations to go awry, which in turn invites the application of the MEDIATOR pattern.

Consider rubber tubs of chemicals at Oozinoz. Tubs are always assigned to a particular machine. You can model this relationship with a table, as Table 10.1 shows.

Table 10.1 shows the **relation** of tubs and machines—the way in which they stand with regard to each other. Mathematically, a relation is a subset of all ordered pairs of objects, so there is a relation of tubs to machines and a relation of machines to tubs. Keeping the Tub

TABLE 10.1 Recording Relational Information in a Table to Preserve Relational Integrity.

TUB	MACHINE
T305	StarPress-2402
T308	StarPress-2402
T377	ShellAssembler-2301
T379	ShellAssembler-2301
T389	ShellAssembler-2301
T001	Fuser-2101
T002	Fuser-2101

column in the table unique guarantees that no tub can appear on two machines at once.

See the sidebar Relational Integrity for a stricter definition of relational consistency in an object model.

Relational Integrity

An object model is *relationally consistent* if every time object **a** points to object **b**, object **b** points to object **a**.

For a more rigorous definition, consider two classes, **Alpha** and **Beta**. Let A represent the set of model objects that are instances of class **Alpha**, and let B represent the set of objects that are instances of class **Beta**. Let **a** and **b** denote members of A and B, and let the *ordered pair* (**a**, **b**) denote that object **a** $\in$ A has a reference to object **b** $\in$ B. This reference may be either a direct reference or one of a set of references, as when object **a** has a **List** object that includes **b**.

The *Cartesian product* A $\times$ B is the set of all possible ordered pairs (**a**, **b**) with **a** $\in$ A and **b** $\in$ B. The sets A and B allow the two Cartesian products A $\times$ B and B $\times$ A. An *object model relation* on A and B is the subset of A $\times$ B that exists in an object model. Let AB denote this subset, and let BA denote the subset of B $\times$ A that exists in the model.

Any binary relation R ⊆ A × B has an *inverse* R⁻¹ ⊆ B × A defined by:

$$(b, a) \in R^{-1} \text{ if and only if } (a, b) \in R$$

The inverse of AB provides the set of references that must occur from instances of B to instances of A if the object model is consistent. In other words, instances of classes **Alpha** and **Beta** are relationally consistent if and only if BA is the inverse of AB.

When you record tub and machine relational information in a table, you can guarantee that each tub is on only one machine by enforcing the restriction that each tub occur only once in the Tub column. One way to do this is to make the Tub column the primary key of the table in a relational database. With this model, as in reality, a tub cannot appear on two machines at once: $(b, a) \in R^{-1}$ if and only if $(a, b) \in R$.

An object model cannot guarantee relational integrity as easily as a relational model can. Consider the MoveATub application. The developer working on its design will eventually stop working with only names and will begin working with Tub objects and Machine objects. When a real tub is near a real machine, the object representing the tub will have a reference to the object representing the machine. Each Machine object will have a collection of Tub objects representing tubs near the machine. Figure 10.4 shows a typical object model.

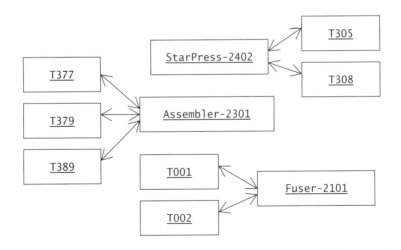

FIGURE 10.4 An object model distributes information about relations.

The arrowheads in Figure 10.4 emphasize that tubs know about machines and that machines know about tubs. The information about the relationship of tubs and machines is now distributed across many objects instead of being in a central table. The distribution of the tub/machine relationship makes the management of the relationship more difficult and makes this management a candidate for application of the MEDIATOR pattern.

Consider a defect that occurred at Oozinoz when a developer began modeling a new machine that included a bar code reader for identifying tubs. After scanning a tub for its ID, the developer set the location of tub t to machine m with the following code:

```
// Tell tub about machine, and machine about tub
t.setMachine(m);
m.addTub(t);
```

CHALLENGE 10.3

Assume that the objects begin as shown in Figure 10.4. Suppose that the object t represents tub T308 and that the object m represents the machine Fuser-2101. Complete the object diagram in Figure 10.5, showing the effects of the code that updates the tub's location. What defect does this reveal?

A solution appears on page 374.

The easiest way to guarantee relational integrity is to pull the relational information back into a single table managed by a mediating object. Instead of having tubs know about machines and machines know about tubs, you can give all these objects a reference to a mediator that keeps a single table of tubs and machines. This "table" can be an instance of the Map class (from java.util). Figure 10.6 shows a class diagram with a mediator in place.

The Tub class has a location that allows for recording which machine a tub is near. The code ensures that a tub can be in only one place at

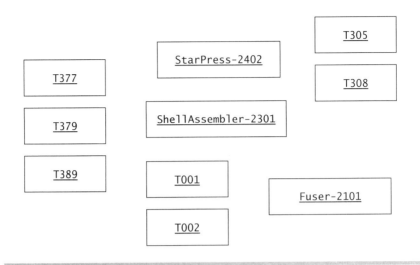

FIGURE 10.5 When completed, this diagram will show the flaw in a developer's code that updates a tub's location.

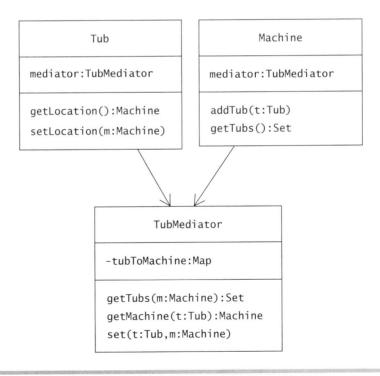

FIGURE 10.6 Tub and Machine objects rely on a mediator to control the relationship between tubs and machines.

one time, using a TubMediator object to manage the tub/machine relation:

```
package com.oozinoz.machine;
public class Tub {
    private String id;
    private TubMediator mediator = null;

    public Tub(String id, TubMediator mediator) {
        this.id = id;
        this.mediator = mediator;
    }



    public Machine getLocation() {
        return mediator.getMachine(this);
    }

    public void setLocation(Machine value) {
        mediator.set(this, value);
    }

    public String toString() {
        return id;
    }

    public int hashCode() {
        // ...
    }

    public boolean equals(Object obj) {
            // ...
    }
}
```

The Tub class's setLocation() method uses a mediator to update a tub's location, delegating responsibility for maintaining relational integrity to the mediator. The Tub class implements the hashCode() and equals() methods so that Tub objects will store properly in a hash table. The detail for this code is as follows:

```
public int hashCode() {
    return id.hashCode();
}
```

```
public boolean equals(Object obj) {
    if (obj == this) return true;

    if (obj.getClass() != Tub.class)
        return false;

    Tub that = (Tub) obj;
    return id.equals(that.id);
}
```

The TubMediator class uses a Map object to store the tub/machine relationship. By storing the relation in a table, the mediator can guarantee that the object model never allows two machines to possess a
single tub:

```
public class TubMediator {
    protected Map tubToMachine = new HashMap();

    public Machine getMachine(Tub t) {
        // Challenge!
    }

    public Set getTubs(Machine m) {
        Set set = new HashSet();
        Iterator i = tubToMachine.entrySet().iterator();
        while (i.hasNext()) {
            Map.Entry e = (Map.Entry) i.next();
            if (e.getValue().equals(m))
                set.add(e.getKey());
        }
        return set;
    }

    public void set(Tub t, Machine m) {
        // Challenge!
    }
}
```

CHALLENGE 10.4

Write the code for the TubMediator methods getMachine() and
set().

A solution appears on page 375.

Rather than introducing a mediator class, you could ensure that tubs never appear on two machines at once by placing the logic inside the code for the Tub and Machine classes. However, this logic pertains to relational integrity and has little to do with how chemical tubs and factory machines work. The logic is also error prone. In particular, a common error would be to move a tub to a new machine, updating the tub and machine, but forgetting to update the machine that was the tub's previous location.

Moving the relation-management code to a mediator lets an independent class encapsulate the logic for how this set of objects interact. In the mediator, it is easy to ensure that changing a Tub object's location automatically moves the tub away from its current machine. The following JUnit test code, from TubTest.java, shows this behavior:

```java
public void testLocationChange() {
    TubMediator mediator = new TubMediator();
    Tub t = new Tub("T403", mediator);
    Machine m1 = new Fuser(1001, mediator);
    Machine m2 = new Fuser(1002, mediator);

    t.setLocation(m1);
    assertTrue(m1.getTubs().contains(t));
    assertTrue(!m2.getTubs().contains(t));

    t.setLocation(m2);
    assertFalse(m1.getTubs().contains(t));
    assertTrue(m2.getTubs().contains(t));
}
```

When you have an object model that is not tied to a relational database, you can use mediators to sustain the relational integrity of your model. Moving the relation-management logic into mediators lets these classes specialize in maintaining relational integrity.

CHALLENGE 10.5

With respect to moving logic out of one class and into a new one, MEDIATOR is similar to other patterns. List two other patterns that may involve refactoring an aspect of behavior out of an existing class or hierarchy.

A solution appears on page 375.

Summary

The MEDIATOR pattern promotes loose coupling, keeping related objects from referring to one another explicitly. MEDIATOR shows up most often in GUI application development, where you don't want to manage the complexity of individual widgets updating one another. The architecture of Java guides you in this direction, encouraging you to define objects that register for GUI events. If you are developing user interfaces with Java, you are probably applying MEDIATOR.

Although it may nudge you into using MEDIATOR when creating a GUI, Java does not require you to move this mediation outside an application class. Doing so can simplify your code. You can let a mediator class concentrate on the interaction between GUI components and let an application class concentrate on component construction.

There are other cases in which you can benefit from introducing a mediator object. For example, you might need a mediator to centralize responsibility for maintaining the relational integrity in an object model. You can apply MEDIATOR whenever you need to define an object that encapsulates how a set of objects interact.

11

PROXY

AN ORDINARY OBJECT does its own work in support of the public inter-face that it advertises. It can happen, though, that a legitimate object cannot live up to this ordinary responsibility. This may occur when an object takes a long time to load, when the object is running on another computer, or when you need to intercept messages to the object. In these cases, a *proxy* object can take the responsibility that a client expects and forward requests appropriately to an underlying target object.

The intent of the PROXY pattern is to control access to an object by providing a surrogate, or placeholder, for it.

A Classic Example: Image Proxies

A proxy object usually has an interface that is nearly identical to the interface of the object it is a proxy, or substitute, for. The proxy does its work by judiciously forwarding requests to the underlying object that the proxy controls access to. A classic example of the PROXY pattern relates to avoiding the expense of loading large images into memory. Suppose that images in an application belong in pages or panels that do not initially display. To avoid loading all the images before they are needed, you might let proxies for the images act as placeholders that load the required images on demand. This section provides an example of an image proxy. But note that designs that use PROXY are sometimes brittle, because they rely on forwarding method calls to underlying objects. This forwarding may create a fragile, high-maintenance design.

Suppose that an Oozinoz engineer is working on an image proxy that will, for performance reasons, show a small, temporary image while a larger image is loading. The engineer has a prototype working

(Figure 11.1). The code for this application is in the ShowProxy class in the app.proxy package. The underlying code that supports the application is in the com.oozinoz.imaging package.

FIGURE 11.1 Three screen shots show a mini-application before, during, and after loading a large image. (Image is in the public domain. Library of Congress, Prints and Photographs Division, Gottscho-Schleisner Collection [LC-G605-CT-00488].)

The user interface displays one of three images: one that indicates that loading has not begun, one that indicates that the real image is loading, or the real image. When the application starts, it shows Absent, a JPEG image that you have built in an image-processing tool. When the user clicks Load, the image changes almost instantly to a prebuilt Loading... image. After a few moments, the desired image appears.

An easy way to display an image saved in, say, a JPEG file is to use an `ImageIcon` object as an argument to a "label" that will show the image:

```
ImageIcon icon = new ImageIcon("images/fest.jpg");
JLabel label = new JLabel(icon);
```

In the application that you are building, you want to pass into `JLabel` a proxy that will forward painting requests to (1) an "absent" image, (2) a "loading" image, or (3) the desired image. The message flow might look like the sequence diagram in Figure 11.2.

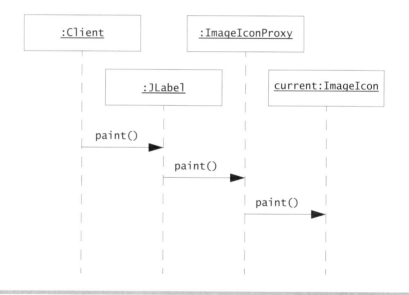

FIGURE 11.2 An `ImageIconProxy` object forwards `paint()` requests to the current `ImageIcon` object.

When the user clicks Load, your code will cause the `ImageIconProxy` object to change its current image to the Loading... image. The proxy will also begin loading the desired image. When the desired image is completely loaded, the `ImageIconProxy` object will change its current image to be the desired image.

To set up a proxy, you can create a subclass of ImageIcon, as Figure 11.3 shows. The code for ImageIconProxy defines two static variables that contain the Absent and Loading... images:

```
static final ImageIcon ABSENT = new ImageIcon(
    ClassLoader.getSystemResource("images/absent.jpg"));

static final ImageIcon LOADING = new ImageIcon(
    ClassLoader.getSystemResource("images/loading.jpg"));
```

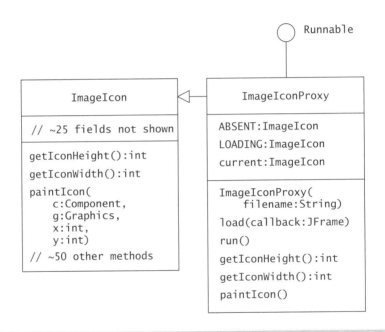

FIGURE 11.3 An ImageIconProxy object can stand in for an ImageIcon object because an ImageIconProxy object *is* an ImageIcon object.

The constructor for ImageIconProxy accepts the name of an image file to eventually load. When an ImageIconProxy object's load() method is called, it sets the image to LOADING and starts a separate thread to load the image. Using a separate thread keeps the application from waiting while the image loads. The load() method accepts a JFrame object that the run() method calls back once the desired image is loaded. The almost-complete code for ImageIconProxy.java is:

```java
package com.oozinoz.imaging;
import java.awt.*;
import javax.swing.*;

public class ImageIconProxy
        extends ImageIcon implements Runnable {
    static final ImageIcon ABSENT = new ImageIcon(
        ClassLoader.getSystemResource("images/absent.jpg"));
    static final ImageIcon LOADING = new ImageIcon(
        ClassLoader.getSystemResource("images/loading.jpg"));
    ImageIcon current = ABSENT;
    protected String filename;
    protected JFrame callbackFrame;

    public ImageIconProxy(String filename) {
        super(ABSENT.getImage());
        this.filename = filename;
    }

    public void load(JFrame callbackFrame) {
        this.callbackFrame = callbackFrame;
        current = LOADING;
        callbackFrame.repaint();
        new Thread(this).start();
    }

    public void run() {
        current = new ImageIcon(
                ClassLoader.getSystemResource(filename));
        callbackFrame.pack();
    }

    public int getIconHeight() { /* Challenge! */ }

    public int getIconWidth() {  /* Challenge! */ }

    public synchronized void paintIcon(
            Component c, Graphics g, int x, int y) {
        // Challenge!
    }
}
```

CHALLENGE 11.1

An `ImageIconProxy` object accepts three image display calls that it must pass on to the current image. Write the code for `getIconHeight()`, `getIconWidth()`, and `paintIcon()` for the `ImageIconProxy` class.

A solution appears on page 376.

Suppose that you get the code working for this small demonstration application. Before you build the real application, which has more than just a Load button, you hold a design review, and the fragility of your design comes to light.

CHALLENGE 11.2

The `ImageIconProxy` class is *not* a well-designed, reusable component. Point out two problems with the design.

A solution appears on page 376.

As you review someone's design, you must concurrently form an understanding of the design and your opinion of the design. When you encounter a developer who feels that he or she is using a specific design pattern, you may disagree about whether the pattern is present. In this example, the PROXY pattern is evident but does not demonstrate that the design is good; in fact, much better designs exist. When the PROXY pattern appears in a design, its presence should be justified, because the use of forwarding can create problems that other designs may avoid. As you read the next section, you should form an opinion about whether PROXY is a desirable choice.

Image Proxies Reconsidered

At this point, you might ask whether design patterns have helped you. You faithfully implemented a pattern, and now you're looking at tearing it out. In fact, this is natural and healthy, although it happens more often in real development than in books. An author—with the help of reviewers—can rethink and replace an inferior design before any reader sees it. In practice, a design pattern can help you get an application running and can facilitate the discussion of your design. In the `ImageIconProxy` example at Oozinoz, the pattern has served its purpose, even though it is much simpler to achieve the effect you desire without a literal implementation of a proxy.

The `ImageIcon` class operates on an `Image` object. Rather than forwarding painting requests to a separate `ImageIcon` object, it is easier to operate on the `Image` object that `ImageIcon` wraps. Figure 11.4 shows an `LoadingImageIcon` class—from `com.oozinoz.imaging`—that has only two methods beyond its constructor: `load()` and `run()`.

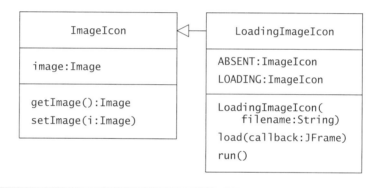

FIGURE 11.4 The `LoadingImageIcon` class works by switching the `Image` object that it holds.

The `load()` method in this revised class still receives a `JFrame` object to call back after the desired image is loaded. When `load()` executes, it calls `setImage()` with the image held by `LOADING`, repaints the frame, and starts a separate thread for itself. The `run()` method, executing in a separate thread, creates a new `ImageIcon` object for the file named in the constructor, calls `setImage()` with the image held by this object, and repacks the frame.

The almost-complete code for `LoadingImageIcon.java` is:

```
package com.oozinoz.imaging;
import javax.swing.ImageIcon;
import javax.swing.JFrame;
```

```
public class LoadingImageIcon
       extends ImageIcon implements Runnable {
    static final ImageIcon ABSENT = new ImageIcon(
            ClassLoader.getSystemResource("images/absent.jpg"));
    static final ImageIcon LOADING = new ImageIcon(
            ClassLoader.getSystemResource("images/loading.jpg"));
    protected String filename;
    protected JFrame callbackFrame;

    public LoadingImageIcon(String filename) {
        super(ABSENT.getImage());
        this.filename = filename;
    }

    public void load(JFrame callbackFrame) {
        // Challenge!
    }

    public void run() {
            // Challenge!
    }
}
```

CHALLENGE 11.3

Fill in the code for load() and run() in LoadingImageIcon.

A solution appears on page 377.

The revised code is less coupled to the design of ImageIcon, relying primarily on getImage() and setImage() rather than on the mechanics of which methods to forward. In fact, no forwarding exists: LoadingImageIcon is a proxy in spirit but not in structure.

The Proxy pattern's reliance on forwarding can create a maintenance burden. For example, should the underlying object change, the Oozinoz team will have to update the proxy. To avoid this burden, you should usually consider alternatives to Proxy, but there will be times when Proxy is the right choice. In particular, when the object for which you need to intercept messages is executing on another machine, there may be no substitute for Proxy.

Remote Proxies

When an object whose method you want to call is running on another computer, you cannot call the method directly, so you must find another way to communicate with it. You could open a socket on the remote machine and devise some protocol to pass messages to the remote object. Ideally, such a scheme would let you pass messages in almost the same way as if the object were local. You should be able to call methods on a proxy object that forwards the calls to the real object on the remote machine. In fact, such schemes have been realized, notably in **CORBA** (Common Object Request Broker Architecture), in ASP.NET (Active Server Pages for .NET), and in Java's **Remote Method Invocation** (RMI).

RMI makes it fairly easy for a client to obtain a proxy object that forwards calls to a desired object that is active on another computer. It is well worth learning about RMI, as it is part of the underpinning of the **Enterprise JavaBeans** (EJB) specification, an important industry standard. Regardless of how industry standards evolve, the role of PROXY in distributed computing will continue into the foreseeable future, and RMI provides a good example of this pattern in action.

To experiment with RMI, you will need a good reference on this topic, such as *Java™ Enterprise in a Nutshell* [Flanagan et al. 2002]. The following example is not a tutorial on RMI but merely points out the presence and value of PROXY within RMI applications. RMI and EJB bring in a number of new design concerns; you can't simply make every object remote and get a reasonable system. We won't go into those challenges; we'll simply explore how RMI is a great example of PROXY.

Suppose that you decide to explore the workings of RMI, making an object's methods available to a Java program running on another computer. The initial development step is to create an interface for the class to which you want to provide remote access. As an experimental project, suppose that you create a `Rocket` interface that is independent of existing code at Oozinoz:

```
package com.oozinoz.remote;
import java.rmi.*;
public interface Rocket extends Remote {
    void boost(double factor) throws RemoteException;
    double getApogee() throws RemoteException;
    double getPrice() throws RemoteException;
}
```

The Rocket interface extends Remote, and the methods in the interface all declare that they throw RemoteException. The reasons for these aspects of the interface lie outside the scope of this book, but any book that teaches RMI should cover them. Your RMI source should also explain that, to act as a server, the implementation of your remote interface can subclass UnicastRemoteObject, as Figure 11.5 shows.

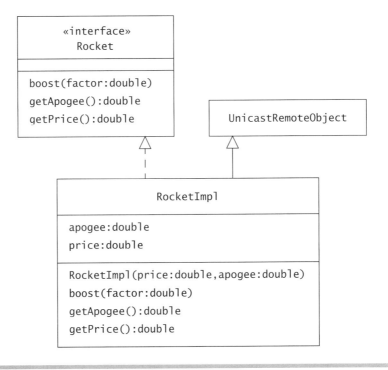

FIGURE 11.5 To use RMI, you can first define the interface you want for messages that pass between computers and then create a subclass of UnicastRemoteObject that implements it.

Your plan is for RocketImpl objects to be active on a server and to be available through a proxy that is active on a client. The code for RocketImpl is simple.

```
package com.oozinoz.remote;
import java.rmi.*;
import java.rmi.server.UnicastRemoteObject;
```

```
public class RocketImpl
        extends UnicastRemoteObject
        implements Rocket {
    protected double price;
    protected double apogee;

    public RocketImpl(double price, double apogee)
        throws RemoteException {
        this.price = price;
        this.apogee = apogee;
    }

    public void boost(double factor) {
        apogee *= factor;
    }

    public double getApogee() {
        return apogee;
    }

    public double getPrice() {
        return price;
    }
}
```

An instance of RocketImpl can be active on one machine and can be accessed by a Java program running on another machine. For this to work, a client needs a proxy for the RocketImpl object. This proxy needs to implement the Rocket interface and must have the additional features required to communicate with a remote object. A great benefit of RMI is that it *automates* the construction of this proxy. To generate the proxy, place the RocketImpl.java file and the Rocket.java interface file below the directory where you will run the RMI registry:

```
c:\rmi>dir /b com\oozinoz\remote
RegisterRocket.class
RegisterRocket.java
Rocket.class
Rocket.java
RocketImpl.class
RocketImpl.java
ShowRocketClient.class
ShowRocketClient.java
```

To create the `RocketImpl` stub that facilitates remote communication, run the RMI compiler that comes with the JDK:

```
c:\rmi> rmic com.oozinoz.remote.RocketImpl
```

Note that the `rmic` executable takes a class name, not the filename, as an argument. Earlier versions of the JDK constructed separate files for use on the client and server machines. As of version 1.2, the RMI compiler creates a single stub file that both the client and server machines need. The `rmic` command creates a `RocketImpl_Stub` class:

```
c:\rmi>dir /b com\oozinoz\remote
RegisterRocket.class
RegisterRocket.java
Rocket.class
Rocket.java
RocketImpl.class
RocketImpl.java
RocketImpl_Stub.class
ShowRocketClient.class
ShowRocketClient.java
```

To make an object active, you must register it with an RMI registry running on the server. The `rmiregistry` executable comes as part of the JDK. When you run the registry, specify the port that the registry will listen to:

```
c:\rmi> rmiregistry 5000
```

With the registry running on the server machine, you can create and register a `RocketImpl` object:

```
package com.oozinoz.remote;
import java.rmi.*;
public class RegisterRocket {
    public static void main(String[] args) {
        try {
            // Challenge!
            Naming.rebind(
                "rmi://localhost:5000/Biggie", biggie);
            System.out.println("Registered biggie");
        } catch (Exception e) {
            e.printStackTrace();
        }
    }
}
```

If you compile and run this code, the program displays a confirmation that the rocket is registered:

```
Registered biggie
```

You need to replace the `//Challenge!` line in the `RegisterRocket` class with code that creates a `biggie` object that models a rocket. The remaining code in the `main()` method registers this object. A description of the mechanics of the `Naming` class is outside the scope of this discussion. However, you should have enough information to create the `biggie` object that this code registers.

CHALLENGE 11.4

Replace the `//Challenge!` line with a declaration and instantiation of the `biggie` object. Define `biggie` to model a rocket with a price of $29.95 and an apogee of 820 meters.

A solution appears on page 377.

Running the `RegisterRocket` program makes a `RocketImpl` object—specifically, `biggie`—available on a server. A client that runs on another machine can access `biggie` if the client has access to the Rocket interface and the `RocketImpl_Stub` class. If you are working on a single machine, you can still test out RMI, accessing the server on `localhost` rather than on another host.

```java
package com.oozinoz.remote;

import java.rmi.*;
public class ShowRocketClient {
    public static void main(String[] args) {
        try {
            Object obj = Naming.lookup(
                "rmi://localhost:5000/Biggie");
```

```
                Rocket biggie = (Rocket) obj;
                System.out.println(
                    "Apogee is " + biggie.getApogee());
            } catch (Exception e) {
                System.out.println(
                    "Exception while looking up a rocket:");
                e.printStackTrace();
            }
        }
    }
}
```

When this program runs, it looks up an object with the registered name of "Biggie." The class that is serving this name is RocketImpl, and the object obj that lookup() returns will be an instance of RocketImpl_Stub class. The RocketImpl_Stub class implements the Rocket interface, so it is legal to cast the object obj as an instance of the Rocket interface. The RocketImpl_Stub class actually subclasses a RemoteStub class that lets the object communicate with a server.

When you run the ShowRocketClient program, it prints out the apogee of a "Biggie" rocket.

```
Apogee is 820.0
```

Through a proxy, the getApogee() call is forwarded to an implementation of the Rocket interface that is active on a server.

CHALLENGE 11.5

Figure 11.6 shows the getApogee() call being forwarded. The rightmost object appears in a bold outline, indicating that it is active outside the ShowRocketClient program. Fill in the class names of the unlabeled objects in this figure.

A solution appears on page 377.

The benefit of RMI is that it lets client programs interact with a local object that is a proxy for a remote object. You define the interface for the object that you want clients and servers to share. RMI supplies the communication mechanics and isolates both server and client from

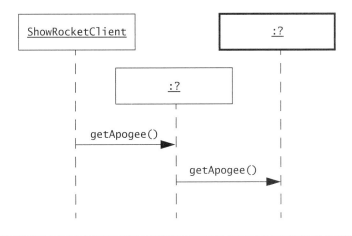

FIGURE 11.6 This diagram, when completed, will show the flow of messages in an RMI-based distributed application.

the knowledge that two implementations of Rocket are collaborating to provide nearly seamless interprocess communication.

Dynamic Proxies

The engineers at Oozinoz occasionally face performance problems. They'd like a way to instrument code without making major changes to the design.

Java has a feature that can help with this: *Dynamic proxies* let you wrap a proxy object around another object. You can arrange for the outer object—the proxy—to intercept all the calls intended for the wrapped object. The proxy will usually pass these calls on to the wrapped object, but you can add code that executes before or after the intercepted calls. Limitations to dynamic proxies prevent you from wrapping any arbitrary object. Under the right conditions, though, dynamic proxies give you complete control over the operation of an object that you want to wrap with a proxy.

Dynamic proxies work with the *interfaces* that an object's class implements. The calls that the proxy can intercept are calls that one of these interfaces defines. If you have a class that implements an interface with methods you want to intercept, you can use dynamic proxies to wrap an instance of that class.

To create a dynamic proxy, you must have a list of the interfaces that you want to intercept. Fortunately, you can usually obtain this list by interrogating the object that you want to wrap, using a line such as:

```
Class[] classes = obj.getClass().getInterfaces();
```

This code establishes that the methods you want to intercept are those that belong to interfaces that an object's class implements. To build a dynamic proxy, you need two other ingredients: a class loader and a class that contains the behavior that you want to execute when your proxy intercepts a call. As with the list of interfaces, you can obtain an appropriate class loader by using the one associated with the object that you want to wrap:

```
ClassLoader loader = obj.getClass().getClassLoader();
```

The last ingredient that you need is the proxy object itself. This object must be an instance of a class that implements the `InvocationHandler` interface in the `java.lang.reflect` package. That interface declares the following operation:

```
public Object invoke(Object proxy, Method m, Object[] args)
    throws Throwable;
```

When you wrap an object in a dynamic proxy, calls intended for the wrapped object are diverted to this `invoke()` operation, in a class that you supply. Your code for the `invoke()` method will probably need to pass each method call on to the wrapped object. You can pass on the invocation with a line such as:

```
result = m.invoke(obj, args);
```

This line uses reflection to pass along the desired call to the wrapped object. The beauty of dynamic proxies is that you can add any behavior you like before or after executing this line.

Suppose that you want to log a warning if a method takes a long time to execute. You might create an `ImpatientProxy` class with the following code:

```
package app.proxy.dynamic;

import java.lang.reflect.*;

public class ImpatientProxy implements InvocationHandler {
    private Object obj;

    private ImpatientProxy(Object obj) {
        this.obj = obj;
    }

    public Object invoke(
            Object proxy, Method m, Object[] args)
            throws Throwable {
        Object result;
        long t1 = System.currentTimeMillis();
        result = m.invoke(obj, args);
        long t2 = System.currentTimeMillis();
        if (t2 - t1 > 10) {
            System.out.println(
                "> It takes " + (t2 - t1)
                + " millis to invoke " + m.getName()
                + "() with");
            for (int i = 0; i < args.length; i++)
                System.out.println(
                    ">     arg[" + i + "]: " + args[i]);
        }
        return result;
    }
}
```

This class implements the invoke() method so that it checks the time it takes for the wrapped object to complete an invoked operation. If that execution time is too long, the ImpatientProxy class prints a warning.

To put an ImpatientProxy object to use, you need to use the Proxy class in the java.lang.reflect package. The Proxy class will need a list of interfaces and a class loader, as well as an instance of

ImpatientProxy. To simplify the creation of a dynamic proxy, we might add the following method to the ImpatientProxy class:

```
public static Object newInstance(Object obj) {
    ClassLoader loader = obj.getClass().getClassLoader();
    Class[] classes = obj.getClass().getInterfaces();
    return Proxy.newProxyInstance(
        loader, classes, new ImpatientProxy(obj));
}
```

This static method creates the dynamic proxy for us. Given an object to wrap, the newInstance() method extracts the object's list of interfaces and class loader. The method instantiates the ImpatientProxy class, passing it the object to wrap. All these ingredients are then passed to the Proxy class's newProxyInstance() method.

The returned object will implement all the interfaces that the wrapped object's class implements. We can cast the returned object to any of these interfaces.

Suppose that you are working with a set of objects, and some operations seem to run slowly for some objects. To find which objects are behaving sluggishly, you can wrap the set in an ImpatientProxy object. The following code shows this example:

```
package app.proxy.dynamic;

import java.util.HashSet;
import java.util.Set;
import com.oozinoz.firework.Firecracker;
import com.oozinoz.firework.Sparkler;
import com.oozinoz.utility.Dollars;

public class ShowDynamicProxy {
    public static void main(String[] args) {
        Set s = new HashSet();
        s = (Set)ImpatientProxy.newInstance(s);
        s.add(new Sparkler(
            "Mr. Twinkle", new Dollars(0.05)));
        s.add(new BadApple("Lemon"));
        s.add(new Firecracker(
            "Mr. Boomy", new Dollars(0.25)));
        System.out.println(
            "The set contains " + s.size() + " things.");
    }
}
```

This code creates a Set object to hold a few items. The code then wraps this set, using an ImpatientProxy object, casting the result of the newInstance() method back to a Set. The result is that the s object behaves just like a set, except that the code in ImpatientProxy will issue a complaint if any method takes too long to execute. For example, when the program calls the set's add() method, our ImpatientProxy object intercepts the call. The ImpatientProxy object passes the call along to the real set but times the result of each call.

Running the ShowDynamicProxy program produces the following output:

```
> It takes 1204 millis to invoke add() with
>      arg[0]: Lemon
The set contains 3 things.
```

The ImpatientProxy code helps us identify which object takes a long time to add to a set. It's the "Lemon" instance of the BadApple class. The BadApple code is as follows:

```
package app.proxy.dynamic;

public class BadApple {
    public String name;

    public BadApple(String name) {
        this.name = name;
    }

    public boolean equals(Object o) {
        if (!(o instanceof BadApple))
            return false;
        BadApple f = (BadApple) o;
        return name.equals(f.name);
    }

    public int hashCode() {
        try {
            Thread.sleep(1200);
        } catch (InterruptedException ignored) {
        }
        return name.hashCode();
    }
```

```
    public String toString() {
        return name;
    }
}
```

The ShowDynamicProxy code uses an ImpatientProxy object to moni-tor calls to a set. There is no connection, though, between sets and ImpatientProxy. Once you write a dynamic proxy class, you can use it to wrap any object, so long as the object is an instance of a class that implements an interface that declares the behavior you want to intercept.

The idea that you should be able to create behavior that runs before and after intercepted method calls is one of the ideas behind aspect-oriented programming. In AOP, an aspect is a combination of advice—code that you want to drop in—and point cuts—definitions of execution points in your code where you want the drop-in code to run. AOP is a book-length topic, but you can get a taste of applying reusable behavior to a variety of objects by experimenting with dynamic proxies.

Dynamic proxies in Java let you wrap an object with a proxy that intercepts the object's calls and that can add behavior before or after passing the call along. This lets you create reusable behavior that you can drop in on an arbitrary object, in a fashion similar to aspect-oriented programming.

Summary

Implementations of the PROXY pattern establish a placeholder object that manages access to a target object. A proxy object can isolate cli-ents from shifts in state of a desired object, as when loading an image requires a discernible duration. A problem with PROXY is that it usu-ally relies on a tight coupling between the placeholder and the prox-ied object. Dynamic proxies in Java will sometimes offer a solution. If an object's class implements interfaces for the methods that you want to intercept, you can wrap the object in a dynamic proxy and arrange for your own logic to execute around or instead of the wrapped object's code.

12

CHAIN OF RESPONSIBILITY

OBJECT-ORIENTED DEVELOPERS strive to keep objects loosely coupled, keeping the responsibility between objects specific and minimal. This lets you introduce change more easily and with less risk of introducing defects. Decoupling occurs naturally in Java, to a degree. Clients see only an object's visible interface and remain isolated from the details of the object's implementation. This arrangement, however, leaves in place the fundamental coupling that the client knows which object has the method the client needs to call. You can loosen the restriction that a client must know which object to use when you can arrange a group objects in a kind of hierarchy that allows each object to either perform an operation or pass the request along to another object.

The intent of the CHAIN OF RESPONSIBILITY **pattern is to avoid coupling the sender of a request to its receiver, by giving more than one object a chance to handle the request.**

An Ordinary Chain of Responsibility

The CHAIN OF RESPONSIBILITY pattern often emerges in real life when a person who is responsible for a task either does it personally or delegates it to someone else. Such a situation occurs at Oozinoz, where engineers are responsible for maintaining the fireworks manufacturing machines.

As described in Chapter 5, COMPOSITE, Oozinoz models machines, lines, bays, and factories as "machine components." This approach allows simple, recursive implementations of operations, such as shutting down all the machines in a bay. It also simplifies the modeling of engineering responsibility in the factory. At Oozinoz, there is always an engineer who is responsible for any particular machine component, although this responsibility may be assigned at different levels.

For example, a complex machine, such as a star press, may have an engineer directly assigned to it. A simpler machine may not have a directly assigned engineer, in which case the engineer responsible for the line or bay that the machine occupies will take on responsibility for the machine.

We would like to avoid forcing client objects to interrogate several objects when seeking the responsible engineer. We can apply CHAIN OF RESPONSIBILITY here, by giving every machine component a `responsible` object. Figure 12.1 shows this design.

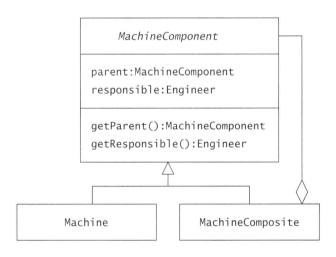

FIGURE 12.1 Every `Machine` or `MachineComposite` object has `parent` and `responsible` associations, inherited from the `MachineComponent` class.

The design reflected in Figure 12.1 allows but does not require each machine component to keep track of its responsible engineer. If a machine does not have a directly assigned engineer, it can pass a request asking for its responsible engineer to be its "parent." In practice, a machine's parent is a line, a line's parent is a bay, and a bay's parent is a factory. At Oozinoz, there is always a responsible engineer somewhere in this chain.

The advantage of this design is that clients of machine components don't have to determine how engineers are assigned. A client can ask any machine component for its responsible engineer. Machine components isolate their clients from knowledge of how responsibilities are assigned. On the other hand, this design has some possible disadvantages.

CHALLENGE 12.1

Point out two weaknesses of the design shown in Figure 12.1.

A solution appears on page 378.

The CHAIN OF RESPONSIBILITY pattern helps to simplify client code when it's not obvious which object in a group should handle a request. If you do not have CHAIN OF RESPONSIBILITY in place, you may come across areas where it will help you migrate your code to a simpler design.

Refactoring to CHAIN OF RESPONSIBILITY

If you find client code that makes probing calls before issuing the request it really wants to make, you may be able to improve the design through refactoring. To apply CHAIN OF RESPONSIBILITY, determine the operation that objects in a group of classes will sometimes be able to support. For example, machine components at Oozinoz can sometimes provide a reference to a responsible engineer. Add the desirable operation to each class in the group, but implement the operation with a chaining strategy for cases in which a specific object needs help in satisfying the request.

Consider the Oozinoz code base's modeling of tools and tool carts. Tools are not part of the MachineComponent hierarchy but are similar to machines in some ways. In particular, tools are always assigned to tool carts, and tool carts have a responsible engineer. Suppose that a visualization shows all the tools and machines in a given bay and has pop-up help that displays the responsible engineer for any chosen item. Figure 12.2 shows the classes involved in finding the engineers who are responsible for selected equipment.

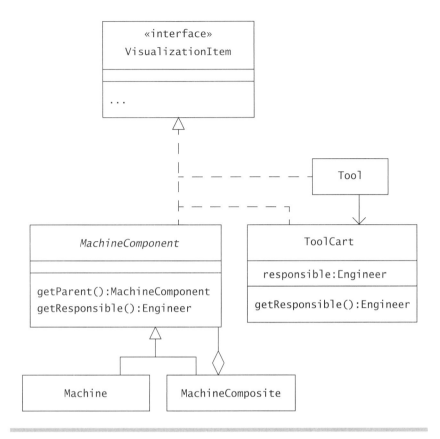

FIGURE 12.2 Items in a simulation include machines, machine composites, tools, and tool carts.

The VisualizationItem interface specifies a few behaviors that classes need in order to participate in the visualization but does not have a getResponsible() method. In fact, not all items in the visualization have direct knowledge of which engineer is responsible for them. When the visualization needs to determine which engineer is responsible for an item, the answer depends on which kind of item is selected. Machines, machine groups, and tool carts have a get-Responsible() method, but tools do not. To see who is responsible for a tool, the code has to see which cart the tool belongs with and then determine who is responsible for the cart. To find the responsible engineer for a simulated item, an application's menu code uses a series of if statements and type testing. These traits are signs that refactoring might be able to improve the code, which is as follows:

```
package com.oozinoz.machine;

public class AmbitiousMenu {
    public Engineer getResponsible(VisualizationItem item) {
        if (item instanceof Tool) {
            Tool t = (Tool) item;
            return t.getToolCart().getResponsible();
        }
        if (item instanceof ToolCart) {
            ToolCart tc = (ToolCart) item;
            return tc.getResponsible();
        }
        if (item instanceof MachineComponent) {
            MachineComponent c = (MachineComponent) item;
            if (c.getResponsible() != null)
                return c.getResponsible();
            if (c.getParent() != null)
                return c.getParent().getResponsible();
        }
        return null;
    }
}
```

The intent of a CHAIN OF RESPONSIBILITY is to relieve callers from knowing which object can handle a request. In this example, the caller is a menu, and the request is to find a responsible engineer. In the current design, the caller has to know which items have a getResponsible() method. You can clean up this code by applying CHAIN OF RESPONSIBIL-ITY, giving all simulated items a responsible party. This moves the requirement for knowing which objects know their engineer into the simulated items and away from the menu.

CHALLENGE 12.2

Redraw the diagram in Figure 12.2, moving the getResponsible() method to VisualizationItem and adding this behavior to Tool.

A solution appears on page 379.

The menu code becomes much simpler once it can ask any selectable item for its responsible engineer, as follows:

```
package com.oozinoz.machine;

public class AmbitiousMenu2 {
    public Engineer getResponsible(VisualizationItem item) {
        return item.getResponsible();
    }
}
```

The implementation of the `getResponsible()` method for each item is simple, too.

CHALLENGE 12.3

Write the code for the `getResponsible()` method for:

A. `MachineComponent`

B. `Tool`

C. `ToolCart`

A solution appears on page 380.

Anchoring a Chain

When you write the `getResponsible()` method for `MachineCompo-nent`, you have to consider that a `MachineComponent` object's parent might be `null`. Alternatively, you can tighten up your object model, insisting that `MachineComponent` objects have a parent that is not `null`. To achieve this, you can add a parent argument to the constructor for `MachineComponent`. (You may even want to throw an exception when the supplied object is `null`, so long as you know where this exception will be caught.) Also consider that some object will be the *root*—a distinguished object that has no parent. One reasonable approach is to create a `MachineRoot` class as a subclass of `Machine-Composite` (not `MachineComponent`). Then you can guarantee that a `MachineComponent` object always has a responsible engineer if

- The constructor(s) for MachineRoot require an Engineer object
- The constructor(s) for MachineComponent require a parent object that is itself a MachineComponent
- Only MachineRoot uses null as the value for its parent

CHALLENGE 12.4

Fill in the constructors in Figure 12.3 to support a design that ensures that every MachineComponent object has a responsible engineer.

A solution appears on page 380.

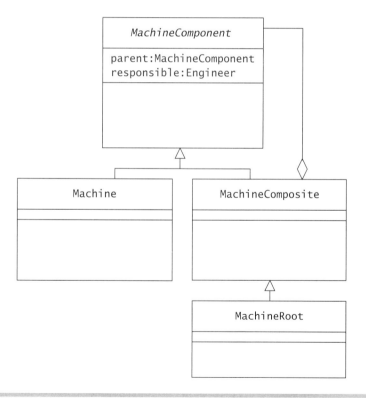

FIGURE 12.3 How can constructors ensure that every MachineComponent object has a responsible engineer?

By anchoring a chain of responsibility, you strengthen the object model and simplify the code. Now you can implement the get-Responsible() method of MachineComponent as

```
public Engineer getResponsible() {
    if (responsible != null)
        return responsible;
    return parent.getResponsible();
}
```

CHAIN OF RESPONSIBILITY without COMPOSITE

CHAIN OF RESPONSIBILITY requires a strategy for ordering the search for an object that can handle a request. Usually, the order to follow will depend on an underlying aspect in the modeled domain. This frequently occurs when there is some kind of composition, as in the Oozinoz machine hierarchy. However, this pattern can apply outside of object models that are composites.

CHALLENGE 12.5

Cite an example in which the CHAIN OF RESPONSIBILITY pattern might occur where the chained objects do not form a composite.

A solution appears on page 382.

Summary

When you apply the CHAIN OF RESPONSIBILITY pattern, you relieve a client from having to know which object in a collection supports a given behavior. By setting up the search for responsibility to occur across objects, you decouple the client from any specific object in the chain.

The CHAIN OF RESPONSIBILITY pattern occurs occasionally when an arbitrary chain of objects can apply a series of various strategies to tackling some problem, such as parsing a user's input. More frequently, this pattern occurs in aggregations, whereby a containment hierarchy provides a natural ordering for a chain of objects. CHAIN OF RESPONSIBILITY leads to simpler code in both the hierarchy and the client.

13

FLYWEIGHT

THE FLYWEIGHT PATTERN provides for sharing an object between clients, creating a responsibility for the shared object that normal objects need not consider. An ordinary object doesn't have to worry much about shared responsibility. Most often, only one client will hold a reference to an object at any one time. When the object's state changes, it's because the client changed it, and the object does not have any responsibility to inform any other clients. Sometimes, though, you will want to arrange for multiple clients to share access to an object.

One incentive for sharing an object among multiple clients occurs when you must manage thousands or tens of thousands of small objects, such as the characters in an online version of a book. In such a case, you may have a performance incentive to safely share these fine-grained objects among many clients. A book needs only one A object, although it needs some way to model where different A's appear.

The intent of the FLYWEIGHT **pattern is to use sharing to support large numbers of fine-grained objects efficiently.**

Immutability

The FLYWEIGHT pattern lets multiple clients share access to a limited number of objects: the flyweights. For this to work, you have to consider that when a client changes the state of an object, the state changes for every client that has access to the object. When multiple clients will share access to an object, the easiest and most common way to keep clients from affecting one another is to restrict clients from introducing any state changes in the shared object. You can achieve this by making an object **immutable**, so that once created, the object cannot change. The most common immutable objects in

Java are instances of the String class. Once you create a string, neither you nor any client with access to the string can change its characters.

CHALLENGE 13.1

Provide a justification of why the creators of Java made String objects immutable, or argue that this was an unwise restriction.

A solution appears on page 382.

When you have large numbers of similar objects, you may want to arrange for shared access to them, but they may not be immutable. In this case, a preliminary step in applying the FLYWEIGHT pattern is to extract the immutable part of an object so that this part can be shared.

Extracting the Immutable Part of a Flyweight

Around Oozinoz, chemicals are as prevalent as characters in a document. The purchasing, engineering, manufacturing, and safety departments are all concerned with directing the flow of thousands of chemicals through the factory. Batches of chemicals are often modeled with instances of the Substance class, shown in Figure 13.1.

The Substance class has better methods for its attributes and also has a getMoles() method that returns the number of **moles**—a count of molecules—in the substance. A Substance object represents a quantity of a particular molecule. Oozinoz uses a Mixture class to model combinations of substances. For example, Figure 13.2 shows an object diagram of a batch of black powder.

Suppose that, given the proliferation of chemicals at Oozinoz, you decide to apply FLYWEIGHT to reduce the number of Substance objects in Oozinoz applications. To treat Substance objects as flyweights, a first step is to separate the class's mutable and immutable parts. Suppose that you decide to refactor the Substance class, extracting its immutable part into a Chemical class.

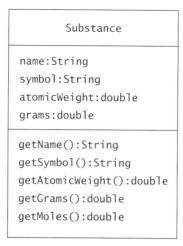

FIGURE 13.1 A Substance object models a physical batch of chemical material.

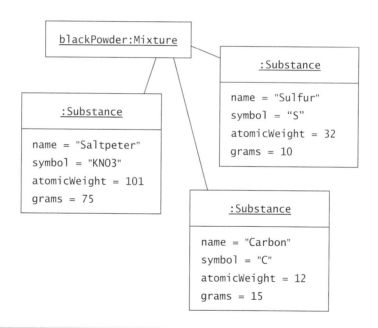

FIGURE 13.2 A batch of black powder contains saltpeter, sulfur, and carbon.

CHALLENGE 13.2

Complete the class diagram in Figure 13.3 to show a refactored
Substance2 class and a new, immutable Chemical class.

A solution appears on page 383.

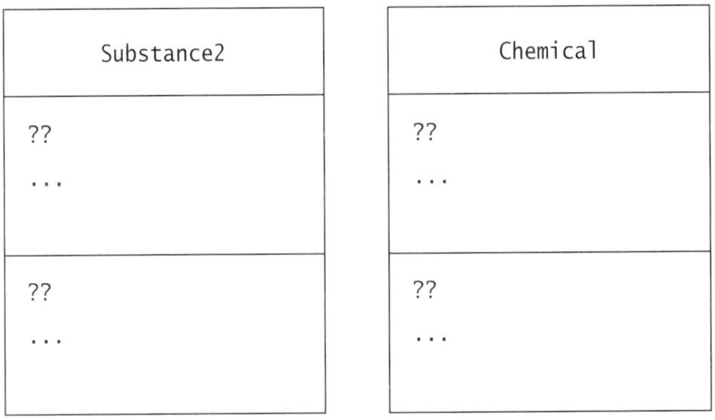

Substance2	Chemical
?? ...	?? ...
?? ...	?? ...

FIGURE 13.3 Complete this diagram to extract the immutable aspects of
Substance2 into the Chemical class.

Sharing Flyweights

Extracting the immutable part of an object is half the battle in applying the FLYWEIGHT pattern. The remaining work includes creating a
flyweight factory that instantiates flyweights and that arranges for
clients to share them. You also have to ensure that clients will use
your factory instead of constructing instances of the flyweight class
themselves.

To make chemicals flyweights, you need some kind of factory, perhaps a ChemicalFactory class, with a static method that returns a
chemical given its name. You might store chemicals in a hash table,
creating known chemicals as part of the factory's initialization.
Figure 13.4 shows a design for a ChemicalFactory.

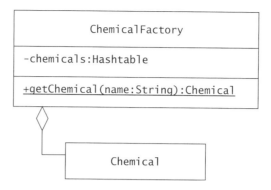

FIGURE 13.4 The ChemicalFactory class is a flyweight factory that returns
Chemical objects.

The code for ChemicalFactory can use a static initializer to store
Chemical objects in a Hashtable:

```java
package com.oozinoz.chemical;
import java.util.*;

public class ChemicalFactory {
    private static Map chemicals = new HashMap();

    static {
      chemicals.put(
            "carbon", new Chemical("Carbon", "C", 12));
      chemicals.put(
                "sulfur", new Chemical("Sulfur", "S", 32));
      chemicals.put(
                "saltpeter", new Chemical("Saltpeter", "KNO3", 101));
      //...
    }

    public static Chemical getChemical(String name) {
      return (Chemical) chemicals.get(name.toLowerCase());
    }
}
```

Having created a factory for chemicals, you now have to take steps to
ensure that other developers use this factory instead of instantiating
the Chemical class themselves. A simple approach is to rely on the
accessibility of the Chemical class.

CHALLENGE 13.3

How can you use the accessibility of the `Chemical` class to discourage other developers from instantiating `Chemical` objects?

A solution appears on page 384.

Access modifiers do not supply the complete control over instantiation that you might want. You might like to ensure that `ChemicalFactory` is absolutely the only class that can create new `Chemical` instances. To achieve this level of control, you can apply an *inner* class, defining the `Chemical` class within `ChemicalFactory`. (See the package `com.oozinoz.chemical2`.)

To access a nested type, clients must specify the enclosing type, with expressions such as the following:

```
ChemicalFactory.Chemical c =
    ChemicalFactory.getChemical("saltpeter");
```

You can simplify the use of a nested class by making `Chemical` an interface and making `ChemicalImpl` the name of the class. The `Chemical` interface can specify three accessor methods, as follows:

```
package com.oozinoz.chemical2;
public interface Chemical {
    String getName();
    String getSymbol();
    double getAtomicWeight();
}
```

Clients will never reference the inner class directly, so you can make it private, ensuring that only `ChemicalFactory2` has access to it.

CHALLENGE 13.4

Complete the following code for `ChemicalFactory2.java`.

A solution appears on page 384.

```
package com.oozinoz.chemical2;
import java.util.*;

public class ChemicalFactory2 {
    private static Map chemicals = new HashMap();

    /* Challenge! */  implements Chemical {
        private String name;
        private String symbol;
        private double atomicWeight;

        ChemicalImpl(
                String name,
                String symbol,
                double atomicWeight) {
            this.name = name;
            this.symbol = symbol;
            this.atomicWeight = atomicWeight;
        }

        public String getName() {
            return name;
        }

        public String getSymbol() {
            return symbol;
        }

        public double getAtomicWeight() {
            return atomicWeight;
        }

        public String toString() {
            return name + "(" + symbol + ")[" +
                atomicWeight + "]";
        }
    }
}
```

```
/* Challenge! */ {
    chemicals.put("carbon",
        factory.new ChemicalImpl("Carbon", "C", 12));
    chemicals.put("sulfur",
        factory.new ChemicalImpl("Sulfur", "S", 32));
    chemicals.put("saltpeter",
        factory.new ChemicalImpl(
            "Saltpeter", "KNO3", 101));
    //...
}

public static Chemical getChemical(String name) {
    return /* Challenge! */
}
}
```

Summary

The FLYWEIGHT pattern lets you share access to objects that may appear in large quantities, such as characters, chemicals, and borders. The flyweight objects must be immutable, a feature that you can establish by extracting the immutable part of the class that you want to share. To ensure that your flyweight objects are shared, you can provide a factory in which clients can find flyweights, and you have to enforce the use of this factory. Access modifiers give you some control over how other developers access your code, but inner classes take this control further, letting you guarantee that a class is accessible by only its containing class. By ensuring that clients use your flyweight factory properly, you can provide safe, shared access to what would otherwise be a multitude of fine-grained objects.

PART III

CONSTRUCTION PATTERNS

14

INTRODUCING CONSTRUCTION

Wʜᴇɴ ʏᴏᴜ ᴄʀᴇᴀᴛᴇ a Java class, you normally provide for the creation of objects of your class by supplying class **constructors**. Constructors are useful, though, only if clients know which class to construct and have values for the parameters that a constructor requires. Several design patterns address cases in which these conditions or other circumstances of ordinary construction do not hold. Before examining designs for cases in which ordinary construction is insufficient, it is useful to review ordinary construction in Java.

A Few Construction Challenges

Constructors are special methods. In many respects, including access modifiers, overloading, and the syntax of parameter lists, constructors are like ordinary methods. On the other hand, a significant number of syntactic and semantic rules govern the use and behavior of constructors.

CHALLENGE 14.1

List four rules that govern the use and behavior of constructors in Java.

A solution appears on page 386.

Java supplies default constructors and default constructor behavior in some cases. First, if a class has no declared constructor, Java will supply a default. This default constructor is equivalent to a public constructor, with no arguments and with no statements in its body.

A second default in Java constructors is that if a constructor declaration does not use a variation of `this()` or `super()` to explicitly invoke another constructor, Java effectively inserts `super()` with no arguments. This may cause surprising results, as in the results of compiling the following code:

```
package app.construction;
public class Fuse {
    private String name;
   // public Fuse(String name) { this.name = name; }
}
```

and

```
package app.construction;
public class QuickFuse extends Fuse { }
```

This code compiles correctly until you remove the `//` comment marks.

CHALLENGE 14.2

Explain the error that will occur if you uncomment the lines that allow the `Fuse` superclass to accept a fuse name in its constructor.

A solution appears on page 386.

The most common way to instantiate objects is by invoking the new operator, but you can also use **reflection**. Reflection provides the ability to work with types and type members as objects. Even if you do not use reflection frequently, you may be able to follow the logic of a working program that relies on reflection, such as the following:

```
package app.construction;
import java.awt.Point;
import java.lang.reflect.Constructor;
public class ShowReflection {
    public static void main(String args[]) {
        Constructor[] cc = Point.class.getConstructors();
        Constructor cons = null;
        for (int i = 0; i < cc.length; i++)
            if (cc[i].getParameterTypes().length == 2)
                cons = cc[i];
```

```
        try {
            Object obj = cons.newInstance(
                new Object[] { new Integer(3), new Integer(4)});
            System.out.println(obj);
        } catch (Exception e) {
            System.out.println("Exception: " + e.getMessage());
        }
    }
}
```

CHALLENGE 14.3

What does the ShowReflection program print out?

A solution appears on page 387.

Reflection lets you achieve results that are otherwise difficult or impossible. To learn more about using reflection, see *Java™ in a Nutshell* [Flanagan 2005].

Summary

Ordinarily, you will furnish classes that you develop with constructors to provide a means for instantiation. These constructors may form a collaborating suite, and every constructor in classes that you write must ultimately also invoke a superclass constructor. The ordinary way to invoke a constructor is with the new operator, but you can also use reflection to instantiate and use objects.

Beyond Ordinary Construction

Java's constructor features provide many alternatives when you design a new class. However, constructors are effective only if the user of your class knows which class to instantiate and knows the required fields for instantiating an object. For example, the choice of which user interface component to compose may depend on whether the program is running on a handheld device or on a larger display. It can also happen that a developer knows which class to instantiate but does not have all the necessary initial values or has them in the wrong format. For example, the developer may need to create an object from a dormant or textual version of an object. In such circumstances, you need to go beyond the use of ordinary Java constructors and apply a design pattern.

The following table describes the intent of patterns that facilitate construction.

If you intend to	Apply the pattern
• Gather the information for an object gradually before requesting its construction	BUILDER
• Defer the decision of which class to instantiate	FACTORY METHOD
• Construct a family of objects that share some trait	ABSTRACT FACTORY
• Specify an object to create by giving an example	PROTOTYPE
• Reconstruct an object from a dormant version that contains only the object's internal state	MEMENTO

The intent of each design pattern is to solve a problem in a context. Construction-oriented patterns are designs that let a client construct a new object through a means other than calling a class's constructor. For example, when you find the initial values for an object gradually, you may want to follow the BUILDER pattern.

15

BUILDER

YOU DON'T ALWAYS have all the information needed for an object when it's time to construct it. It is especially convenient to allow step-by-step construction of a target object when you acquire the parameters for a constructor gradually, as happens with parsers and may happen with a user interface. Or, you might simply want to reduce the size of a class whose construction is relatively complicated but has little to do with the main focus of the class.

The intent of the BUILDER pattern is to move the construction logic for an object outside the class to be instantiated.

An Ordinary Builder

A common situation in which you can benefit from BUILDER occurs when data that defines a desired object is embedded in a text string. As your code looks through, or *parses*, the data, you need to store the data as you find it. Whether your parser is XML based or handcrafted, you may not initially have enough data to construct a legitimate target object. The solution that BUILDER provides is to store the data in an intermediate object until the program is ready to ask the storage object to construct, or *build*, the target object from the data extracted from text.

Suppose that in addition to manufacturing fireworks, Oozinoz occasionally puts on fireworks displays. Travel agencies send e-mail reservation requests that look like this:

```
Date, November 5, Headcount, 250, City, Springfield,
DollarsPerHead, 9.95, HasSite, False
```

As you might guess, this protocol originated in the days before **Extensible Markup Language** (XML), but it has thus far proved sufficient.

The request tells when a potential customer wants us to put on a display and in what city. The request also specifies the minimum head-count that the customer will guarantee and the amount of money per guest that the customer will pay. The customer in this example wants to put on a show for 250 guests and is willing to pay $9.95 per guest, or a total of $2,487.50 for our services. The travel agent has also indicated that the customer does not have a site in mind for our display.

The task at hand is to parse the textual request and create a Reservation object that represents it. We might approach this task by creating an empty Reservation object and setting its parameters as our parser encounters them. This causes the problem that a given Reservation object may or may not represent a valid request. For example, we might finish reading the text of a request and then realize that it is missing a date.

To ensure that Reservation objects are always valid requests, we can use a ReservationBuilder class. The ReservationBuilder object can store a reservation request's attributes as a parser finds them and then build a Reservation object, verifying its validity. Figure 15.1 shows the classes we need for this design.

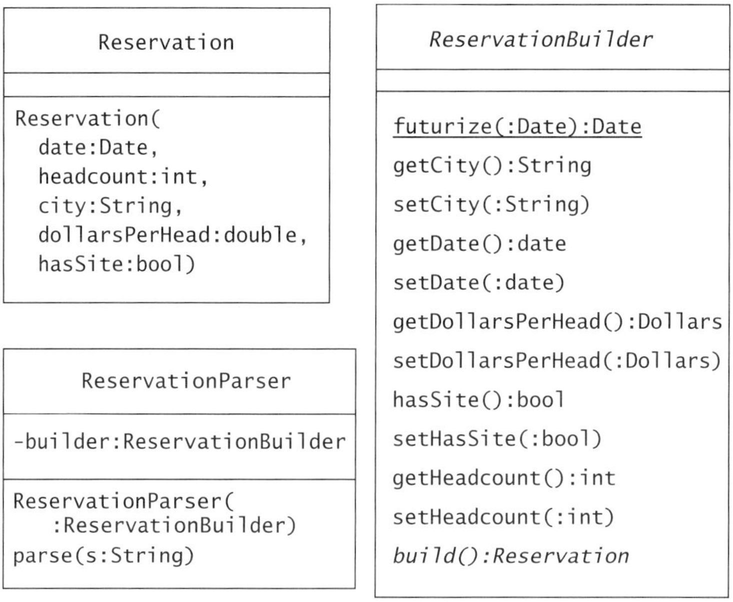

```
┌─────────────────────────────┐     ┌─────────────────────────────┐
│        Reservation          │     │     ReservationBuilder      │
├─────────────────────────────┤     ├─────────────────────────────┤
│                             │     │                             │
├─────────────────────────────┤     │ futurize(:Date):Date        │
│ Reservation(                │     │ getCity():String            │
│   date:Date,                │     │ setCity(:String)            │
│   headcount:int,            │     │ getDate():date              │
│   city:String,              │     │ setDate(:date)              │
│   dollarsPerHead:double,    │     │ getDollarsPerHead():Dollars │
│   hasSite:bool)             │     │ setDollarsPerHead(:Dollars) │
│                             │     │ hasSite():bool              │
└─────────────────────────────┘     │ setHasSite(:bool)           │
                                     │ getHeadcount():int          │
┌─────────────────────────────┐     │ setHeadcount(:int)          │
│      ReservationParser      │     │ build():Reservation         │
├─────────────────────────────┤     └─────────────────────────────┘
│ -builder:ReservationBuilder │
├─────────────────────────────┤
│ ReservationParser(          │
│    :ReservationBuilder)     │
│ parse(s:String)             │
└─────────────────────────────┘
```

FIGURE 15.1 A builder class offloads construction logic from a domain class and can accept initialization parameters gradually, as a parser discovers them.

The `ReservationBuilder` class is abstract, as is its `build()` method. We will create concrete `ReservationBuilder` subclasses that vary in how aggressively they try to create a `Reservation` object given incomplete data. The `ReservationParser` class constructor accepts a builder to pass information to. The `parse()` method pulls information out of a reservation string and passes it to a builder, as follows:

```
public void parse(String s) throws ParseException {
    String[] tokens = s.split(",");
    for (int i = 0; i < tokens.length; i += 2) {
        String type = tokens[i];
        String val = tokens[i + 1];

        if ("date".compareToIgnoreCase(type) == 0) {
            Calendar now = Calendar.getInstance();
            DateFormat formatter = DateFormat.getDateInstance();
            Date d = formatter.parse(
                val + ", " + now.get(Calendar.YEAR));
            builder.setDate(ReservationBuilder.futurize(d));
        } else if ("headcount".compareToIgnoreCase(type) == 0)
            builder.setHeadcount(Integer.parseInt(val));
        else if ("City".compareToIgnoreCase(type) == 0)
            builder.setCity(val.trim());
        else if ("DollarsPerHead".compareToIgnoreCase(type)==0)
            builder.setDollarsPerHead(
                new Dollars(Double.parseDouble(val)));
        else if ("HasSite".compareToIgnoreCase(type) == 0)
            builder.setHasSite(val.equalsIgnoreCase("true"));
    }
}
```

The `parse()` code uses a `String.split()` method to split up, or *tokenize*, the input string. The code expects a reservation to be a comma-separated list of information types and values. The `String.compareToIgnoreCase()` method makes the comparison disregard case. When it finds the word `"date"`, the parser parses the following value and moves the date into the future. The `futurize()` method moves a date's year forward until the date lies in the future. This ensures, for example, that a date of `"November 5"` will parse into the next November 5th. As you review the code, you may begin to notice several areas where the parser can go astray, beginning with the initial tokenization of the reservation string.

> **CHALLENGE 15.1**
>
> The regular expression object used by the `split(s)` call divides a comma-separated list into individual strings. Suggest an improvement to this regular expression—or to the entire approach—that will make the parser better at recognizing a reservation's information.
>
> *A solution appears on page 387.*

Building under Constraints

You want to ensure that invalid `Reservation` objects are never instantiated. Specifically, suppose that every reservation must have a non-`null` date and city. Suppose too that a business rule says that Oozinoz will not perform for fewer than 25 people or for less than $495.95. We might want to record these limits in a database, but for now we will record them as constants in the Java code, as follows:

```
public abstract class ReservationBuilder {
    public static final int MINHEAD = 25;
    public static final Dollars MINTOTAL = new Dollars(495.95);
        // ...
}
```

To avoid creating an instance of `Reservation` when a request is invalid, you might place business logic checks and exception throwing in the constructor for `Reservation`. But this logic is fairly independent of the normal function of a `Reservation` object once it is created. Introducing a builder will make the `Reservation` class simpler, leaving it with methods that concentrate on behavior other than construction. Using a builder also creates an opportunity to validate the parameters of a `Reservation` object with different reactions to invalid parameters. Finally, moving the construction job to a `ReservationBuilder` subclass lets construction occur gradually as the parser finds a reservation's attributes. Figure 15.2 shows concrete `ReservationBuilder` subclasses that differ in how forgiving they are regarding invalid parameters.

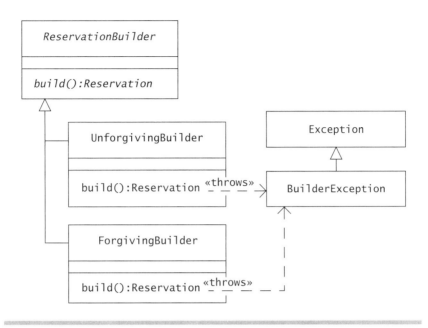

FIGURE 15.2 Builders may differ in how likely they are to throw an exception given an incomplete reservation string.

The diagram in Figure 15.2 brings out an advantage of applying the BUILDER pattern: By separating the construction logic from the Reservation class itself, we can treat construction as an entirely separate task and can even create a separate hierarchy of approaches for building. Differences in builder behavior may have little to do with reservation logic. For example, the builders in Figure 15.2 differ in how likely they are to throw a BuilderException. Code that uses a builder will look something like this:

```
package app.builder;
import com.oozinoz.reservation.*;

public class ShowUnforgiving {
    public static void main(String[] args) {
        String sample =
            "Date, November 5, Headcount, 250, "
            + "City, Springfield, DollarsPerHead, 9.95, "
            + "HasSite, False";
```

```
ReservationBuilder builder = new UnforgivingBuilder();
try {
    new ReservationParser(builder).parse(sample);
    Reservation res = builder.build();
    System.out.println("Unforgiving builder: " + res);
} catch (Exception e) {
    System.out.println(e.getMessage());
}
    }
}
```

Running this program prints out a `Reservation` object:

```
Date: Nov 5, 2001, Headcount: 250, City: Springfield,
Dollars/Head: 9.95, Has Site: false
```

Given a reservation request string, the code instantiates a builder and a parser and asks the parser to parse the string. As it reads the string, the parser passes the reservation attributes to the builder, using the builder's `set` methods.

After parsing, the code asks the builder to build a valid reservation. This example simply prints out an exception's message text rather than taking a more significant action as you would in a real application.

CHALLENGE 15.2

The `build()` method of the `UnforgivingBuilder` class throws a `BuilderException` if the date or city is `null`, if the headcount is too low, or if the total cost of the proposed reservation is too low. Write the code for the `build()` method according to these specifications.

A solution appears on page 388.

A Forgiving Builder

The `UnforgivingBuilder` class rejects requests that are anything less than fully formed. A better business decision might be to make reasonable changes to requests that are missing certain details about the reservation.

Suppose that an Oozinoz analyst asks you to set the headcount for an event to the minimum if this attribute is missing. Similarly, if the dollars/head value is missing, the builder should set it to be high enough so that the total take is above our minimum. These requirements are simple enough, but the design requires some skill. For example, what should the builder do if a reservation string supplies a dollars/head value but does not supply a headcount value?

CHALLENGE 15.3

Write a specification for `ForgivingBuilder.build()`, focusing on how the builder can handle missing values for headcount or dollars/head.

A solution appears on page 389.

CHALLENGE 15.4

After reviewing your approach, write the code for the `ForgivingBuilder` class's `build()` method.

A solution appears on page 389.

The classes `ForgivingBuilder` and `UnforgivingBuilder` let you guarantee that `Reservation` objects are always valid. Your design also gives you flexibility about what action to take when there is a problem in constructing a reservation.

Summary

The BUILDER pattern separates the construction of a complex object from its representation. This has the immediate effect of making a complex target class simpler. It lets a builder class focus on the proper construction of an object, leaving the target class to focus on the operation of a valid instance. This is especially useful when you want to ensure the validity of an object before instantiating it and don't want the associated logic to appear in the target class's constructors. A builder also accommodates step-by-step construction, which often occurs when you create an object by parsing text.

16

FACTORY METHOD

WHEN YOU DEVELOP a class, you usually provide class constructors to let clients of your class instantiate it. Sometimes, though, a client that needs an object does not or should not know which of several possible classes to instantiate.

The intent of FACTORY METHOD is to let a class developer define the interface for creating an object while retaining control of which class to instantiate.

A Classic Example: Iterators

The ITERATOR pattern provides a way to access the elements of a collection sequentially. (See Chapter 28, ITERATOR.) But the way iterators are created often uses a FACTORY METHOD. Java JDK version 1.2 introduced a Collection interface that includes an iterator() method; all collections implement this operation. The iterator() isolates its caller from knowing which class to instantiate.

An iterator() method creates an object that returns a sequence of the elements of a collection. For example, the following code creates and prints out the contents of a list:

```java
package app.factoryMethod;
import java.util.*;

public class ShowIterator {
    public static void main(String[] args) {
        List list = Arrays.asList(
            new String[] {
                "fountain", "rocket", "sparkler"});

        Iterator iter = list.iterator();
        while (iter.hasNext())
            System.out.println(iter.next());
    }
}
```

CHALLENGE 16.1

What is the actual class of the Iterator object in this code?

A solution appears on page 390.

The FACTORY METHOD pattern relieves a client from the burden of knowing which class to instantiate.

Recognizing FACTORY METHOD

You might think that any method that creates and returns a new object is a "factory" method. In object-oriented programming, however, methods that return new objects are common, and not every such method is an instance of the FACTORY METHOD pattern.

CHALLENGE 16.2

Name two commonly used methods in the Java class libraries that return a new object.

A solution appears on page 391.

The fact that a method creates a new object does not in itself make it an example of the FACTORY METHOD pattern. A FACTORY METHOD is an operation that both creates an object and isolates a client from knowing which class to instantiate. In FACTORY METHOD, you will find several classes that implement the same operation, returning the same abstract type but internally instantiating different classes that implement the type. When a client requests a new object, the precise class of the object that is created depends on the behavior of the factory object receiving the creation request.

CHALLENGE 16.3

The class javax.swing.BorderFactory sounds like it *ought* to be an example of the Factory Method pattern. Explain how the intent of the Factory Method pattern is *different* from the intent of the BorderFactory class.

A solution appears on page 391.

Taking Control of Which Class to Instantiate

The ordinary way for a client to instantiate a class is to use one of the class's constructors. But sometimes, a client that needs an object doesn't know exactly which class to create. This happens with iterators; the class of the iterator that a client needs depends on the type of collection that the client wants to walk through. It also happens frequently in application code.

Suppose that Oozinoz wants to start letting customers buy fireworks on credit. Early in the design of the credit authorization system, you accept responsibility for developing a CreditCheckOnline class that checks whether a customer can maintain a certain amount of credit with Oozinoz.

As you begin development, you realize that sometimes the credit agency will be offline. The analyst on the project determines that in this situation, the business wants you to bring up a dialog for the call center representative and make a credit decision, based on a few questions. To handle this, you create a CreditCheckOffline class, and you get this working to specification. Initially, you design the classes as Figure 16.1 shows. The creditLimit() method accepts a customer's identification number and returns that customer's credit limit.

With the classes in Figure 16.1, you can provide credit limit information whether or not the credit agency is online. The problem now is that the user of your classes needs to know which class to instantiate. But **you** are the one who knows whether the agency is up!

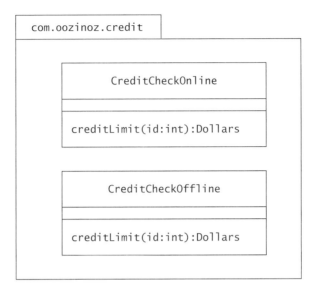

FIGURE 16.1 You can instantiate one of these classes to check a customer's credit, depending on whether the online credit agency is up.

In this scenario, you need to commit to the interface for creating an object but keep control of which class to instantiate. One solution is to change both classes to implement a standard interface and create a factory method that returns an object of that type. Specifically, you might

- Make `CreditCheck` a Java interface that includes the `creditLimit()` method

- Change both credit check classes to declare that they implement the `CreditCheck` interface

- Create a `CreditCheckFactory` class that provides a `createCreditCheck()` method that returns an object whose type is `CreditCheck`

When you implement `createCreditCheck()`, you will use your knowledge of the credit agency's status to decide which class to instantiate.

CHALLENGE 16.4

Draw a class diagram that establishes a way for this new scheme to create a credit-checking object while retaining control of which class to instantiate.

A solution appears on page 391.

By applying FACTORY METHOD, you let the user of your services call the `createCreditCheck()` method to get a credit-checking object that works whether or not the credit agency is online.

CHALLENGE 16.5

Assume that the `CreditCheckFactory` class has an `isAgencyUp()` method that tells whether the credit agency is available, and write the code for `createCreditCheck()`.

A solution appears on page 391.

FACTORY METHOD in Parallel Hierarchies

The FACTORY METHOD pattern often appears when you use parallel hierarchies to model a problem domain. A **parallel hierarchy** is a pair of class hierarchies in which each class in one hierarchy has a corresponding class in the other hierarchy. Parallel hierarchies usually emerge when you decide to move a subset of behavior out of an existing hierarchy.

Consider the construction of aerial shells, as illustrated in Chapter 5, COMPOSITE. To build these shells, Oozinoz uses the machines that the diagram in Figure 16.2 models.

To make a shell, we mix chemicals in a mixer and pass them to a star press, which extrudes individual stars. We pack stars into a shell around a core of black powder and place this over a lifting charge,

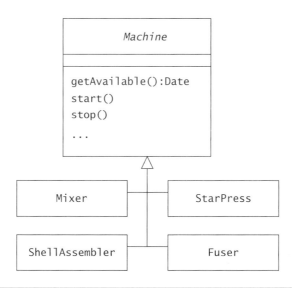

FIGURE 16.2 The Machine hierarchy contains logic for controlling physical machines and for planning.

using a shell assembler. We use a fuser to insert the fusing that will ignite both the lifting charge and the shell core.

Suppose that you want the getAvailable() method to forecast when a machine will complete its current processing and be available for more work. This method may require several supporting, private methods, adding up to quite a bit of logic to add to each of our machine classes. Rather than adding the planning logic to the Machine hierarchy, you might prefer to have a separate MachinePlanner hierarchy. You need a separate planner class for most machine types, but mixers and fusers are always available for additional work. For these classes, you can use a BasicPlanner class.

CHALLENGE 16.6

Fill in the diagram of a Machine/MachinePlanner parallel hierarchy in Figure 16.3.

A solution appears on page 393.

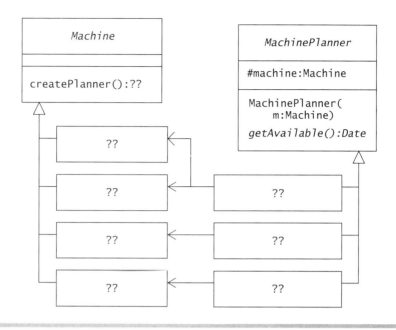

FIGURE 16.3 Slim down the Machine hierarchy by moving planning logic to a parallel hierarchy.

CHALLENGE 16.7

Write a createPlanner() method for the Machine class to return a BasicPlanner object, and write a createPlanner() method for the StarPress class.

A solution appears on page 394.

Summary

The intent of the FACTORY METHOD pattern is to let a service provider relieve clients from knowing which class to instantiate. This pattern occurs in the Java class library, notably in the iterator() method in the Collection interface.

FACTORY METHOD often appears in client code, occurring any time that you need to isolate clients from knowing exactly which class to instantiate. This need for isolation occurs when the decision of which class to instantiate depends on a factor that the client is unaware of, such as the status of an online credit bureau. You may also encounter FACTORY METHOD when you introduce a parallel class hierarchy to keep a set of classes from becoming bloated with many different aspects of behavior. FACTORY METHOD lets you connect parallel hierarchies by letting subclasses in one hierarchy determine which class to instantiate in the corresponding hierarchy.

17

ABSTRACT FACTORY

SOMETIMES, YOU WANT to provide for object creation while still retaining control of which class to instantiate. In such circumstances, you can apply the FACTORY METHOD pattern with a method that uses an outside factor to determine which class to instantiate. Sometimes, the factor that controls which object to instantiate can be thematic, running across several classes.

The intent of ABSTRACT FACTORY, **or** KIT, **is to allow the creation of families of related or dependent objects.**

A Classic Example: GUI Kits

GUI kits provide the classic example of the ABSTRACT FACTORY pattern. A GUI kit is an object that is an abstract factory, supplying GUI controls to a client that is building a user interface. Each GUI kit object determines how buttons, text areas, and other controls appear. A **kit** establishes a specific look-and-feel, including background colors, shapes, and other aspects of GUI design that run across the family of controls that the kit provides. You might establish a single look-and-feel for an entire system. You can also use look-and-feel changes to reflect changes in versions of the application, changes in company standard graphics, or simply improvements over time. ABSTRACT FACTORY lets you put look-and-feel to work, making your applications easier to learn and use. The Oozinoz UI class, shown in Figure 17.1, provides an example.

Subclasses of the UI class can override any particular element of the user control factory. An application that builds a GUI from an instance of the UI class can later produce a different look-and-feel by building from an instance of a subclass of UI. For example, Oozinoz uses a Visualization class to help engineers lay out new equipment lines. This visualization appears as in Figure 17.2.

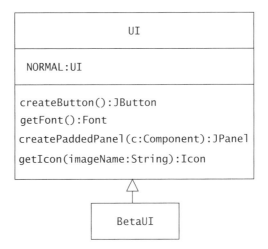

FIGURE 17.1 Instances of the `UI` and `BetaUI` classes are abstract factories that create families of GUI controls.

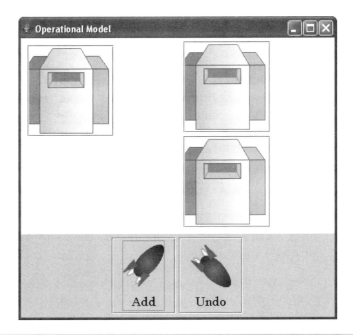

FIGURE 17.2 This visualization adds machines at the top-left location of the panel and lets a user drag machines into place. Users can undo either drags or adds.

The visualization in Figure 17.2 lets the user add machines and drag them around the factory floor. (The executable that shows this visualization is the ShowVisualization program in the app.abstractFactory directory.) The application gets its buttons from a UI object that the Visualization class accepts in its constructor. Figure 17.3 shows the Visualization class.

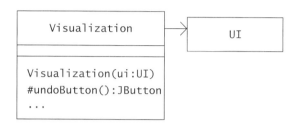

FIGURE 17.3 The Visualization class builds a GUI, using a UI factory object.

The Visualization class builds its GUI, using a UI object. For example, the code for the undoButton() method is as follows:

```
protected JButton undoButton() {
    if (undoButton == null) {
        undoButton = ui.createButtonCancel();
        undoButton.setText("Undo");
        undoButton.setEnabled(false);
        undoButton.addActionListener(mediator.undoAction());
    }
    return undoButton;
}
```

This code creates a cancel button and changes its text to Undo. The UI class determines the size and placement of the image and text on the button. The button-producing code of the UI class is as follows:

```
public JButton createButton() {
    JButton button = new JButton();
    button.setSize(128, 128);
    button.setFont(getFont());
    button.setVerticalTextPosition(AbstractButton.BOTTOM);
    button.setHorizontalTextPosition(AbstractButton.CENTER);
    return button;
}
```

```
public JButton createButtonOk() {
    JButton button = createButton();
    button.setIcon(getIcon("images/rocket-large.gif"));
    button.setText("Ok!");
    return button;
}

public JButton createButtonCancel() {
    JButton button = createButton();
    button.setIcon(getIcon("images/rocket-large-down.gif"));
    button.setText("Cancel!");
    return button;
}
```

To produce a different look-and-feel for the visualization, we can create a subclass that overrides some of the elements of the UI factory class. We can pass an instance of this GUI factory to the Visualization class's constructor.

Suppose that we release a version of the Visualization class with new features, and while this code is in beta test, we want to change the user interface. Let's say that we want fonts to be italicized and that in place of the rocket images, we want to use cherry-large.gif and cherry-large-down.gif images. The code for a BetaUI class will look something like the following:

```
public class BetaUI extends UI {
    public BetaUI () {
        Font oldFont = getFont();
        font = new Font(
            oldFont.getName(),
            oldFont.getStyle() | Font.ITALIC,
            oldFont.getSize());
    }

    public JButton createButtonOk() {
        // Challenge!
    }

    public JButton createButtonCancel() {
        // Challenge!
    }
}
```

CHALLENGE 17.1

Complete the code for the `BetaUI` class.

A solution appears on page 394.

The following code runs the visualization with the new look-and-feel:

```
package app.abstractFactory;
// ...
public class ShowBetaVisualization {
    public static void main(String[] args) {
        JPanel panel = new Visualization(new BetaUI());
        SwingFacade.launch(panel, "Operational Model");
    }
}
```

This program runs the visualization with the look shown in
Figure 17.4. Instances of the `UI` and `BetaUI` classes supply different

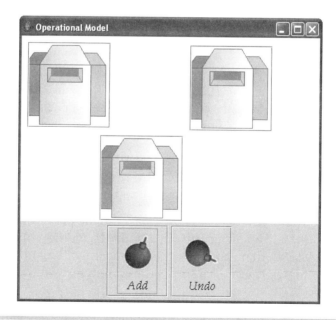

FIGURE 17.4 With no code changes to the `Visualization` class, the application
shows the new look-and-feel provided by the `BetaUI` class.

families of GUI controls to provide different looks to a GUI application. Although this is a useful application of ABSTRACT FACTORY, the design is somewhat fragile. In particular, the BetaUI class depends on the ability to override the creation methods and to have access to certain protected instance variables—notably font—of the UI class.

CHALLENGE 17.2

Suggest a design change that would still allow for the development of a variety of GUI control factories but that would reduce the reliance of subclasses on method modifiers in the UI class.

A solution appears on page 395.

ABSTRACT FACTORY frees a client from knowing which classes to instantiate when it needs new objects. In this regard, ABSTRACT FACTORY is similar to a set of FACTORY METHODS. In some cases, a FACTORY METHOD design may grow into an ABSTRACT FACTORY design.

Abstract Factories and Factory Method

Chapter 16, FACTORY METHOD, introduced a pair of classes that implement the CreditCheck interface. The CreditCheckFactory class instantiates one of these classes when a client calls its create-CreditCheck() method. Which class the factory instantiates depends on whether the usual credit agency is up and running. This design isolates other developers from the status of the credit agency. Figure 17.5 shows the CreditCheckFactory class and the current implementations of the CreditCheck interface.

The CreditCheckFactory class usually provides credit agency information about a customer's credit. In addition, the credit package has classes that can look up shipping and billing information for a customer. Figure 17.5 shows the current com.oozinoz.credit package.

Now suppose that a requirements analyst tells you that Oozinoz wants to start servicing customers in Canada. To do business in Canada, you will use a different credit agency and different data sources to determine shipping and billing information.

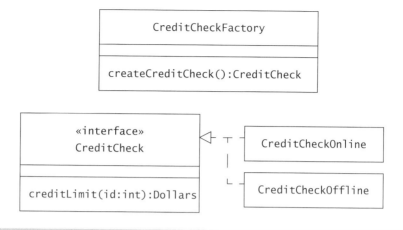

FIGURE 17.5 A FACTORY METHOD design that isolates clients from knowledge of which class to instantiate for performing credit checks

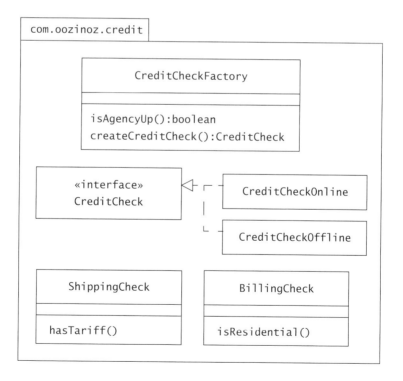

FIGURE 17.6 Classes in this package check a customer's credit, shipping address, and billing address.

When a customer calls, the call center application needs a *family* of objects to perform a variety of checks. The family to use depends on whether the call is from Canada or from the United States. You can apply the Abstract Factory pattern to provide for the creation of these object families.

Expanding to Canada will nearly double the number of classes that support credit checks. Suppose that you decide to maintain these classes in three packages. The credit package will now contain three "check" interfaces and one abstract factory class. This class will have three creation methods that supply appropriate objects for checking credit, billing, and shipping information. You will also put Credit-CheckOffline in this package, assuming that you can use this class for offline checks regardless of a call's origin. Figure 17.7 shows the new contents of the com.oozinoz.credit package.

To implement the interfaces in credit with concrete classes, you can introduce two new packages: com.oozinoz.credit.ca and com.oozinoz.credit.us. Each of these can contain a concrete version of the factory class and classes to implement each of the interfaces in credit.

CHALLENGE 17.3

Complete the diagram in Figure 17.8, which shows the classes in com.oozinoz.credit.ca and their relation to classes and interfaces in credit.

A solution appears on page 396.

The concrete factory classes for Canadian and U.S. calls are fairly simple. They return the Canadian or U.S. versions of the "check" interfaces, with the exception that both concrete factories return a CreditCheckOffline object if the local credit agency is offline. As in the previous chapter, the CreditCheckFactory class has an isAgencyUp() method that tells whether the credit agency is available.

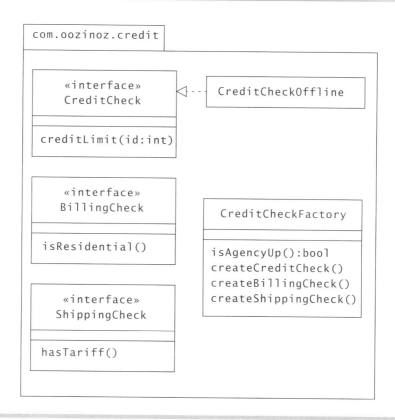

FIGURE 17.7 The revised package contains primarily interfaces and an abstract factory class.

CHALLENGE 17.4

Complete the code for CheckFactoryCanada.cs:

```
package com.oozinoz.credit.ca;

import com.oozinoz.credit.*;

public class CheckFactoryCanada extends CreditCheckFactory {
    // Challenge!
}
```

A solution appears on page 397.

At this point, you have a design that applies the ABSTRACT FACTORY pattern to provide for the creation of families of objects that conduct checks of different kinds of customer information. An instance of the abstract CreditCheckFactory class will be either a CheckFactory-Canada class or a CheckFactoryUS class. These objects are abstract factories, capable of creating billing, shipping, and credit check objects that are appropriate for the country the factory object represents.

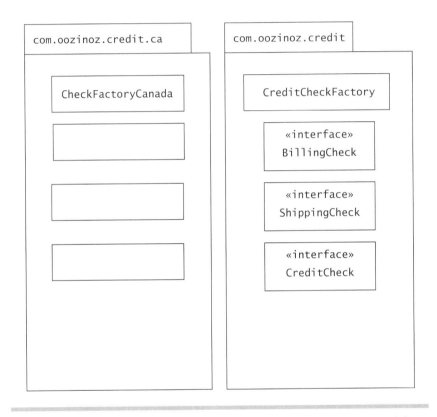

FIGURE 17.8 Show the classes in the com.oozinoz.credit.ca package, and show their relationships to classes in com.oozinoz.credit.

Packages and Abstract Factories

Speaking loosely, a package usually contains a *family* of classes, and an abstract factory produces a *family* of objects. In the previous example, you used separate packages to support abstract factories for Canada and the United States, with a third package that provides common interfaces for the objects the factories produce.

CHALLENGE 17.5

Write down an argument supporting the decision to place each factory and its related classes in a separate package. Or, argue that another approach is superior.

A solution appears on page 397.

Summary

The ABSTRACT FACTORY pattern lets you arrange for a client to create objects that are part of a family of related or dependent objects. A classic application of this pattern is for look-and-feel families—kits—of GUI controls. Other themes that run across a family of objects are possible, such as a customer's country of residence. As with FACTORY METHOD, ABSTRACT FACTORY isolates clients from knowing which class to instantiate. ABSTRACT FACTORY lets you provide a client with a factory that produces objects that are related by a common theme.

18

PROTOTYPE

When you develop a class, you ordinarily furnish it with constructors to let client applications instantiate it. In some circumstances, you may decide to isolate users of your class from directly calling a constructor. The construction-oriented patterns covered so far — Builder, Factory Method, and Abstract Factory—all provide this isolation. These patterns establish methods that instantiate an appropriate class on a client's behalf. The Prototype pattern also conceals object creation from clients but uses a different approach.

The intent of the Prototype pattern is to provide new objects by copying an example rather than by bringing forth new, uninitialized instances of a class.

Prototypes as Factories

Suppose that you are using the Abstract Factory pattern at Oozinoz to provide user interfaces for several different contexts. Figure 18.1 shows the user interface factories that might evolve.

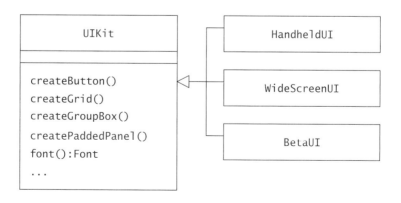

FIGURE 18.1 Three abstract factories, or kits, produce different user interface look-and-feels.

The users at Oozinoz enjoy the productivity that results from applying the right user interface in the right context. The problem you face is that they want several more user interface kits, and it's becoming burdensome to create a new class for each context your users envision. To halt the proliferation of user interface factory classes, a developer at Oozinoz suggests applying the PROTOTYPE pattern as follows.

- Drop the subclasses of UIKit.

- Let each *instance* of UIKit become a user interface factory that works by handing out copies of prototypical controls.

- Place the code that creates new UIKit objects in static methods on the UIKit class.

With this design, a UIKit object will have a complete set of prototypical instance variables: a button object, a grid object, a padded panel object, and so on. The code that creates a new UIKit object will set the values of these prototypical controls to produce the desired look-and-feel. The create-() methods will return copies of these prototypical controls.

For example, we can create a static handheldUI() method on the UI class. This method will instantiate UIKit, set this object's instance variables to values that are appropriate for a handheld display, and return the object for use as a GUI kit.

CHALLENGE 18.1

A PROTOTYPE design will cut down on the number of classes that Oozinoz uses to maintain multiple GUI kits. Name two other pros or cons of this design approach.

A solution appears on page 398.

The normal way to create an object is to invoke a class constructor. The PROTOTYPE pattern offers a flexible alternative, letting you determine at runtime which object to use as a model for the new one. However, the PROTOTYPE approach in Java does not allow new objects to have methods different from those of their parent. You may need to evaluate the advantages and disadvantages of a prototyping scheme, and you may want to experiment with PROTOTYPE to see whether it suits your needs. To use PROTOTYPE, you'll need to master the mechanics of copying objects in Java.

Prototyping with Clones

The intent of the PROTOTYPE pattern is to provide new objects by copying an example. When you copy an object, the new object will have the same attributes and behavior as its parent. The new object may also inherit some or all of the parent object's data values. For example, a copy of a padded panel should have the same padding value as the original.

An important question to ask is: When you copy an object, does the copy operation provide copies of the original object's attribute values, or does the copy share these values with the original? As a developer, it is easy to forget to ask this question or to answer it incorrectly. Defects commonly arise when developers make mistaken assumptions about the mechanics of copying. Many classes in the Java class libraries offer support for copying, but as a developer, you must understand how copying works, especially if you want to use PROTOTYPE.

CHALLENGE 18.2

The `Object` class includes a `clone()` method that all objects inherit. If you're not familiar with this method, look it up in online help or other documentation. Then write in your own words what this method does.

A solution appears on page 399.

CHALLENGE 18.3

Suppose that the `Machine` class had two attributes: an integer ID and a `Location`, where `Location` is a separate class.

Draw an object diagram that shows a `Machine` object, its `Location` object, and any other objects that result from invoking `clone()` on the `Machine` object.

A solution appears on page 399.

The clone() method makes it easy to add a copy() method to a class. For example, you might create a class of cloneable panels with the following code:

```
package com.oozinoz.ui;
import javax.swing.JPanel;

public class OzPanel extends JPanel implements Cloneable {
    // dangerous!
    public OzPanel copy() {
        return (OzPanel) this.clone();
    }
    // ...
}
```

The copy() method in this code makes cloning publicly available and casts the copy to the appropriate type. The problem with this code is that the clone() method will create copies of all the attributes of a JPanel object, regardless of whether you understand the function of those attributes. Note that the attributes of the JPanel class include the attributes of all its ancestors, as Figure 18.2 highlights.

As Figure 18.2 suggests, the OzPanel class inherits a large number of properties from the Component class, and these are often the only attributes that you need to copy when working with GUI objects.

CHALLENGE 18.4

Write an OzPanel.copy2() method that copies a panel without relying on clone(). Assume that the only attributes that are important to a copy are background, font, and foreground.

A solution appears on page 400.

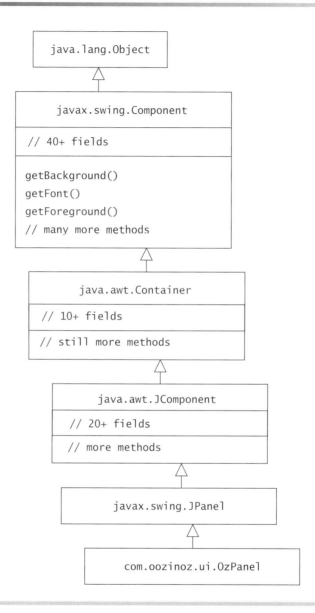

FIGURE 18.2 The OzPanel class inherits a large number of fields and variables from its superclasses.

Summary

The PROTOTYPE pattern lets a client create new objects by copying an example. A major difference between calling a constructor and copying an object is that a copy typically includes some of the state of the original object. You can use this to your advantage, particularly when different "classes" of objects differ only in their attributes and not in their behaviors. In such a case, you can create new classes at runtime by crafting prototypical objects for a client to copy.

When you need to create a copy, the `Object.clone()` method can help, but you must remember that this method creates a new object with the same fields. This object may not be a suitable copy, and any difficulties related to deeper copying are your responsibility. If a prototypical object has too many fields, you can create a copy by instantiating a new object and setting its fields to match only the aspects of original object that you need to copy.

19

MEMENTO

SOMETIMES, THE OBJECT you want to create is one that existed previously. This occurs when you want to let a user undo operations, revert to an earlier version of work, or resume previously suspended work.

The intent of the MEMENTO pattern is to provide storage and restoration of an object's state.

A Classic Example: Using Memento for Undo

Chapter 17, ABSTRACT FACTORY, introduced a visualization application that lets users perform operational modeling experiments with material flow through a factory. Suppose that the functionality for the Undo button has not yet been implemented. We can apply the MEMENTO pattern to make the Undo button work.

A **memento** is an object that holds state information. In the visualization application, the state we need to preserve is that of the application. Whenever adding or moving a machine, a user should be able to undo that change by clicking Undo. To add the undo function to the visualization, we will need to decide how to capture the state of the application in a memento. We will also have to decide when to capture this state, and how to restore the application to a previously captured state. When the application starts up, it appears as in Figure 19.1.

The visualization starts up in an empty state, which *is* a state. Any time that the visualization is in this empty state, the Undo button should be disabled. After a few adds and drags, the visualization might appear as in Figure 19.2.

The state that we need to capture in a memento consists of a list of the locations of the machines that the user has placed. We can keep a

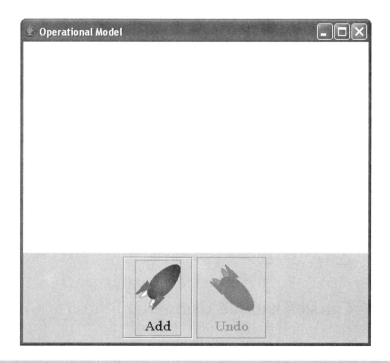

FIGURE 19.1 When the visualization application starts up, the work panel is blank, and the Undo button is disabled.

stack of these mementos, popping one each time the user clicks Undo.

- Each time the user adds or moves a machine in the visualization, your code will create a memento of the simulated factory and add it to a stack.

- Each time the user clicks the Undo button, your code will pop the most recent memento and then restore the simulation to the state stored at the top of the stack.

When your visualization starts up, you will stack an initial, empty memento and never pop it, to ensure that the top of the stack is always a valid memento. Any time the stack contains only one memento, you disable the Undo button.

We might write the code for this program in a single class, but we expect to add features that support operational modeling and other

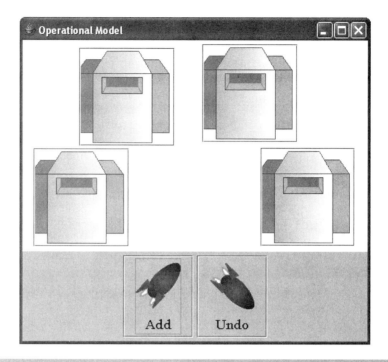

FIGURE 19.2 Users can add and rearrange machines in the visualization.

features that your users may request. Eventually, the application may grow large, so it is wise to use an MVC design that you can build on. Figure 19.3 shows a design that moves the work of modeling the factory into a separate class.

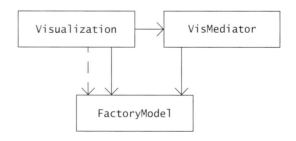

FIGURE 19.3 This design divides the application's work into separate classes for modeling the factory, providing GUI elements, and handling a user's clicks.

This design lets you first focus on developing a FactoryModel class that has no GUI controls and no dependency on the GUI.

The FactoryModel class is at the center of our design. It is responsible for maintaining the current configuration of machines and for maintaining mementos of previous configurations.

Each time a client asks the factory to add or move a machine, the factory will create a copy—a memento—of its current locations and push this onto its stack of mementos. In this example, we do not need a special Memento class. Each memento is merely a list of points: the list of machine locations at a particular time.

The factory model must provide events that let clients register interest in changes to the factory state. This lets the visualization GUI inform the model of changes that the user makes. Suppose that you want the factory to let clients register for the events of adding a machine and dragging a machine. Figure 19.4 shows a design for a FactoryModel class.

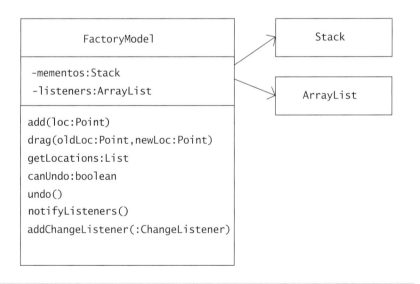

FIGURE 19.4 The FactoryModel class maintains a stack of factory configurations and lets clients register for notification of changes in the factory.

The design in Figure 19.4 calls for the FactoryModel class to provide clients with the ability to register for notification of several events.

For example, consider the event of adding a machine. Any registered ChangeListener object will be notified of this change:

```
package com.oozinoz.visualization;
// ...
public class FactoryModel {
    private Stack mementos;

    private ArrayList listeners = new ArrayList();

    public FactoryModel() {
        mementos = new Stack();
        mementos.push(new ArrayList());
    }
    //...
}
```

The constructor starts off the factory's initial configuration as an empty list. The remaining methods in the class maintain the stack of machine configuration mementos and fire events that correspond to any changes. For example, to add a machine to the current configuration, a client can call the following method:

```
public void add(Point location) {
    List oldLocs = (List) mementos.peek();
    List newLocs = new ArrayList(oldLocs);
    newLocs.add(0, location);
    mementos.push(newLocs);
    notifyListeners();
}
```

This code creates a new list of machine locations and pushes the list on the stack of mementos that the factory model maintains. A subtlety here is that the code ensures that the new machine is first in this list. This is a clue to the visualization that a picture of this machine should appear in front of any other machines that the picture may overlap.

A client that registers for the change notification might update its view of the factory model by rebuilding itself entirely on receiving any event from the factory model. The factory model's latest configuration is always available from getLocations(), whose code is as follows:

```
public List getLocations() {
    return (List) mementos.peek();
}
```

The undo() method of the FactoryModel class lets a client change the model of machine locations to be a previous version. When this code executes, it also calls notifyListeners().

CHALLENGE 19.1

Write the code for the FactoryModel class's undo() method.

A solution appears on page 400.

An interested client can provide undo support by registering as a listener, supplying a method that rebuilds the client's view of the factory. The Visualization class is one such client.

The MVC design in Figure 19.3 separates the tasks of translating user actions from the tasks of maintaining the GUI. The Visualization class creates its GUI controls but passes off the handling of GUI events to a mediator. The VisMediator class translates GUI events into appropriate changes in the factory model. When the model changes, the GUI may need to update. The Visualization class registers for the notification that the FactoryModel class provides. Note the division of responsibility.

- The visualization changes factory events into GUI changes.

- The mediator translates GUI events into factory changes.

Figure 19.5 shows the three collaborating classes in more detail.

Suppose that while dragging a machine image, a user accidentally drops it in the wrong spot and clicks Undo. To be able to handle this click, the visualization registers the mediator for notification of but-

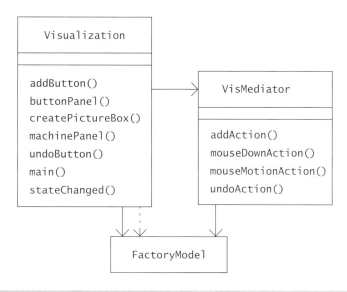

FIGURE 19.5 The mediator translates GUI events into factory model changes, and the visualization reacts to factory events to update the GUI.

ton events. The code for the Undo button in the Visualization class is:

```
protected JButton undoButton() {
    if (undoButton == null) {
        undoButton = ui.createButtonCancel();
        undoButton.setText("Undo");
        undoButton.setEnabled(false);
        undoButton.addActionListener(mediator.undoAction());
    }
    return undoButton;
}
```

This code passes responsibility for handling a click to the mediator. The mediator informs the factory model of any requested changes. The mediator translates an undo request to a factory change with the following code:

```
private void undo(ActionEvent e) {
        factoryModel.undo();
}
```

The factoryModel variable in this method is an instance of Factory-
Model that the Visualization class creates and passes the mediator in
the VisMediator class's constructor. We have already examined the
FactoryModel class's pop() command. The flow of messages that
occurs when the user clicks Undo appears in Figure 19.6.

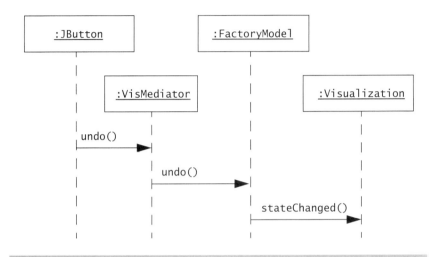

FIGURE 19.6 This diagram shows the message flow that occurs when the user clicks
Add.

When the FactoryModel class pops its current configuration, expos-
ing the previous configuration it stored as a memento, the undo()
method notifies any ChangeListeners. The Visualization class registers for this in its constructor:

```
public Visualization(UI ui) {
    super(new BorderLayout());
    this.ui = ui;
    mediator = new VisMediator(factoryModel);
    factoryModel.addChangeListener(this);
    add(machinePanel(), BorderLayout.CENTER);
    add(buttonPanel(), BorderLayout.SOUTH);
}
```

For each machine location in the factory model, the visualization
maintains a Component object that it creates with its createPicture-
Box() method. The stateChanged() method must clear all the picture box controls from the machine panel, and re-add new picture

boxes from the current set of locations in the factory model. The `stateChanged()` method must also disable the Undo button if the factory has only a single memento left on its stack.

CHALLENGE 19.2

Write the `stateChanged()` method for the `Visualization` class.

A solution appears on page 401.

The MEMENTO pattern lets you save and restore an object's state. A common use of MEMENTO is related to providing undo support in applications. In some applications, as in the factory visualization example, the repository for the information you need to store can be another object. In other cases, you may need to store mementos in a more durable form.

Memento Durability

A memento is a tiny repository that saves an object's state. You can create a memento by using another object, a string, or a file. The anticipated duration between the storage and reconstruction of an object has an effect on the strategy that you can use in designing a memento. The time that elapses can be moments, hours, days, or years.

CHALLENGE 19.3

Write down two reasons that might drive you to save a memento in a file rather than as an object.

A solution appears on page 402.

Persisting Mementos Across Sessions

A **session** occurs when a user runs a program, conducts transactions in the program, and exits. Suppose that your users want to be able to save a simulation in one session and restore it in another session. This ability is a matter normally referred to as **persistent storage**. Persistent storage fulfills the intent of the MEMENTO pattern and is a natural extension to the undo functionality you have already implemented.

Suppose that you subclass the Visualization class with a Visualization2 class that has a menu bar with a File menu with Save As... and Restore From... items:

```
package com.oozinoz.visualization;

import javax.swing.*;
import com.oozinoz.ui.SwingFacade;
import com.oozinoz.ui.UI;

public class Visualization2 extends Visualization {
    public Visualization2(UI ui) {
        super(ui);
    }

    public JMenuBar menus() {
        JMenuBar menuBar = new JMenuBar();

        JMenu menu = new JMenu("File");
        menuBar.add(menu);

        JMenuItem menuItem = new JMenuItem("Save As...");
        menuItem.addActionListener(mediator.saveAction());
        menu.add(menuItem);

        menuItem = new JMenuItem("Restore From...");
        menuItem.addActionListener(
            mediator.restoreAction());
        menu.add(menuItem);

        return menuBar;
    }

    public static void main(String[] args) {
        Visualization2 panel = new Visualization2(UI.NORMAL);
        JFrame frame = SwingFacade.launch(
            panel, "Operational Model");
        frame.setJMenuBar(panel.menus());
        frame.setVisible(true);
    }
}
```

This code requires the addition of saveAction() and restore-Action() methods to the VisMediator class. The MenuItem objects cause these actions to be called when the menu is selected. When the Visualization2 class runs, the GUI appears as in Figure 19.7.

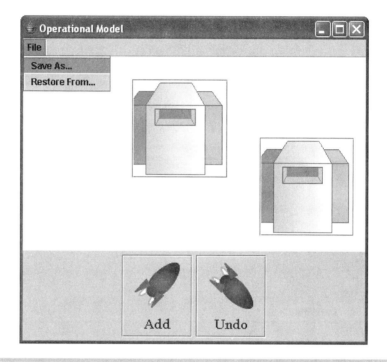

FIGURE 19.7 The addition of a File menu lets a user save a memento that the application can later restore from.

An easy way to store an object, such as the factory model's topmost configuration, is to serialize it. The code for the saveAction() method in the VisMediator class might appear as follows:

```
public ActionListener saveAction() {
    return new ActionListener() {
        public void actionPerformed(ActionEvent e) {
            try {
                VisMediator.this.save((Component)e.getSource());
```

```
            } catch (Exception ex) {
                System.out.println(
                    "Failed save: " + ex.getMessage());
        }
    }};
}

public void save(Component source) throws Exception {
    JFileChooser dialog = new JFileChooser();
    dialog.showSaveDialog(source);

    if (dialog.getSelectedFile() == null)
        return;

    FileOutputStream out = null;
    ObjectOutputStream s = null;
    try {
        out = new FileOutputStream(dialog.getSelectedFile());
        s = new ObjectOutputStream(out);
        s.writeObject(factoryModel.getLocations());
    } finally {
        if (s != null) s.close();
    }
}
```

CHALLENGE 19.4

Write the code for the `restoreAction()` method of the `VisMediator` class.

A solution appears on page 402.

Design Patterns states the intent of the MEMENTO pattern as, "Without violating encapsulation, capture and externalize an object's internal state so that the object can be restored to this state later" (p. 283).

CHALLENGE 19.5

In this case, we used Java serialization to write to a file in binary format. Suppose that we had written it to XML format (textual) instead. Write a short statement of whether, in your opinion, saving a memento in textual form would violate encapsulation.

A solution appears on page 403.

You should understand what a developer means in saying that he or she creates mementos by storing an object's data via serialization or via writing to an XML file. That's the point of design patterns: By using a common vocabulary, we can readily discuss design concepts and their application.

Summary

The Memento pattern lets you capture an object's state so you can restore the object later. The means of storage may depend on whether you need to be able to restore an object after a few clicks and key-strokes or after days or years. The most common reason for saving and restoring objects during an application session is the support of undo operations. In such a case, you can store an object's state in another object. To let an object persist across sessions, you can save the memento through object serialization or other means.

PART IV

OPERATION PATTERNS

20

INTRODUCING OPERATIONS

WHEN YOU WRITE a Java method, you produce a fundamental unit of work that is a level up from writing a statement. Your methods have to participate in an overall design, architecture, and test plan, but writing methods is central to object-oriented programming. Ironically, despite the central role of methods, it is easy to get confused about what methods are and how methods function. This confusion may stem from the tendency of many developers—and authors—to mix the meaning of the words *method* and *operation*. Further, the concepts of *algorithm* and *polymorphism* are more abstract than methods and yet are ultimately realized by methods.

Having a clear understanding of the terms *algorithm, polymorphism, method,* and *operation* will help you understand several design patterns. In particular, STATE, STRATEGY, and INTERPRETER all work by implementing an operation in methods across several classes, but such observations are useful only if we agree on the meaning of *method* and *operation*.

Operations and Methods

Of the many terms that relate to the work that a class may be called on to perform, it is especially useful to distinguish *operation* from *method*. The UML defines the difference between an operation and a method as follows.

- An **operation** is a specification of a service that can be requested from an instance of a class.

- A **method** is an implementation of an operation.

Note that the meaning of **operation** is a level of abstraction up from the idea of **method**.

An operation specifies something that a class does and specifies the interface for calling on this service. Multiple classes may implement the same operation in different ways. For example, many classes implement the `toString()` operation, each in its own way. Every class that implements an operation implements it with a method. That method contains—or *is*—the code that makes the operation work for that class.

The definitions of *method* and *operation* help to clarify the structure of many design patterns. Because design patterns are a level up from classes and methods, it is no surprise that operations feature prominently in many patterns. For example, COMPOSITE arranges for operations to apply to both items and groups. PROXY lets an intermediary that has the same operations as a target object interpose itself to manage access to the target.

CHALLENGE 20.1

Use the words **operation** and **method** to explain how CHAIN OF RESPONSIBILITY implements an operation.

A solution appears on page 403.

In Java, a method declaration includes a *header* and a *body*. A method's **body** is the series of instructions that can be called into action by invoking the method's signature. A method's **header** includes the method's return type and signature and may include modifiers and a throws clause. The form of a method header is:

modifiers return-type signature throws-clause

CHALLENGE 20.2

Write down as many of the nine Java method modifiers as you can.

An answer appears on page 403.

Signatures

On the surface, the meaning of **operation** is similar to the meaning of **signature**. Both words refer to the interface into a method. When you write a method, it becomes available for invocation according to its signature. Section 8.4.2 of the *Java™ Language Specification* [Arnold and Gosling 1998] says:

> The signature of a method consists of the name of the method and the number and types of formal parameters to the method.

Note that a method's signature does not include its return type, although if a method declaration overrides the declaration of another method, a compile-time error occurs if they have different return types.

CHALLENGE 20.3

The method `Bitmap.clone()` returns `Object`, even though the method always returns an instance of the `Bitmap` class. Would it still compile if its return type were declared as a `Bitmap`?

An answer appears on page 404.

A signature specifies which method is invoked when a client makes a call. An *operation* is a specification of a service that can be requested. The meanings of the terms *signature* and *operation* are similar, yet the words are not synonyms. The difference between the meaning of these terms is mainly in the context in which they apply. The term operation applies when discussing the idea that methods in different classes may have the same interface. The term *signature* applies when discussing the rules that govern how Java matches a method call to a method in the receiving object. A signature depends on a method's name and parameters but not on the method's return type.

Exceptions

In *Illness as Metaphor,* Susan Sontag observes: "Everyone who is born holds dual citizenship, in the kingdom of the well and in the kingdom of the sick" (Sontag 1978, p. 35). This metaphor applies to methods as well as to people: Instead of returning normally, methods may throw an exception or may call another method that causes an exception to be thrown. When a method returns normally, program control returns to the point just after the method call. A different set of rules applies in the kingdom of exceptions.

When an exception is thrown, the Java execution environment must find a containing `try/catch` statement that matches the exception. The `try/catch` statement may exist in the method that throws the exception, in the method that called the current method, or in the method that called the previous method, and so on, back through the current stack of method calls. If no matching `try/catch` statement is found, the programs stops; it crashes.

Any method can throw an exception with a `throw` statement. For example:

```
throw new Exception("Good Luck!");
```

If your application uses a method that throws an exception that you haven't planned for, your application can unceremoniously crash. To prevent this sort of behavior, you need to have an architectural plan that species the points that catch and react appropriately to exceptions in your application. You might think that it's a bother to have to declare the possibility of throwing an exception. C#, for example, does not require methods to declare exceptions. C++ allows an exception specification to appear but doesn't require the compiler to check callers against it.

CHALLENGE 20.4

Unlike Java, C# does not require methods to declare any exceptions that they might throw. Write down your opinion of whether this is an improvement on Java's rules.

A solution appears on page 404.

Algorithms and Polymorphism

Algorithms and polymorphism are important ideas in programming, but it can be difficult to explain what we mean by these terms. If you want to show someone a method, you can edit the source code for a class and point to lines of code. Occasionally, an algorithm may exist entirely within one method, but an algorithm's work often relies on the interplay of several methods. In *Introduction to Algorithms* [Cormen, Leiserson, and Rivest 1990, p. 1], say:

> An *algorithm* is any well-defined computational procedure that takes some value, or set of values, as input and produces some value, or set of values, as output.

An **algorithm** is a procedure—a sequence of instructions—that accepts inputs and produces output. A single method may be an algorithm: It accepts inputs—its parameter list—and produces as output its return value. However, many algorithms require more than one method to execute in an object-oriented program. For example, the isTree() algorithm in Chapter 5, COMPOSITE, requires four methods, as Figure 20.1 shows.

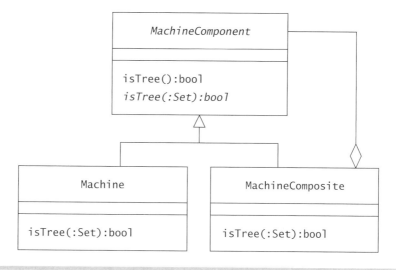

FIGURE 20.1 Four isTree() methods collaborate to effect the algorithm for determining whether an instance of MachineComponent is a tree.

> **CHALLENGE 20.5**
>
> How many algorithms, how many operations, and how many methods does Figure 20.1 depict?
>
> *An answer appears on page 405.*

Algorithms get something done. They may appear as part of a method, or they may involve many methods. In OO computing, algorithms that require more than one method often rely on *polymorphism* to allow multiple implementations of a single operation. **Polymorphism** is the principle that method invocation depends on both the operation invoked and the class of the invocation receiver. For example, you might ask which method executes when Java encounters the expression `m.isTree()`. The answer is, *it depends*. If m is an instance of `Machine`, Java will invoke `Machine.isTree()`. If m is an instance of `MachineComposite`, Java will invoke `MachineComposite.isTree()`. Informally, polymorphism means that the right method gets invoked for the right type of object. Many patterns use polymorphism, which in some cases ties directly to the intent of the pattern.

Summary

Although it is common to intermingle the meanings of *operation, method, signature,* and *algorithm,* preserving their distinctions makes it easier to describe important concepts. An operation is, like a signature, a specification of a service. The word *operation* applies when talking about the idea that many methods may have the same interface. The word *signature* applies when discussing method lookup rules. A method definition includes its signature—its name and parameter list—along with modifiers, return type, and the method's body. A method *has* a signature and *implements* an operation.

The normal way to invoke a method is to call it. The normal way for a method to conclude is for it to return, but any method will stop executing when it encounters an unhandled exception.

An *algorithm* is a procedure that accepts inputs and produces outputs. Methods accept inputs, produce outputs, and contain a procedural method body, and some authors may refer to a method body as an "algorithm." However, an algorithm's procedure may involve many operations and methods, or it may exist as part of another method. The word *algorithm* best applies when you are discussing a procedure that produces a result.

Many design patterns involve distributing an operation across several classes. You can also say that these patterns rely on *polymorphism,* the principle that method selection depends on the class of the object that receives a method call.

Beyond Ordinary Operations

Different classes can implement an operation in different ways. In other words, Java supports polymorphism. The power of this seemingly simple idea appears in several design patterns.

If you intend to	Apply the pattern
• Implement an algorithm in a method, deferring the definition of some steps of the algorithm so that subclasses can redefine them	TEMPLATE METHOD
• Distribute an operation so that each class represents a different state	STATE
• Encapsulate an operation, making implementations interchangeable	STRATEGY
• Encapsulate a method call in an object	COMMAND
• Distribute an operation so that each implementation applies to a different type of composition	INTERPRETER

Operation-oriented patterns address contexts in which you need more than one method, usually with the same signature, to participate in a design. For example, the TEMPLATE METHOD pattern allows subclasses to implement methods that adjust the effect of a procedure defined in a superclass.

TEMPLATE METHOD

ORDINARY METHODS HAVE bodies that define a sequence of instructions. It is also quite ordinary for a method to invoke methods on the current object and on other objects. In this sense, ordinary methods are "templates" that outline a series of instructions for the computer to follow. The TEMPLATE METHOD pattern, however, involves a more specific type of template.

When you write a method, you may want to define the outline of an algorithm while allowing for the fact that there may be differences in how you want to implement certain steps. In this case, you can define the method but leave some steps as abstract methods, as stubbed-out methods, or as methods defined in a separate interface. This produces a more rigid "template" that specifically defines which steps of an algorithm other classes can or must supply.

The intent of TEMPLATE METHOD is to implement an algorithm in a method, deferring the definition of some steps of the algorithm so that other classes can redefine them.

A Classic Example: Sorting

Sorting algorithms are ancient and highly reusable. Suppose that a prehistoric woman devised a method for sorting arrows by the sharpness of their heads. Perhaps she lined up the arrows and made a series of left-to-right sweeps, switching each arrow with one on its left if the left arrowhead was sharper. Having worked out this algorithm, she may then have realized that she could reapply the method to sort the arrows by their flight distance or by any other attribute.

Sorting algorithms vary in approach and speed, but every sorting algorithm relies on the primitive step of comparing two items, or attributes. If you have a sorting algorithm and can compare an attribute of any two items, your sorting algorithm will let you sort a collection of items by that attribute.

Sorting is an ancient example of TEMPLATE METHOD. It is a procedure that lets us change one critical step—the comparison of two objects— to reuse the algorithm for various attributes of various collections of objects.

In recent times, sorting probably reigns as the most frequently reim- plemented algorithm, with implementations likely outnumbering the number of existing programmers. But unless you are sorting a huge collection, there is no reason to write your own sorting algorithm.

The `Arrays` and `Collections` classes provide a `sort()` method, which are static, and take an array to sort as an argument, and take an optional `Comparator`. The `ArrayList` class's `sort()` method is an instance method that sorts the recipient of the `sort()` message. In other regards, these methods share a common strategy that depends on `Comparable` and `Comparator` interfaces, shown in Figure 21.1.

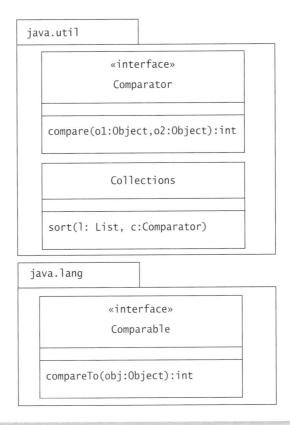

FIGURE 21.1 The `sort()` method in the `Collections` class uses the interfaces shown here.

The sort() methods in the Arrays and Collections classes allow you to provide an instance of a Comparator interface if you choose. If you use a sort() method without providing such an instance, the method will rely on the compareTo() method of the Comparable interface. An exception will occur if you attempt to sort items without providing a Comparator instance if the items do not implement the Comparable interface. But note that most basic types, such as String, do implement Comparable.

The sort() methods provide an example of TEMPLATE METHOD; the class libraries provide an algorithm that lets you supply one critical step: comparing two items. The compare() method returns a number less than, equal to, or greater than 0. These values correspond to the idea that, in a sense that you define, object o1 is less than, equal to, or greater than object o2. For example, the following code sorts a collection of rockets by their apogees and then by their names. (The rocket constructor accepts the name, mass, price, apogee, and thrust of the rocket.)

```
package app.templateMethod;

import java.util.Arrays;
import com.oozinoz.firework.Rocket;
import com.oozinoz.utility.Dollars;

public class ShowComparator {
    public static void main(String args[]) {
        Rocket r1 = new Rocket(
            "Sock-it", 0.8, new Dollars(11.95), 320, 25);
        Rocket r2 = new Rocket(
            "Sprocket", 1.5, new Dollars(22.95), 270, 40);
        Rocket r3 = new Rocket(
            "Mach-it", 1.1, new Dollars(22.95), 1000, 70);
        Rocket r4 = new Rocket(
            "Pocket", 0.3, new Dollars(4.95), 150, 20);
        Rocket[] rockets = new Rocket[] { r1, r2, r3, r4 };

        System.out.println("Sorted by apogee: ");
        Arrays.sort(rockets, new ApogeeComparator());
        for (int i = 0; i < rockets.length; i++)
            System.out.println(rockets[i]);
```

```
            System.out.println();
            System.out.println("Sorted by name: ");
            Arrays.sort(rockets, new NameComparator());
            for (int i = 0; i < rockets.length; i++)
                System.out.println(rockets[i]);
    }
}
```

Here are the comparators ApogeeComparator:

```
package app.templateMethod;

import java.util.Comparator;
import com.oozinoz.firework.Rocket;

public class ApogeeComparator implements Comparator {
    // Challenge!
}
```

and NameComparator:

```
package app.templateMethod;

import java.util.Comparator;
import com.oozinoz.firework.Rocket;

public class NameComparator implements Comparator {
    // Challenge!
}
```

The program printout depends on how Rocket implements toString() but shows the rockets sorted both ways:

```
Sorted by apogee:
Pocket
Sprocket
Sock-it
Mach-it

Sorted by name:
Mach-it
Pocket
Sock-it
Sprocket
```

> **CHALLENGE 21.1**
>
> Fill in the missing code in the `ApogeeComparator` and `NameComparator` classes so that the program will sort a collection of rockets correctly.
>
> *A solution appears on page 405.*

Sorting is a general algorithm that, except for one step, has nothing to do with the specifics of your domain or application. The critical step is the comparison of items. No sorting algorithm includes, for example, a step that compares the apogees of two rockets; an application needs to supply that step. The `sort()` methods and the `Comparator` interface let you supply a specific step to a general sorting algorithm.

TEMPLATE METHOD is not restricted to the case in which only the missing step is domain specific. Sometimes, the entire algorithm applies to a specific application domain.

Completing an Algorithm

The TEMPLATE METHOD pattern is similar to the ADAPTER pattern in that both patterns allow one developer to simplify and specify the way in which another developer's code completes a design. In ADAPTER, one developer may specify the interface for an object that a design requires. A second developer creates an object that provides the interface that the design expects but using the services of an existing class with a different interface. In TEMPLATE METHOD, one developer may provide a general algorithm, whereas a second developer supplies a key step of the algorithm. Consider the Aster star press that Figure 21.2 shows.

A **star press** from Aster Corporation accepts empty metal molds and presses fireworks stars into them. The machine has **hoppers** that dispense the chemicals that the machine mixes into a paste and presses into the molds. When the machine shuts down, it stops working on the mold in the processing area and ushers any molds on its input conveyor through the processing area to the output, without actually processing the molds. Then the machine discharges its current batch of paste and flushes its processing area with water. The machine

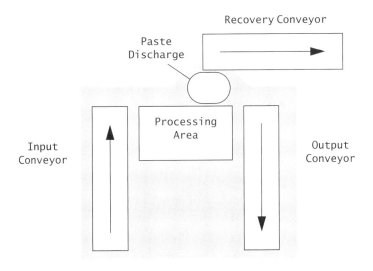

FIGURE 21.2 An Aster star press comes with input and output conveyors that move star press molds. Oozinoz adds a recovery conveyor that saves discarded star press paste.

orchestrates all this activity by using an onboard computer and the AsterStarPress class shown in Figure 21.3.

The Aster star press is smart and independent and aware that it may be running in a smart factory with which it must communicate. For example, the shutDown() method informs the factory if the mold it was processing is left incomplete:

```
public void shutdown() {
    if (inProcess()) {
        stopProcessing();
        markMoldIncomplete(currentMoldID);
    }
    usherInputMolds();
    dischargePaste();
    flush();
}
```

The markMoldIncomplete() method and the AsterStarPress class are abstract. At Oozinoz, you create a subclass that implements the required method and download this code to the star press computer. You can implement markMoldIncomplete() by passing the informa-

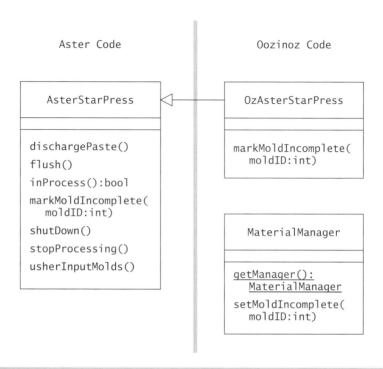

FIGURE 21.3 Star presses from Aster Corporation come with an abstract class that you must subclass to work at Oozinoz.

tion about the incomplete mold to the MaterialManager singleton that tracks material status.

CHALLENGE 21.2

Write the code for the markMoldIncomplete() method of the OzAsterStarPress class:

```
public class OzAsterStarPress extends AsterStarPress {
    public void markMoldIncomplete(int id) {
        // Challenge!
    }
}
```

A solution appears on page 406.

The Aster star press developers are well aware of how fireworks factories work and have done a good job of communicating with the factory at the right processing points. Nonetheless, it can happen that you need to establish communication at a point that the Aster developers have not foreseen.

TEMPLATE METHOD Hooks

A **hook** is a method call that a developer places in code to give other developers a chance to insert code at a specific spot in a procedure. When you are adapting another developer's code and need control at a point where you don't currently have it, you can request a hook. An obliging developer can add a method call at the point you need it. The developer will also usually supply a stubbed-out version of the hook method so that other clients need not necessarily override the hook method.

Consider the Aster star press that discharges its chemical paste and flushes itself with water when shutting down. The press has to discharge this paste to keep it from drying and clogging the machine. At Oozinoz, you recover this paste so that you can dice it for use as tiny stars in Roman candles. (A **Roman candle** is a stationary tube that contains a mixture of explosive charges, sparks, and stars.) After the star press discharges the paste, you arrange for a robot to move the paste to a separate conveyor, as Figure 21.2 shows. It is important to remove the paste before the machine flushes its processing area with water. The problem is that you want to gain control between the two statements in the `shutdown()` method:

```
dischargePaste();
flush();
```

You might override `dischargePaste()` with a method that adds a call to collect the paste.

```
public void dischargePaste() {
    super.dischargePaste();
    getFactory().collectPaste();
}
```

This method effectively inserts a step after discharging paste. The added step uses a `Factory` singleton to collect discarded paste. When the `shutdown()` method executes, the factory robot will now collect discarded paste before the `shutdown()` method flushes the press. Unfortunately, the `dischargePaste()` code is now dangerous, because paste collection is a surprising side effect. Developers at Aster will certainly be unaware that you're defining `dischargePaste()` in this way. If they modify their code to discharge paste at a time you don't want to collect it, an error will occur.

Developers usually strive to solve problems by writing code. But here the challenge is to solve a problem by communicating with other developers.

CHALLENGE 21.3

Write a note to the developers at Aster, asking for a change that will let you safely collect discarded star paste before the machine flushes its processing area.

A solution appears on page 406.

The step that a subclass supplies in TEMPLATE METHOD may be required to complete the algorithm or may be an optional step that hooks in a subclass's code, often at another developer's request. Although the intent of the pattern is to let a separate class define part of an algorithm, you can also apply TEMPLATE METHOD when you refactor an algorithm that appears in multiple methods.

Refactoring to TEMPLATE METHOD

When TEMPLATE METHOD is at work, you will find classes in a hierarchy where a superclass provides the outline of an algorithm and subclasses provide certain steps of the algorithm. You may introduce this arrangement, refactoring to TEMPLATE METHOD, when you find similar algorithms in different methods. (*Refactoring* is the process of transforming programs into equivalent programs with a better design.) Consider the `Machine` and `MachinePlanner` parallel hierarchy that you worked with in Chapter 16, FACTORY METHOD. As Figure 21.4 shows, the `Machine` class provides a `createPlanner()` method as a FACTORY METHOD that returns an appropriate subclass of `MachinePlanner`.

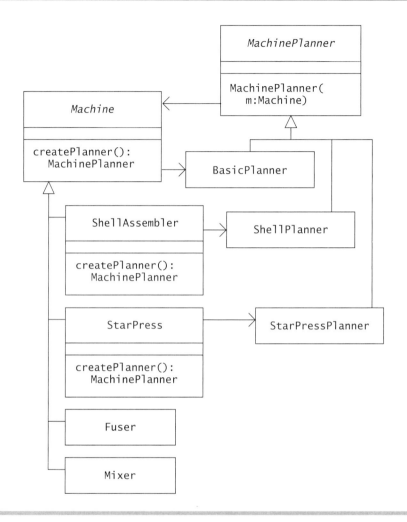

FIGURE 21.4 A Machine object can create an appropriate MachinePlanner instance for itself.

Two of the subclasses of Machine instantiate specific subclasses from the MachinePlanner hierarchy when asked to create a planner. These classes—ShellAssembler and StarPress—have a common problem in that they want to create a MachinePlanner only on demand.

Looking at the code for these classes, you might notice that the subclasses use similar techniques for lazy-initializing a planner. For example, the ShellAssembler class has a getPlanner() method that lazy-initializes a planner member:

```
public ShellPlanner getPlanner() {
    if (planner == null)
        planner = new ShellPlanner(this);
    return planner;
}
```

In the ShellPlanner class, planner is of type ShellPlanner. The StarPress class also has a planner member but declares it to be of type StarPressPlanner. The getPlanner() method of the StarPress class also lazy-initializes the planner attribute:

```
public StarPressPlanner getPlanner() {
    if (planner == null)
        planner = new StarPressPlanner(this);
    return planner;
}
```

The other subclasses of Machine have similar approaches to creating a planner only when it is first needed. This presents a refactoring opportunity, letting you clean up and reduce the amount of code that you maintain. Suppose that you decide to provide the Machine class with a planner attribute of type MachinePlanner, removing this attribute from subclasses and eliminating the existing getPlanner() methods.

CHALLENGE 21.4

Write the code for the getPlanner() method in the Machine class.

A solution appears on page 406.

You can often refactor your code into an instance of TEMPLATE METHOD by abstracting the outline of the similar methods, moving the outline method up to a superclass, and letting subclasses supply only the step where they differ in their implementation of the algorithm.

Summary

The intent of TEMPLATE METHOD is to define an algorithm in a method, leaving some steps abstract, stubbed out, or defined in an interface, so that other classes can fill them in.

TEMPLATE METHOD may function as a contract between developers. One developer supplies the outline of an algorithm, and another developer supplies a certain step of the algorithm. This may be a step that lets the algorithm complete, or it may be a step that the algorithm developer includes to hook in your code at specific points in the procedure.

The intent of TEMPLATE METHOD does not imply that you will always write the template method in advance of defining subclasses. You may discover similar methods in an existing hierarchy. In this case, you may be able to distill the outline of an algorithm and move it up to a superclass, applying TEMPLATE METHOD to simplify and organize your code.

22

STATE

T<small>HE</small> <small>STATE</small> OF an object is a combination of the current values of its attributes. When you call an object's `set-` method or assign a value to one of the object's fields, you are changing the object's state. Objects also commonly change their own state as their methods execute.

We sometimes use the word *state* to refer to a single, changing attribute of an object. For example, we may say that the state of a machine is up or down. In such a case, the changeable part of an object's state may be the most prominent aspect of its behavior. As a result, logic that depends on the object's state may spread through many of the class's methods. Similar or identical logic may appear many times, creating a maintenance burden.

One way to counter the spread of state-specific logic is to introduce a new group of classes, with each class representing a different state. Then you can place state-specific behavior into each of these classes.

The intent of the S<small>TATE</small> **pattern is to distribute state-specific logic across classes that represent an object's state.**

Modeling States

When you model an object whose state is important, you may find that you have a particular variable that tracks how the object should behave, depending on its state. This variable may appear in complex, cascading `if` statements that focus on how to react to the events that an object can experience. The problem with this approach to modeling state is not only that `if` statements can become complex but also that when you adjust how you model the state, you often have to adjust `if` statements in several methods. The S<small>TATE</small> pattern offers a cleaner, simpler approach, using a distributed operation. S<small>TATE</small> lets you model states as objects, encapsulating state-specific logic in separate classes. To see STATE at work, it will help to first look at a system that models states without using the STATE pattern. In the next section, we refactor this code to investigate whether the STATE pattern can improve the design.

Consider the Oozinoz software that models the state of a carousel door. A **carousel** is a large, smart rack that accepts material through a doorway and stores the material according to a bar code ID on it. The door operates with a single button. If the door is closed, touching the button makes the door start opening. Touching the button again before the door opens makes it start closing. If the door opens all the way, it will automatically begin closing after a 2-second time-out. You can prevent this by touching the button again when the door is open. Figure 22.1 shows the states and transitions of the carousel's door.

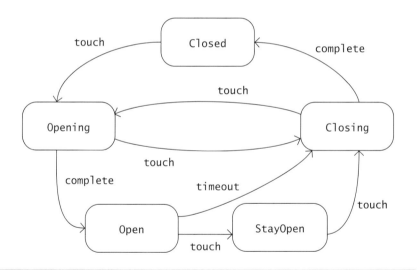

FIGURE 22.1 A carousel door provides one-touch control with a single button that changes the door's state.

The diagram in Figure 22.1 is a UML *state machine*. Such diagrams can be much more informative than a corresponding textual description.

CHALLENGE 22.1

Suppose that you open the door and place a material bin in the doorway. Is there a way to make the door begin closing without waiting for it to time out?

A solution appears on page 407.

You can supply the carousel software with a Door object that the carousel software will update with state changes in the carousel. Figure 22.2 shows the Door class.

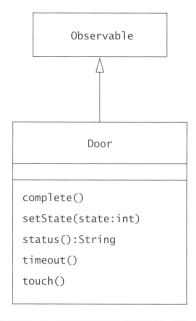

FIGURE 22.2 The Door class models a carousel door, relying on state-change events sent by the carousel machine.

The Door class is Observable so that clients, such as a GUI, can display the status of a door. The class definition establishes the states that a door can enter:

```
package com.oozinoz.carousel;
import java.util.Observable;

public class Door extends Observable {
    public final int CLOSED = -1;
    public final int OPENING = -2;
    public final int OPEN = -3;
    public final int CLOSING = -4;
    public final int STAYOPEN = -5;

    private int state = CLOSED;

    // ...
}
```

(You might choose to use an enumerated type if you're using Java 5.) Not surprisingly, a textual description of the state of a door depends on the door's state:

```
public String status() {
    switch (state) {
        case OPENING:
            return "Opening";
        case OPEN:
            return "Open";
        case CLOSING:
            return "Closing";
        case STAYOPEN:
            return "StayOpen";
        default:
            return "Closed";
    }
}
```

When a user touches the carousel's one-touch button, the carousel generates a call to a Door object's touch() method. The Door code for a state transition mimics the information in Figure 22.1:

```
public void touch() {
    switch (state) {
        case OPENING:
```

```
        case STAYOPEN:
            setState(CLOSING);
            break;
        case CLOSING:
        case CLOSED:
            setState(OPENING);
            break;
        case OPEN:
            setState(STAYOPEN);
            break;
        default:
            throw new Error("can't happen");
    }
}
```

The setState() method of the Door class notifies observers of the door's change:

```
private void setState(int state) {
    this.state = state;
    setChanged();
    notifyObservers();
}
```

CHALLENGE 22.2

Write the code for the complete() and timeout() methods of the Door class.

Solutions appear on page 407.

Refactoring to STATE

The code for Door is somewhat complex because the use of the state variable is spread throughout the class. In addition, you might find it difficult to compare the state-transition methods, particularly touch(), with the state machine in Figure 22.1. The STATE pattern can help you to simplify this code. To apply STATE in this example, make each state of the door a separate class, as shown in Figure 22.3.

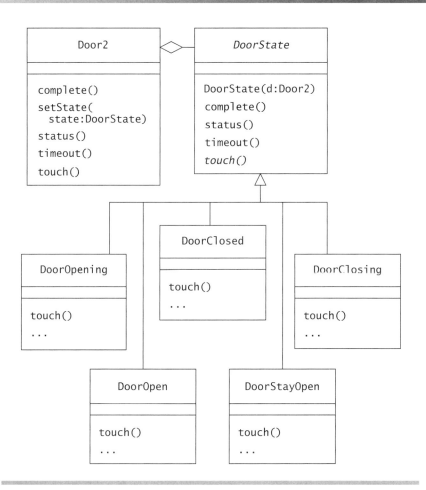

FIGURE 22.3 This diagram shows a door's states as classes in an arrangement that mirrors the door's state machine.

The refactoring shown in Figure 22.3 creates a special class for each state that the door might be in. Each of these classes contains the logic for responding to a touch of the one-touch button while the door is in a specific state. For example, the file DoorClosed.java contains the following code:

```
package com.oozinoz.carousel;
public class DoorClosed extends DoorState {
    public DoorClosed(Door2 door) {
        super(door);
    }
```

```
        public void touch() {
            door.setState(door.OPENING);
        }
}
```

The touch() method in the DoorClosed class informs a Door2 object of the door's new state. The Door2 object is the object received by the DoorClosed constructor. The design at play here requires each state object to hold a reference to a Door2 object so that the state object can inform the door of state transitions. This design approach requires a state object to refer to a particular door, so a state object can apply only to a single door. The next section addresses how to modify this design so that a single set of states would suffice for any number of doors. The current design requires the generation of a Door2 object to be accompanied by the creation of a suite of states that belong to the door:

```
package com.oozinoz.carousel;
import java.util.Observable;

public class Door2 extends Observable {
  public final DoorState CLOSED = new DoorClosed(this);
  public final DoorState CLOSING = new DoorClosing(this);
  public final DoorState OPEN = new DoorOpen(this);
  public final DoorState OPENING = new DoorOpening(this);
  public final DoorState STAYOPEN = new DoorStayOpen(this);

  private DoorState state = CLOSED;
  // ...
}
```

The abstract DoorState class requires subclasses to implement touch(). This is consistent with the state machine, in which every state has a touch() transition. The DoorState class stubs out other transitions, so that subclasses can override or ignore irrelevant messages:

```
package com.oozinoz.carousel;

public abstract class DoorState {
    protected Door2 door;

    public abstract void touch();

    public void complete() { }
```

```
public void timeout() { }

public String status() {
    String s = getClass().getName();
    return s.substring(s.lastIndexOf('.') + 1);
}

public DoorState(Door2 door) {
    this.door = door;
}
}
```

Note that the status() method works for all the states and is much simpler than its predecessor before refactoring.

The new design doesn't change the role of a Door2 object in receiving state changes from the carousel, but now the Door2 object simply passes these changes to its current state object:

```
package com.oozinoz.carousel;
import java.util.Observable;

public class Door2 extends Observable {
    // variables and constructor ...

    public void touch() {
        state.touch();
    }

    public void complete() {
        state.complete();
    }

    public void timeout() {
        state.timeout();
    }

    public String status() {
        return state.status();
    }

    protected void setState(DoorState state) {
        this.state = state;
        setChanged();
        notifyObservers();
    }
}
```

The touch(), complete(), timeout(), and status() methods show the role of polymorphism in this design. Each of these methods is still a kind of switch. In each case, the operation is fixed, but the class of the receiver—the class of state—varies. The rule of polymorphism is that the method that executes depends on the operation signature and the class of the receiver. What happens when you call touch()? The answer depends on the door's state. The code still effectively performs a switch, but by relying on polymorphism, the code is simpler than before.

The setState() method in the Door2 class is now used by subclasses of DoorState. These subclasses closely resemble their counterparts in the state machine in Figure 22.1. For example, the code for DoorOpen handles calls to touch() and timeout(), the two transitions from the Open state in the state machine:

```
package com.oozinoz.carousel;
public class DoorOpen extends DoorState {
    public DoorOpen(Door2 door) {
        super(door);
    }

    public void touch() {
        door.setState(door.STAYOPEN);
    }

    public void timeout() {
        door.setState(door.CLOSING);
    }
}
```

CHALLENGE 22.3

Write the code for DoorClosing.java.

A solution appears on page 407.

The new design leads to much simpler code, but you might feel a bit dissatisfied that the "constants" that the Door class uses are in fact local variables.

Making States Constant

The STATE pattern moves state-specific logic across classes that represent an object's state. However, STATE does not specify how to manage communication and dependencies between the state objects and the central object to which they apply. In the previous design, each state class accepted a Door object in its constructor. The state objects retain this object and use it to update the door's state. This is not necessarily a bad design, but it does create the effect that instantiating a Door object causes the instantiation of a complete set of DoorState objects. You might prefer a design that created a single, static set of DoorState objects and require the Door state to manage all updates resulting from state changes.

One approach to making the state objects constant is to have the state classes simply identify the next state, leaving it to the Door class to update its state variable. In this design, the Door class's touch() method, for example, updates the state variable as follows:

```
public void touch() {
    state = state.touch();
}
```

Note that the Door class's touch() method's return type is void. Subclasses of DoorState will also implement touch(), but these implementations will provide a DoorState value in their returns. For example, the DoorOpen class's touch() method now reads as follows:

```
public DoorState touch() {
    return DoorState.STAYOPEN;
}
```

In this design, the DoorState objects do not retain a reference to a Door object, so the application needs only a single instance of each DoorState object.

Another approach to making the DoorState objects constants is to pass around the central Door object during state transitions. You can add a Door parameter to the complete(), timeout(), and touch() state-change methods. These methods receive the central Door object as a parameter and update its state without retaining a reference to it.

CHALLENGE 22.4

Complete the class diagram in Figure 22.4 to show a design that lets DoorState objects be constants and that passes around a Door object during state transitions.

A solution appears on page 408.

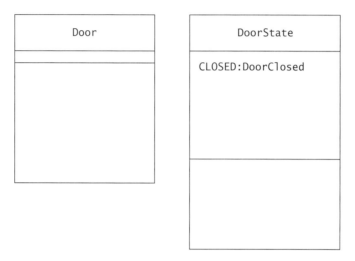

FIGURE 22.4 Complete this diagram to show a design that makes door states constants.

When you apply the STATE pattern, you have complete freedom in how your design arranges for the communication of state changes. The state classes can retain a reference to the central object whose state is being modeled. Alternatively, you can pass this object around during transitions. You can also make the state subclasses mere information providers that determine the next state but that do not update the central object. Which approach you use may depend on the context of your application or on aesthetics.

If your states will be used by different threads, make sure that your state-transition methods are synchronized to ensure that there are no conflicts when two threads try to change state at the same time.

The power of the STATE pattern is that the logic for any given state is centralized in a single class.

Summary

Generally speaking, the state of an object depends on the collective value of the object's instance variables. In some cases, most of an object's attributes are fairly static once set, and one attribute is dynamic and plays a prominent role in the class's logic. This attribute may represent the state of the entire object and may even be named `state`.

A dominant state variable may occur when an object is modeling a real-world entity whose state is important, such as a transaction or a machine. In such a case, logic that depends on the object's state may appear in many methods. You may be able to simplify such code by moving state-specific behavior to a hierarchy of state objects. This lets each state class contain the behavior for one state in the domain. It also allows the state classes to correspond directly to states in a state machine.

To handle transitions between states, you can let the central object retain references to a set of states. Or, in state-transition calls, you can pass around the central object whose state is changing. You can also make the state classes information providers that only indicate a following state without updating the central object. Regardless of how you manage state transitions, the STATE pattern simplifies your code by distributing an operation across a collection of classes that represent an object's various states.

23

STRATEGY

A STRATEGY IS A plan, or approach, for achieving an aim given certain input conditions. A strategy is thus similar to an algorithm, a procedure that produces an output from a set of inputs. Usually, there is more latitude in how a strategy pursues its goal than in an algorithm. This latitude also means that strategies often appear in groups, or families, of alternatives.

When multiple strategies appear in a computer program, the code may become complex. The logic that surrounds the strategies must select a strategy, and this selection code may itself become complex. The execution of various strategies may also lie along different code paths but in code that all resides in a single method. If the choice and execution of various strategies lead to complex code, you can apply the STRATEGY pattern to clean it up.

The strategic operation defines the inputs and outputs of a strategy but leaves implementation up to the individual classes. Classes that implement the various approaches implement the same operation and are thus interchangeable, presenting different strategies but the same interface to clients. The STRATEGY pattern allows a family of strategies to coexist without their code intermingling. STRATEGY also separates the logic for selecting a strategy from the strategies themselves.

The intent of STRATEGY is to encapsulate alternative approaches, or strategies, in separate classes that each implement a common operation.

Modeling Strategies

The STRATEGY pattern helps to organize and simplify code by encapsulating different approaches to a problem in different classes. To see STRATEGY at work, it is useful to first look at a program that models strategies without applying STRATEGY. In the next section, we refactor this code, applying STRATEGY to improve the quality of the code.

Consider the Oozinoz advertising policy that suggests a firework to purchase when the customer visits the Oozinoz Web site or calls into the call center. Oozinoz uses two commercial off-the-shelf recommendation engines to help choose the right item to offer a customer. The `Customer` class chooses and applies one of these engines to decide on which firework to recommend to a customer.

One of the recommendation engines, the `Re18` engine, suggests a purchase based on the customer's similarity to other customers. For this to work, the customer must have registered and given information about preferences regarding fireworks and other entertainments.

If the customer has not registered, Oozinoz uses another vendor's `LikeMyStuff` engine that suggests a purchase based on the customer's recent purchases. If there is not enough data for either engine to function, the advertising software picks a firework at random. However, a special promotion can override all these considerations to promote a specific firework that Oozinoz wants to sell. Figure 23.1 shows the classes that collaborate to suggest a firework to a customer.

The `LikeMyStuff` and `Re18` engines both accept a `Customer` object, and both suggest something to advertise to the customer. Both engines are configured at Oozinoz to work for fireworks, although `LikeMyStuff` requires a database, and `Re18` works entirely from an object model. The code for `getRecommended()` in class `Customer` mirrors Oozinoz's advertising policies:

```
public Firework getRecommended() {
    // if promoting a particular firework, return it
    try {
        Properties p = new Properties();
        p.load(ClassLoader.getSystemResourceAsStream(
            "config/strategy.dat"));
        String promotedName = p.getProperty("promote");

        if (promotedName != null) {
            Firework f = Firework.lookup(promotedName);
            if (f != null) return f;
        }
```

```
        } catch (Exception ignored) {
            // If resource is missing or it failed to load,
            // fall through to the next approach.
        }

        // if registered, compare to other customers
        if (isRegistered()) {
            return (Firework) Rel8.advise(this);
        }

        // check spending over the last year
        Calendar cal = Calendar.getInstance();
        cal.add(Calendar.YEAR, -1);
        if (spendingSince(cal.getTime()) > 1000)
            return (Firework) LikeMyStuff.suggest(this);

        // oh well!
        return Firework.getRandom();
    }
```

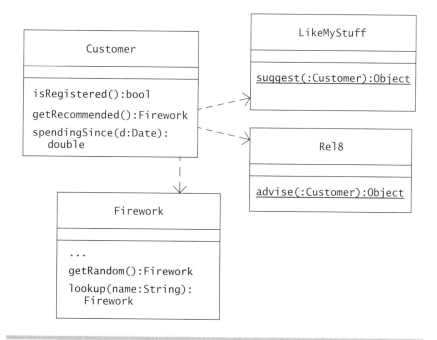

FIGURE 23.1 The Customer class relies on other classes for its recommendations, including two off-the-shelf recommendation engines.

This code is in the `com.oozinoz.recommendation` package of the Oozinoz code base available from `www.oozinoz.com`. The `getRecommended()`
method expects that if a promotion is on, it will be named in a
`strategy.dat` file in a `config` directory. Such a file would look as
follows:

```
promote=JSquirrel
```

It there is no such file, the `getRecommended()` code will use the `Rel8`
engine if the customer is registered. If there is no promotion strategy
file and the customer is not registered, the code will use the `Like-
MyStuff` engine if the customer has spent a certain amount of money
in the past year. If no better recommendation is possible, the code
selects and recommends a firework at random. The method works,
and you might feel that this is not the worst code you've ever seen.
But we can certainly make it better.

Refactoring to STRATEGY

The `getRecommended()` method presents several problems. First, it's
long—so long that comments have to explain its various parts. Short
methods are easy to understand, seldom need explanation, and are
usually preferable to long methods. In addition, the `getRecom-
mended()` method both chooses a strategy and executes it; these are
two different and separable functions. You can clean up this code by
applying STRATEGY. To do so, let us

- Create an interface that defines the strategic operation

- Implement the interface with classes that represent each strategy

- Refactor the code to select and use an instance of the right strategy class

Suppose that you create an `Advisor` interface, as shown in Figure 23.2.

The `Advisor` interface declares that a class that implements the interface can accept a customer and recommend a firework. The next step
in refactoring the `Customer` class's `getRecommended()` code is to create
classes that each represent one of the recommendation strategies.
Each class will provide a different implementation of the `recom-
mend()` method that the `Advisor` interface specifies.

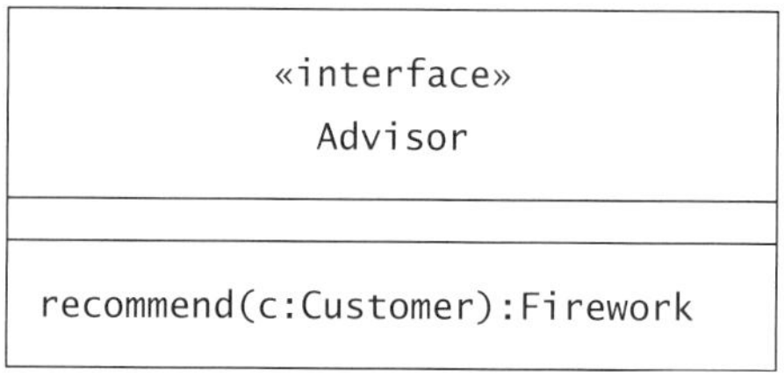

```
┌─────────────────────────────────────────────┐
│                 «interface»                   │
│                  Advisor                      │
├─────────────────────────────────────────────┤
│                                               │
├─────────────────────────────────────────────┤
│  recommend(c:Customer):Firework              │
└─────────────────────────────────────────────┘
```

FIGURE 23.2 The `Advisor` interface defines an operation that various classes can implement with different strategies.

CHALLENGE 23.1

Fill in the class diagram in Figure 23.3, which shows the recommendation logic refactored into a collection of strategy classes.

A solution appears on page 409.

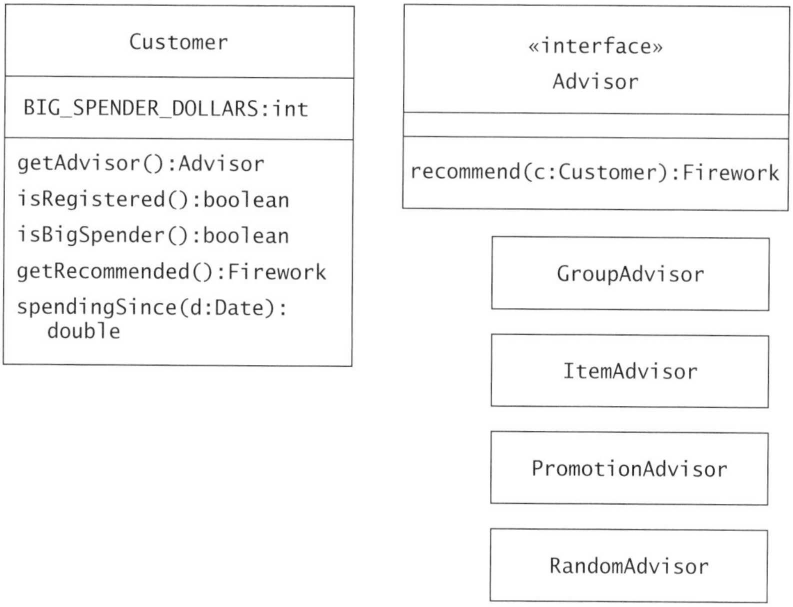

```
┌──────────────────────────────┐    ┌─────────────────────────────────┐
│          Customer            │    │            «interface»           │
├──────────────────────────────┤    │             Advisor              │
│  BIG_SPENDER_DOLLARS:int     │    ├─────────────────────────────────┤
├──────────────────────────────┤    │                                  │
│  getAdvisor():Advisor        │    ├─────────────────────────────────┤
│  isRegistered():boolean      │    │  recommend(c:Customer):Firework  │
│  isBigSpender():boolean      │    └─────────────────────────────────┘
│  getRecommended():Firework   │
│  spendingSince(d:Date):      │         ┌─────────────────────────┐
│     double                   │         │      GroupAdvisor        │
└──────────────────────────────┘         └─────────────────────────┘

                                         ┌─────────────────────────┐
                                         │       ItemAdvisor        │
                                         └─────────────────────────┘

                                         ┌─────────────────────────┐
                                         │     PromotionAdvisor     │
                                         └─────────────────────────┘

                                         ┌─────────────────────────┐
                                         │      RandomAdvisor       │
                                         └─────────────────────────┘
```

FIGURE 23.3 Complete this diagram to show a refactoring of the recommendation software, with strategies appearing as implementations of a common interface.

With the strategy classes in place, the next step is to move code from the existing getRecommended() method of the Customer class into the new classes. The two simplest classes will be GroupAdvisor and Item-Advisor. They must simply wrap calls into the off-the-shelf recommendation engines. Interfaces can define only instance methods, so GroupAdvisor and ItemAdvisor must be instantiated to support the Advisor interface. However, only one such object is ever necessary, so we'll let Customer own a single static instance of each. Figure 23.4 shows a design for these classes.

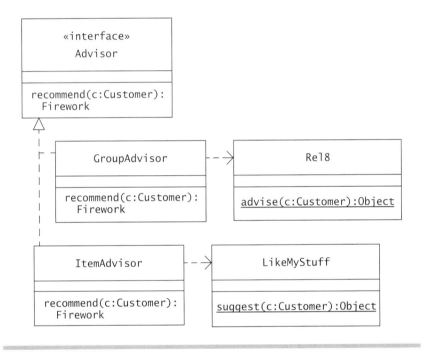

FIGURE 23.4 Implementations of the Advisor interface provide the strategic recommend() operation, relying on off-the-shelf engines.

The advisor classes translate calls to recommend() into the interfaces that the underlying engines require. For example, the GroupAdvisor class translates calls to recommend() into the advise() interface that the Rel8 engine requires:

```
public Firework recommend(Customer c) {
    return (Firework) Rel8.advise(c);
}
```

CHALLENGE 23.2

In addition to Strategy, what pattern appears in the `GroupAdvisor`
and `ItemAdvisor` classes?

A solution appears on page 409.

The `GroupAdvisor` and `ItemAdvisor` classes work by translating a call
to the `recommend()` method into a call to a recommendation engine.
We also need to create a `PromotionAdvisor` class and a `RandomAdvi-`
`sor` class, which we do by refactoring code from the current `getRec-`
`ommended()` method of the `Customer` class. As with the `GroupAdvisor`
and `ItemAdvisor` classes, the remaining classes will each offer the
`recommend()` operation.

The constructor for `PromotionAdvisor` should investigate whether a
promotion is on. You might then supply this class with a `hasItem()`
method that indicates whether there is a promoted item:

```java
public class PromotionAdvisor implements Advisor {
    private Firework promoted;

    public PromotionAdvisor() {
        try {
            Properties p = new Properties();
            p.load(ClassLoader.getSystemResourceAsStream(
                "config/strategy.dat"));
            String promotedFireworkName = p.getProperty("promote");
            if (promotedFireworkName != null)
                promoted = Firework.lookup(promotedFireworkName);
        } catch (Exception ignored) {
            // Resource not found or failed to load
            promoted = null;
        }
    }

    public boolean hasItem() {
        return promoted != null;
    }

    public Firework recommend(Customer c) {
        return promoted;
    }
}
```

The RandomAdvisor class is simple:

```
public class RandomAdvisor implements Advisor {
    public Firework recommend(Customer c) {
        return Firework.getRandom();
    }
}
```

The refactoring of Customer separates the *selection* of a strategy from the *use* of the strategy. An advisor attribute of a Customer object holds the current choice of the strategy to apply. The refactored Customer2 class lazy-initializes this attribute with logic that reflects Oozinoz's advertising policies:

```
private Advisor getAdvisor() {
    if (advisor == null) {
        if (promotionAdvisor.hasItem())
            advisor = promotionAdvisor;
        else if (isRegistered())
            advisor = groupAdvisor;
        else if (isBigSpender())
            advisor = itemAdvisor;
        else
            advisor = randomAdvisor;
    }
    return advisor;
}
```

CHALLENGE 23.3

Write the new code for Customer.getRecommended().

A solution appears on page 410.

Comparing STRATEGY and STATE

The refactored code consists almost entirely of simple methods in simple classes. This is an advantage in its own right and makes adding new strategies easy. The refactoring relies primarily on the idea of distributing an operation across a related group of classes. In this regard, STRATEGY is identical to STATE. In fact, some developers wonder whether these are really different patterns.

On the one hand, the differences in modeling states and strategies may seem subtle. Certainly, the reliance on polymorphism makes STATE and STRATEGY appear almost identical structurally.

On the other hand, in the real world, strategies and states are clearly different ideas. This real difference leads to different problems in modeling states and strategies. For example, transitions are important when modeling states but are usually irrelevant when choosing a strategy. Another difference is that STRATEGY might allow a client to select or provide a strategy, an idea that rarely applies to STATE.

STATE and STRATEGY have different intents, so we'll continue to regard them as distinct patterns. But you should be aware that not everybody recognizes that distinction.

Comparing STRATEGY and TEMPLATE METHOD

Chapter 21, TEMPLATE METHOD, described sorting as an example of the TEMPLATE METHOD pattern. You can use the `sort()` algorithm from the `Arrays` or `Collection` classes to sort any list of objects, so long as you supply a step to compare two objects. But you might argue that when you supply a comparison step to a sorting algorithm, you are changing the strategy. For instance, if you are selling rockets, presenting them sorted by price is a different marketing strategy from presenting them sorted by thrust.

CHALLENGE 23.4

Provide an argument that the `Arrays.sort()` method provides an example of TEMPLATE METHOD or that it is an example of STRATEGY.

A solution appears on page 410.

Summary

Logic that models alternative strategies may appear in a single class, often in a single method. Such methods may be too complicated and may mix strategy-selection logic with the execution of a strategy.

To simplify such code, create a group of classes, one for each strategy. Define an operation and distribute it across these classes. This lets each class encapsulate one strategy, creating simpler code. You also need to arrange for the client that uses a strategy to be able to select one. This selection code may be complex even after refactoring, but you should be able to reduce this code so that it is nearly equivalent to pseudocode that describes strategy selection in the problem domain.

Typically, a client will hold a selected strategy in a context variable. This makes the execution of a strategy a simple matter of forwarding the strategic operation call to the context, using polymorphism to execute the right strategy. By encapsulating alternative strategies in separate classes that each implement a common operation, the STRATEGY pattern lets you create clean, simple code that models a family of approaches to solving a problem.

24

COMMAND

THE ORDINARY WAY to cause a method to execute is to call it. There may be times, though, when you cannot control the timing of or the context in which a method should execute. In these situations, you can encapsulate a method inside an object. By storing the information necessary for invoking a method in an object, you can pass the method as a parameter, allowing a client or a service to determine when to invoke the method.

The intent of the COMMAND pattern is to encapsulate a request in an object.

A Classic Example: Menu Commands

Toolkits that support menus usually apply the COMMAND pattern. Each menu item is outfitted with an object that knows how to behave when the user clicks the item. This design keeps GUI logic and application logic separate. The Swing library takes this approach, allowing you to associate an `ActionListener` with each `JMenuItem`.

How can you arrange for a class to call a method of yours when the user clicks? The answer is to use polymorphism: Make the name of the operation fixed, and let the implementation vary. For `JMenuItem`, the operation is `actionPerformed()`. When the user makes a choice, a `JMenuItem` calls the `actionPerformed()` method of any object that has registered as a listener.

CHALLENGE 24.1

The mechanics of Java menus make it easy to apply the COMMAND
pattern but do not require that you organize your code as
commands. In fact, it is common to develop an application in
which a single object listens to all the events in a GUI. What pattern
does that follow?

A solution appears on page 410.

When you develop a Swing application, you may want to register a
single listener for all the GUI events, especially if the GUI components interact. For menus, however, this is not the usual pattern to
follow. If you were to use a single object to listen to menus, it would
have to sort out which GUI object generated the event. Instead, if you
have many menu items that take independent actions, it may be better to apply COMMAND.

When a user selects a menu item, it calls the `actionPerformed()`
method. When you create the menu item, you can attach an `Action-
Listener` to it, with an `actionPerformed()` method specific to the
behavior of the particular command. Rather than define a new class
to implement this one little behavior, it is common to use an anonymous class.

Consider the `Visualization2` class from the `com.oozinoz.visual-
ization` package. This class provides a menu bar with a File menu
that lets the user save and restore visualizations of a simulated Oozinoz factory. This menu has menu items Save As... and Restore From. ...
The code that creates those menu items registers listeners that wait
for the user to choose them. The listeners implement the `action-
Performed()` method by calling the `save()` and `load()` methods of
the `Visualization2` class:

```
package com.oozinoz.visualization;
import java.awt.event.*;
import javax.swing.*;
import com.oozinoz.ui.*;
```

```
public class Visualization2 extends Visualization {
    public static void main(String[] args) {
        Visualization2 panel = new Visualization2(UI.NORMAL);
        JFrame frame =
            SwingFacade.launch(panel, "Operational Model");
        frame.setJMenuBar(panel.menus());
        frame.setVisible(true);
    }

    public Visualization2(UI ui) {
        super(ui);
    }

    public JMenuBar menus() {
        JMenuBar menuBar = new JMenuBar();

        JMenu menu = new JMenu("File");
        menuBar.add(menu);

        JMenuItem menuItem = new JMenuItem("Save As...");
        menuItem.addActionListener(new ActionListener() {
            // Challenge!
        });
        menu.add(menuItem);

        menuItem = new JMenuItem("Restore From...");
        menuItem.addActionListener(new ActionListener() {
            // Challenge!
        });
        menu.add(menuItem);

        return menuBar;
    }

    public void save() { /* omitted */ }
    public void restore() { /* omitted */ }
}
```

CHALLENGE 24.2

Fill in the code for the anonymous subclasses of `ActionListener`,
overriding the `actionPerformed()` method. Note that this method
expects an `ActionEvent` argument.

A solution appears on page 411.

When you outfit a menu with commands, you are plugging your commands into a context provided by another developer: the Java menu framework. In other cases of COMMAND, you will take the role of the context developer, providing the context in which commands will execute. For example, you might want to provide a timing service that records how long methods take to execute.

Using COMMAND to Supply a Service

Suppose that you want to let developers time how long a method takes to execute. Suppose that we have a Command interface whose essence is:

```
public abstract void execute();
```

and that you have a CommandTimer class:

```
package com.oozinoz.utility;

import com.oozinoz.robotInterpreter.Command;

public class CommandTimer {
    public static long time(Command command) {
        long t1 = System.currentTimeMillis();
        command.execute();
        long t2 = System.currentTimeMillis();
        return t2 - t1;
    }
}
```

You could test the time() method with a JUnit test, something like the following. Note that this is not an exact test; it could fail if the timer is "jittery."

```
package app.command;

import com.oozinoz.robotInterpreter.Command;
import com.oozinoz.utility.CommandTimer;

import junit.framework.TestCase;
```

```
public class TestCommandTimer extends TestCase {
    public void testSleep() {
        Command doze = new Command() {
            public void execute() {
                try {
                    Thread.sleep(
                        2000 + Math.round(10 * Math.random()));
                } catch (InterruptedException ignored) {
                }
            }
        };

        long actual = // Challenge!

        long expected = 2000;
        long delta = 5;
        assertTrue(
            "Should be " + expected + " +/- " + delta + " ms",
            expected - delta <= actual
        && actual <= expected + delta);
    }
}
```

CHALLENGE 24.3

Complete the assignment statement that sets the value for actual in such a way that the doze command is timed.

A solution appears on page 412.

Command **Hooks**

Chapter 21, Template Method, introduced the Aster star press, a smart machine that includes code that relies on Template Method. The star press's code lets you override a method that marks a mold as incomplete if it is in process when the press shuts down.

The AsterStarPress class is abstract, requiring you to subclass it with a class that has a markMoldIncomplete() method. The shutDown()

method of `AsterStarPress` relies on this method to ensure that your
domain object knows that the mold is incomplete:

```
public void shutdown() {
    if (inProcess()) {
        stopProcessing();
        markMoldIncomplete(currentMoldID);
    }
    usherInputMolds();
    dischargePaste();
    flush();
}
```

You might find it inconvenient to subclass `AsterStarPress` with a
class that you have to move to the star press's onboard computer.
Suppose that you ask the developers at Aster to provide the hook in a
different way, using the COMMAND pattern. Figure 24.1 shows a `Hook`
command that the `AsterStarPress` class can use, letting you parameterize the star press code at runtime.

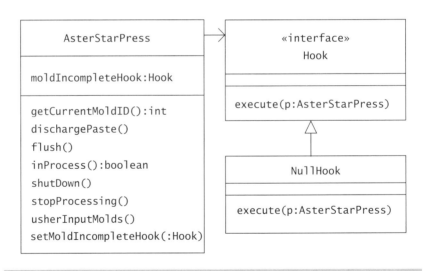

FIGURE 24.1 A class can provide a hook—a way to insert custom code—by invoking a supplied command at a specific point in a procedure.

In the original `AsterStarPress` class, the `shutDown()` method relied
on a step that subclasses would provide. In the new design, the

shutDown() method now uses a hook to execute client code after processing stops but before completing the shutdown process:

```
public void shutDown() {
    if (inProcess()) {
        stopProcessing();
        // Challenge!
    }
    usherInputMolds();
    dischargePaste();
    flush();
}
```

CHALLENGE 24.4

Complete the code for the new shutDown() method.

A solution appears on page 413.

This example demonstrates another pattern, NULL OBJECT [Woolf 1998], that is only slightly less well known than those in *Design Patterns*. This pattern lets us avoid a null-pointer check by introducing a default object that has no effect. (See *Refactoring* [Fowler et al. 1999] for an explanation of how to introduce this pattern into your code.)

The COMMAND pattern affords an alternative design to a TEMPLATE METHOD for hooks and is similar in intent, or structure, to several other patterns.

COMMAND in Relation to Other Patterns

COMMAND is similar to the INTERPRETER pattern. The two patterns are compared in the next chapter. COMMAND is also similar to a pattern in which a client knows when an action is required but doesn't know exactly which operation to call.

CHALLENGE 24.5

Which pattern addresses the situation in which a client knows *when* to create an object but doesn't know which class to instantiate?

A solution appears on page 414.

In addition to bearing similarities to other patterns, COMMAND often collaborates with other patterns. For example, you might combine COMMAND and MEDIATOR in an MVC design. Chapter 19, MEMENTO, shows an example of this. The Visualization class handles GUI control logic but passes off to a mediator any model-related logic. For example, the Visualization class uses the following code to lazy-initialize its Undo button:

```
protected JButton undoButton() {
    if (undoButton == null) {
        undoButton = ui.createButtonCancel();
        undoButton.setText("Undo");
        undoButton.setEnabled(false);
        undoButton.addActionListener(mediator.undoAction());
    }
    return undoButton;
}
```

This code applies COMMAND, packaging an undo() method in an instance of the ActionListener class. This code also applies MEDIATOR, letting a central object mediate events that pertain to an underlying object model. For the undo() method to work, the mediator code has to restore a previous version of the simulated factory, bringing up the opportunity to apply one more pattern that often accompanies COMMAND.

CHALLENGE 24.6

Which pattern provides for the storage and restoration of an object's state?

A solution appears on page 414.

Summary

The COMMAND pattern lets you encapsulate a request in an object, allowing you to manage method calls as objects, passing them and invoking them when the timing or conditions are right. A classic example of the usefulness of COMMAND comes with menus. Menu items know **when** to execute an action but don't know which method to call. COMMAND lets you parameterize a menu with the method calls that correspond to menu labels.

Another use for COMMAND is to allow the execution of client code in the context of a service. A service often runs code both before and after invoking client code. Finally, in addition to controlling the timing or context in which a method executes, the COMMAND pattern can provide a clean mechanism for providing hooks, allowing optional client code to execute as part of an algorithm.

COMMAND encapsulates a request in an object, so you can manipulate it as you would any other object. Perhaps because this idea is so fundamental, COMMAND has interesting relationships to several other patterns. COMMAND can provide an alternative to TEMPLATE METHOD, and COMMAND often collaborates with MEDIATOR and MEMENTO.

25

INTERPRETER

As with the COMMAND pattern, the INTERPRETER pattern produces an executable object. The patterns differ in that INTERPRETER involves the creation of a class hierarchy in which each class implements, or *interprets,* a common operation in a way that matches the class's name. In this regard, INTERPRETER is similar to the STATE and STRATEGY patterns. In INTERPRETER, STATE, and STRATEGY, a common operation appears throughout a collection of classes, with each class implementing the operation in a different way.

The INTERPRETER pattern is also similar to the COMPOSITE pattern, which defines a common interface for individual items and groups of items. COMPOSITE does not require different, interesting ways of forming groups, although it allows this. For example, the `ProcessComponent` hierarchy in Chapter 5, COMPOSITE, allows sequences and alternations of process flows. In INTERPRETER, the idea that there are different types of composition is essential. (An INTERPRETER is often layered on top of a COMPOSITE structure.) The way that a class composes other components helps define how an INTERPRETER class will implement an operation.

Interpreter is a challenging pattern to understand. You may want to review COMPOSITE, as we'll make free use of it in this chapter.

The intent of the INTERPRETER pattern is to let you compose executable objects according to a set of composition rules that you define.

An INTERPRETER Example

The robots that Oozinoz uses to move material along a processing line come with an **interpreter** that controls the robot and that has limited control of machines on the line. You might think of interpreters as being for programming languages, but the INTERPRETER pattern has at its heart a collection of classes that allow for the composition of instructions. The Oozinoz robot interpreter comes as a hierarchy of classes that encapsulate robot commands. At the head of the hierarchy is an abstract Command class. Distributed across the hierarchy is an execute() operation. Figure 25.1 shows the Robot class and two of the commands that the robot interpreter supports.

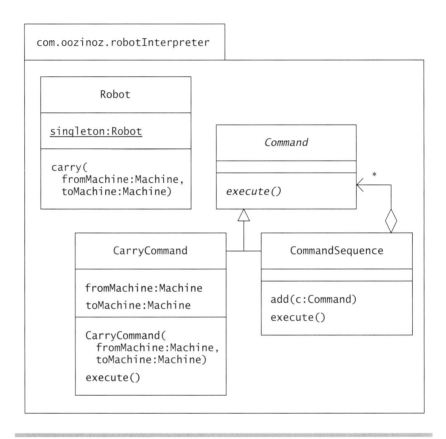

FIGURE 25.1 An interpreter hierarchy provides for runtime programming of a factory robot.

A glance at Figure 25.1 might suggest that the COMMAND pattern is at work in this design, with a Command class at the top of the hierarchy. However, the COMMAND pattern has the intent of encapsulating a method in an object. The Command hierarchy in Figure 25.1 doesn't do that. Rather, this hierarchy's design requires that Command subclasses reinterpret the meaning of the `execute()` operation. This is the intent of INTERPRETER: to allow you to compose executable objects.

A typical INTERPRETER hierarchy will include more than two subclasses, and we will extend the Command hierarchy shortly. The two classes shown in Figure 25.1 are sufficient for an initial example, as follows:

```
package app.interpreter;
import com.oozinoz.machine.*;
import com.oozinoz.robotInterpreter.*;

public class ShowInterpreter {
    public static void main(String[] args) {
        MachineComposite dublin = OozinozFactory.dublin();
        ShellAssembler assembler =
        (ShellAssembler) dublin.find("ShellAssembler:3302");
        StarPress press = (StarPress) dublin.find("StarPress:3404");
        Fuser fuser = (Fuser) dublin.find("Fuser:3102");

        assembler.load(new Bin(11011));
        press.load(new Bin(11015));

        CarryCommand carry1 = new CarryCommand(assembler, fuser);
        CarryCommand carry2 = new CarryCommand(press, fuser);

        CommandSequence seq = new CommandSequence();
        seq.add(carry1);
        seq.add(carry2);

        seq.execute();
    }
}
```

This demonstration code causes a factory robot to move two bins of material from operational machines to an unload buffer. The code works with a machine composite returned by the `dublin()` method of the `OozinozFactory` class. This data model represents a factory planned for a new Oozinoz facility in Dublin, Ireland. The code locates three machines within this factory, loads material bins onto two of them, and then builds up commands from the Command hierarchy. The last statement of the program calls the `execute()` method of a CommandSequence object. This causes the robot to take the actions contained in the `seq` command.

A CommandSequence object interprets the execute() operation by forwarding the call to each subcommand:

```
package com.oozinoz.robotInterpreter;

import java.util.ArrayList;
import java.util.List;

public class CommandSequence extends Command {
    protected List commands = new ArrayList();

    public void add(Command c) {
        commands.add(c);
    }

    public void execute() {
        for (int i = 0; i < commands.size(); i++) {
            Command c = (Command) commands.get(i);
            c.execute();
        }
    }
}
```

The CarryCommand class interprets the execute() operation by interacting with the factory's robot to move a bin from one machine to another:

```
package com.oozinoz.robotInterpreter;
import com.oozinoz.machine.Machine;

public class CarryCommand extends Command {
    protected Machine fromMachine;
    protected Machine toMachine;

    public CarryCommand(
            Machine fromMachine, Machine toMachine) {
        this.fromMachine = fromMachine;
        this.toMachine = toMachine;
    }

    public void execute() {
        Robot.singleton.carry(fromMachine, toMachine);
    }
}
```

The CarryCommand class is designed to work specifically within the domain of a robot-controlled factory line. We can easily imagine other domain-specific classes, such as a StartUpCommand class or a ShutdownCommand class, for controlling machines. It would also be useful to have a command for a ForCommand class that executes a command across a given collection of machines. Figure 25.2 shows these extensions to the Command hierarchy.

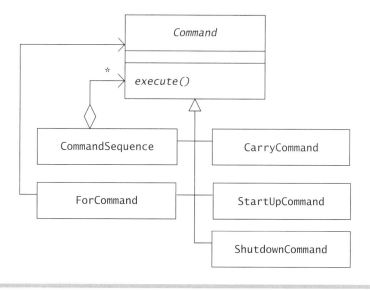

FIGURE 25.2 The INTERPRETER pattern allows for many subclasses to reinterpret the meaning of a common operation.

Part of the design for a ForCommand class is immediately clear. The constructor for this class would presumably accept a collection of machines and a COMMAND object to execute as the body of a for loop. The more difficult part of this design comes in the connection of the loop and the body. Java 5 has an extended for statement that establishes a variable that receives a new value each time the body executes. We'll emulate that approach. Consider the statement:

```
for (Command c: commands)
    c.execute();
```

Java links the c identifier that the for statement declares with the c variable in the loop's body. To create an INTERPRETER class that emulates this, we need an approach for handling and evaluating variables. Figure 25.3 shows a Term hierarchy that does so.

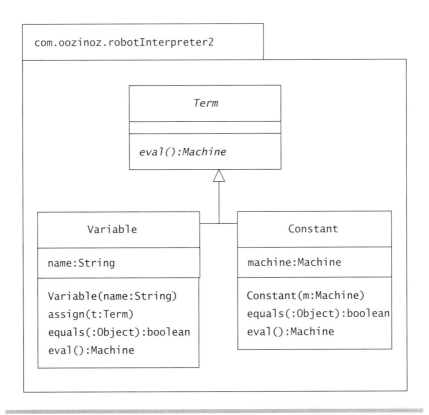

FIGURE 25.3 The Term hierarchy allows for variables that can evaluate to machines.

The Term hierarchy is similar to the Command hierarchy in that a common operation (eval()) appears throughout the hierarchy. You might argue that this hierarchy is itself an example of INTERPRETER, although it does not show composition classes, such as CommandSequence, that usually accompany INTERPRETER.

The Term hierarchy lets us name individual machines as constants and lets us assign variables to these constants or to other variables. It also lets us make domain-specific INTERPRETER classes more flexible. For example, the StartUpCommand code can arrange to work with a Term object rather than with a specific machine, as follows:

```
package com.oozinoz.robotInterpreter2;
import com.oozinoz.machine.Machine;

public class StartUpCommand extends Command {
    protected Term term;

    public StartUpCommand(Term term) {
        this.term = term;
    }

    public void execute() {
        Machine m = term.eval();
        m.startup();
    }
}
```

Similarly, to add flexibility to the CarryCommand class, we can modify it to work with Term objects, as follows:

```
package com.oozinoz.robotInterpreter2;

public class CarryCommand extends Command {
    protected Term from;
    protected Term to;

    public CarryCommand(Term fromTerm, Term toTerm) {
        from = fromTerm;
        to = toTerm;
    }

    public void execute() {
        Robot.singleton.carry(from.eval(), to.eval());
    }
}
```

Once we design the Command hierarchy to work with terms, we can write the ForCommand class so that it sets the value of a variable and executes a body command in a loop:

```
package com.oozinoz.robotInterpreter2;

import java.util.List;
import com.oozinoz.machine.Machine;
import com.oozinoz.machine.MachineComponent;
import com.oozinoz.machine.MachineComposite;

public class ForCommand extends Command {
    protected MachineComponent root;
    protected Variable variable;
    protected Command body;

    public ForCommand(
            MachineComponent mc, Variable v, Command body) {
        this.root = mc;
        this.variable = v;
        this.body = body;
    }

    public void execute() {
        execute(root);
    }

    private void execute(MachineComponent mc) {
        if (mc instanceof Machine) {
            // Challenge!
            return;
        }

        MachineComposite comp = (MachineComposite) mc;
        List children = comp.getComponents();
        for (int i = 0; i < children.size(); i++) {
            MachineComponent child =
                (MachineComponent) children.get(i);
            execute(child);
        }
    }
}
```

The execute() code in the ForCommand class uses casting to walk through a machine component tree. Chapter 28, ITERATOR, reviews faster and more elegant techniques for iterating over a composite. For the INTERPRETER pattern, the important point is to properly interpret the execute() request for each node in the tree.

CHALLENGE 25.1

Complete the code for the execute() method of the ForCommand class.

A solution appears on page 415.

The ForCommand class lets us begin to compose "programs," or "scripts," of commands for the factory. For example, here is a program that composes an interpreter object that shuts down all the machines in a factory:

```
package app.interpreter;

import com.oozinoz.machine.*;
import com.oozinoz.robotInterpreter2.*;

class ShowDown {
    public static void main(String[] args) {
        MachineComposite dublin = OozinozFactory.dublin();
        Variable v = new Variable("machine");
        Command c = new ForCommand(
            dublin, v, new ShutDownCommand(v));
        c.execute();
    }
}
```

When this program calls the execute() method, the ForCommand object c interprets the execute() by traversing the provided machine component and, for each machine:

- Sets the value of the variable v

- Calls the execute() operation of the provided ShutDownCommand object

If we add classes that control the flow of logic, such as an IfCommand class and a WhileCommand, we can build a rich interpreter. These classes will require a way to model a Boolean condition. For example, we might need a way to model whether a machine variable is equal to a particular machine. We might introduce a new hierarchy of terms, but it may be simpler to borrow an idea from the C language: Let null represent falsity and anything else represent truth. With this idea in mind, we can extend the Term hierarchy, as Figure 25.4 shows.

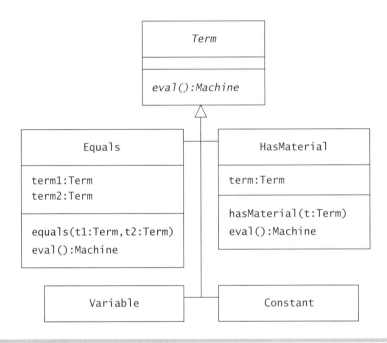

FIGURE 25.4 The Term hierarchy includes classes that model Boolean conditions.

The Equals class compares two terms and returns null to indicate false. A reasonable design is to have the eval() method of the Equals class return one of its terms if the terms are equal, as follows:

```
package com.oozinoz.robotInterpreter2;
import com.oozinoz.machine.Machine;
public class Equals extends Term {
    protected Term term1;
    protected Term term2;
```

```
    public Equals(Term term1, Term term2) {
        this.term1 = term1;
        this.term2 = term2;
    }

    public Machine eval() {
        Machine m1 = term1.eval();
        Machine m2 = term2.eval();
        return m1.equals(m2) ? m1 : null;
    }
}
```

The HasMaterial class extends the idea of the value of a Boolean class to a domain-specific example, with code as follows:

```
package com.oozinoz.robotInterpreter2;

import com.oozinoz.machine.Machine;

public class HasMaterial extends Term {
    protected Term term;

    public HasMaterial(Term term) {
        this.term = term;
    }

    public Machine eval() {
        Machine m = term.eval();
        return m.hasMaterial() ? m : null;
    }
}
```

Now that we have added the idea of Boolean terms to our interpreter package, we can add flow-control classes, as Figure 25.5 shows.

The NullCommand class is useful for when we need a command that does nothing, as when the else branch of an if command is empty:

```
package com.oozinoz.robotInterpreter2;
public class NullCommand extends Command {
    public void execute() {
    }
}
```

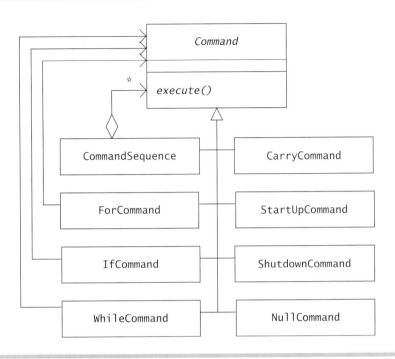

FIGURE 25.5 We can provide for a richer interpreter by adding logical flow-control classes to the interpreter hierarchy.

```
package com.oozinoz.robotInterpreter2;

public class IfCommand extends Command {
    protected Term term;
    protected Command body;
    protected Command elseBody;

    public IfCommand(
            Term term, Command body, Command elseBody) {
        this.term = term;
        this.body = body;
        this.elseBody = elseBody;
    }

    public void execute() {
        // Challenge!
    }
}
```

CHALLENGE 25.2

Complete the code in the `execute()` method of the IfCommand class.

A solution appears on page 415.

CHALLENGE 25.3

Write the code for the `WhileCommand` class.

A solution appears on page 416.

You might put your `WhileCommand` class to use with an interpreter that unloads a star press:

```
package app.interpreter;

import com.oozinoz.machine.*;
import com.oozinoz.robotInterpreter2.*;

public class ShowWhile {
    public static void main(String[] args) {
        MachineComposite dublin = OozinozFactory.dublin();
        Term starPress = new Constant(
            (Machine) dublin.find("StarPress:1401"));
        Term fuser = new Constant(
            (Machine) dublin.find("Fuser:1101"));

        starPress.eval().load(new Bin(77));
        starPress.eval().load(new Bin(88));

        WhileCommand command = new WhileCommand(
            new HasMaterial(starPress),
            new CarryCommand(starPress, fuser));
        command.execute();
    }
}
```

The command object is an interpreter that interprets execute() to mean unload all the bins from star press 1401.

CHALLENGE 25.4

Close this book and write down a short explanation of the difference between COMMAND and INTERPRETER.

A solution appears on page 416.

We can add more classes to the interpreter hierarchy for more types of control or for other domain-specific tasks. We can also extend the Term hierarchy. For example, it might be useful to have a Term subclass that finds an unload buffer that is near another machine.

Users of the Command and Term hierarchies can compose arbitrarily rich, complex "programs" of execution. For example, it is not too difficult to create an object that, when it executes, unloads all the material from all the machines, except unload buffers, in a factory. We might sketch this program in pseudocode, as follows:

```
for (m in factory)
    if (not (m is unloadBuffer))
        ub = findUnload for m
        while (m hasMaterial)
            carry (m, ub)
```

If we write Java code to perform these tasks, the Java code will be more voluminous and less straightforward than the pseudocode. So why not change the pseudocode into real code by creating a parser that reads a domain-specific language for manipulating material in our factory and creates interpreter objects for us?

Interpreters, Languages, and Parsers

The INTERPRETER pattern addresses how interpreters work but does not specify how you should instantiate or compose them. In this chapter, you have built new interpreters "manually" by writing lines of Java code. But a more common way to create a new interpreter is with a parser. A **parser** is an object that can recognize text and decompose its structure according to a set of rules into a form suitable for further processing. For example, you can write a parser that will create a machine command interpreter object that corresponds to a textual program in the pseudocode presented earlier.

At this writing, there are only a few tools for parser writing in Java and only a few books on the topic. To find whether more support is available, try searching the Web for "Java parser tools." Most parser toolkits include a parser generator. To use a generator, you use a special syntax to describe the pattern, or **grammar,** of your language, and the tool generates a parser from your description. The generated parser will recognize instances of your language. Or, rather than using a parser-generator tool, you can write a general-purpose parser by applying the INTERPRETER pattern. *Building Parsers with Java™* [Metsker 2001] explains this technique, with examples in Java.

Summary

The INTERPRETER patterns lets you compose executable objects from a class hierarchy that you create. Each class in the hierarchy implements a common operation that usually has a necessarily vague name, such as `execute()`. Often, though not shown in the previous examples, that method gets an additional "context" object passed in that stores significant state.

Each class's name usually implies how the class implements, or interprets, the common operation. Each class either defines a way of composing commands or is a terminal command that causes some action.

Interpreters are often accompanied by a design for introducing variables and for Boolean or arithmetic expressions. Interpreters also often partner with a parser to create a little language that simplifies the creation of new interpreter objects.

PART V

EXTENSION PATTERNS

26

INTRODUCING EXTENSIONS

When you program in Java, you do not begin from scratch, you "inherit" all the power of the Java class libraries. You also usually inherit the code of your predecessors and coworkers. When you're not reorganizing or improving this legacy code, you're extending it. You might say that programming in Java *is* extension.

If you've ever inherited a codebase, you may have grumbled about its quality. But is the new code you're adding really better? The answer is sometimes subjective, but this chapter reviews a few principles of object-oriented software development that you can use to assess your work.

In addition to normal techniques for extending a codebase, you may be able to apply design patterns to add new behavior. After a look at principles for object-oriented design in ordinary development, this chapter reviews earlier patterns that contain an element of extension and introduces the remaining extension-oriented patterns in this section.

Principles of Object-Oriented Design

Stone bridges have been around for thousands of years, and we have a lot of time-tested, agreed-upon principles for designing them. Object-oriented programming has been around for perhaps 50 years, so it's not surprising that we do not have the same level of principles for object-oriented design. We do, however, have excellent forums for discussing prospective principles. One of the best is the Portland Pattern Repository at www.c2.com [Cunningham]. If you browse this Web site, you will find a few principles that have shown value in assessing OO designs. One principle in particular that you should consider in your designs is the Liskov Substitution Principle (LSP).

The Liskov Substitution Principle

New classes should be logical, consistent extensions of their super-classes, but what does it mean to be *logical* and *consistent*? A Java com-piler will ensure a certain level of consistency, but many principles of consistency will elude a compiler. One rule that may help improve your designs is the **Liskov Substitution Principle** [Liskov 1987], which can be paraphrased as follows: *An instance of a class should func-tion as an instance of its superclass.*

Basic LSP compliance is built into OO languages, such as Java. For example, it is valid to refer to an `UnloadBuffer` object as a `Machine`, as `UnloadBuffer` is a subclass of `Machine`:

```
Machine m = new UnloadBuffer(3501);
```

Some aspects of LSP compliance require human-level intelligence, or at least more intelligence than today's compilers possess. Consider the class hierarchies shown in Figure 26.1.

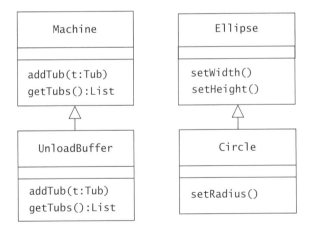

FIGURE 26.1 This diagram applies to the questions: Is an unload buffer a machine? Is a circle an ellipse?

An unload buffer is certainly a machine, but modeling this fact in a class hierarchy can lead to problems. In the case of machines at Oozi-noz, every machine except an unload buffer can receive a tub of chemicals. Because nearly every machine can accept chemical tubs and can report on the collection of tubs that it has nearby, it is useful to move this behavior up into the `Machine` class. But it's a mistake to invoke `addTub()` or `getTubs()` on an `UnloadBuffer` object. If it's a mistake, should we throw exceptions if these methods are called?

Suppose that another developer writes a method that interrogates all the machines in a bay to create a complete list of all the chemical tubs in that bay. When it encounters an unload buffer, this code will encounter an exception if the `getTubs()` method in the `UnloadBuffer` class throws one. This is a strong violation of LSP: Use an `UnloadBuffer` object as a `Machine` object, and your program may crash! Suppose that instead of throwing an exception, we decide to simply ignore calls to `getTubs()` and `addTub()` in the `UnloadBuffer` class. This still violates LSP: If you add a tub to a machine, the tub may disappear!

Violating LSP is not always a design flaw. In the case of Oozinoz machines, you have to weigh the value of letting the `Machine` class have behaviors that apply to most machines against the disadvantages of violating LSP. The important point is to be aware of LSP and to be able to articulate why other design considerations may warrant a breach of LSP.

CHALLENGE 26.1

A circle is certainly a special case of an ellipse, or is it? Say whether the relationship of the `Ellipse` and `Circle` classes in Figure 26.1 is a violation of LSP.

A solution appears on page 416.

The Law of Demeter

In the late 1980s, members of the Demeter Project at Northeastern University attempted to codify rules that would ensure the good health of object-oriented programs. The project team referred to these rules as the **Law of Demeter** (LOD). Karl Lieberherr and Ian Holland [1989] provided a thorough summary of the rules in "Assuring Good Style for Object-Oriented Programs," which states: "Informally, the law [of Demeter] says that each method can send messages to only a limited set of objects: to argument objects, to the [this] pseudovariable, and to the immediate subparts of [this]." The paper goes on to give formal definitions of the law. It is easier to point out violations of LoD than to fully grasp the law's intent.

Suppose that you have a `MaterialManager` object with a method that receives a `Tub` object as a parameter. `Tub` objects have a `Location` property that returns the `Machine` object that represents where the tub is placed. Suppose that in the `MaterialManager` method, you need to know whether this machine is up and available. You might find yourself writing the following code in your method:

```
if (tub.getLocation().isUp()) {
    //...
}
```

This code violates LoD because it invokes a method—sends a message—to `tub.getLocation()`. The `tub.getLocation()` object is not a parameter, not `this`—the `MaterialManager` object whose method is executing—and not an attribute of `this`.

CHALLENGE 26.2

Explain why the expression `tub.getLocation().isUp()` might be viewed as unhealthy.

A solution appears on page 417.

This challenge may trivialize the value of LoD, if the challenge suggests that LoD means only that expressions of the form `a.b.c` are bad. In fact, Lieberherr and Holland hope that LoD will go further and answer affirmatively the question, Is there some formula or rule that you can follow to write good object-oriented programs? It is well worth reading the original papers that explain LoD. Like the Liskov Substitution Principle, the Law of Demeter will help you write better code if you know the rules, generally follow them, and know when your designs merit a violation of the rules.

You may find that by following a set of guidelines, your extensions will automatically generate good code. But to many practitioners, OO development is still an art. The artful extension of a codebase appears to result from a set of practices acquired by artisans who are still only beginning to articulate and codify their art. **Refactoring** refers to a collection of tools for code modification that can improve a codebase's quality without altering its functionality.

Removing Code Smells

You may believe that the Liskov Substitution Principle and the Law of Demeter may prevent you from ever writing bad code. But more likely, you will use these principles to find bad code and fix it. This is normal practice: Write code that runs, then improve its quality by finding and fixing quality problems. But how exactly do you find problems? The answer, according to some, is **smell.** In *Refactoring: Improving the Design of Existing Code,* Fowler et al. [1999] describe 22 such indications that code quality can be improved through one or more corresponding refactorings.

This book has used refactoring many times to reorganize and improve existing code by applying a pattern. But you need not always apply a design pattern when refactoring. Any time that a method's code smells, the code may merit refactoring.

CHALLENGE 26.3

Provide an example of a method that smells—that cries out for improvement—without violating either LSP or LoD.

A solution appears on page 417.

Beyond Ordinary Extensions

Many design patterns, including many that this book has already covered, have a purpose that relates to extending behavior. Extension-oriented patterns often clarify the roles of two developers. For example, in the ADAPTER pattern, a developer may provide a useful service along with an interface for objects that want to use the service.

CHALLENGE 26.4

Fill in the blanks in the following table, which gives examples of using design patterns to extend the behavior of a class or an object.

Example	Pattern at Play
A fireworks simulation designer establishes an interface that defines the behaviors your object must possess in order to participate in the simulation.	ADAPTER
A toolkit that lets you compose executable objects at runtime.	?
?	TEMPLATE METHOD
?	COMMAND
A code generator inserts behavior that provides the illusion that an object executing on another machine is local.	?
?	OBSERVER
A design lets you define abstract operations that depend on a well-defined interface and lets you add new drivers that fulfill the interface.	?

A solution appears on page 418.

In addition to the patterns already covered, three patterns remain whose intent applies primarily to extension.

If you intend to	Apply the pattern
• Let developers compose an object's behavior dynamically	DECORATOR
• Provide a way to access the elements of collection sequentially	ITERATOR
• Let developers define a new operation for a hierarchy without changing the hierarchy classes	VISITOR

Summary

Writing code is primarily a matter of extension to provide new features, followed by reorganization that improves the quality of the code. A complete, objective technique for assessing code quality does not exist, but some principles of good OO code have been proposed.

The Liskov Substitution Principle suggests that an instance of a class should function as an instance of its superclass. You should be aware of and able to justify any violations of LSP in your code. The Law of Demeter is a collection of rules that help to reduce the dependencies between classes and that help lead to cleaner code.

Martin Fowler et al. [1999] have organized a large collection of indicators, or smells, that suggest that code is of imperfect quality. Each smell is subject to one or more refactorings, some of which include refactoring to a design pattern. Many design patterns serve as techniques for clarifying, simplifying, or facilitating extension.

27

DECORATOR

To extend a codebase, you ordinarily add new classes or methods to it. Sometimes, though, you want to compose an object with new behavior at runtime. The INTERPRETER pattern, for example, lets you compose an executable object whose behavior changes radically, depending on how you compose it. In some cases, you may need small variations in behavior and want to be able to mix them together. The DECORATOR pattern addresses this need.

The intent of DECORATOR is to let you compose new variations of an operation at runtime.

A Classic Example: Streams and Writers

The Java class libraries provide a classic example of the DECORATOR pattern in the overall design of input and output streams. A **stream** is a serial collection of bytes or characters, such as those that appear in a document. In Java, Writer classes are one approach to supporting streams. Some writer classes have constructors that accept another writer, so that you create a writer from a writer. This sort of slim composition is the typical structure of DECORATOR. The DECORATOR pattern is at work in Java writers. But, as we shall see, with a small amount of code, we can leverage DECORATOR to greatly expand our ability to mix in variations of the read and write operations of streams.

For an example of DECORATOR in Java, consider the following code, which creates a small text file:

```
package app.decorator;
import java.io.*;

public class ShowDecorator {
    public static void main(String[] args)
            throws IOException {
        FileWriter file = new FileWriter("sample.txt");
        BufferedWriter writer = new BufferedWriter(file);
        writer.write("a small amount of sample text");
```

```
        writer.newLine();
        writer.close();
    }
}
```

Running this program will produce a `sample.txt` file that contains a small amount of sample text. The program uses a `FileWriter` object to create a new file. The program wraps this object inside a `Buffered-Writer` object. The main point to note in the program is that we can compose one stream from another: The code composes a `Buffered-Writer` object from a `FileWriter` object.

At Oozinoz, salespeople have a need to format custom messages from text in the product database. These messages don't use a variety of fonts or styles, but the salespeople want a little formatting to spruce them up. To support this project, we'll build a framework of decorators. These decorator classes will let us compose a large variety of output filters.

To develop a collection of filter classes, it is useful to first create an abstract class that defines the operations you want your filters to support. By selecting operations that already exist in the `Writer` class, you can create, almost effortlessly, a class that inherits all its behavior from `Writer`. Figure 27.1 shows this design.

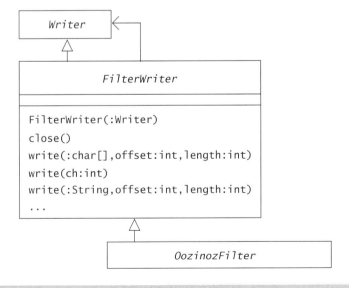

FIGURE 27.1 The `OozinozFilter` class will be the parent for classes that decorate output character streams.

We will define a filter class that accepts a writer in its constructor and that mixes in new behaviors in its `write()` methods.

To create a toolkit of composable output streams, the next step is to introduce a filter superclass that has several critical attributes. The filter class will

- Accept in its constructor a `Writer` object

- Act as the superclass of a filter hierarchy

- Provide default implementations of all `Writer` methods except `write(:int)`

Figure 27.2 shows this design.

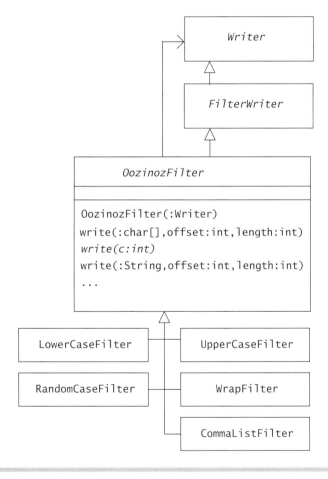

FIGURE 27.2 The `OozinozFilter` class constructor will accept an instance of any subclass of `Writer`.

The OozinozFilter class meets its design goals with a small amount of code:

```
package com.oozinoz.filter;
import java.io.*;
public abstract class OozinozFilter extends FilterWriter {
    protected OozinozFilter(Writer out) {
        super(out);
    }

    public void write(char cbuf[], int offset, int length)
                throws IOException {
        for (int i = 0; i < length; i++)
            write(cbuf[offset + i]);
    }

    public abstract void write(int c) throws IOException;

    public void write(String s, int offset, int length)
            throws IOException {
        write(s.toCharArray(), offset, length);
    }
}
```

This code is all we need to start putting DECORATOR to work. Subclasses of OozinozFilter can supply new implementations of write(:int) that modify a character before passing it on to the underlying stream's write(:int) method. The other methods in the Oozinoz-Filter class supply the behavior that subclasses will usually want. The class simply leaves close() and flush() calls to its parent (FilterWriter). The OozinozFilter class also interprets write(:char[]) in terms of the write(:int) method that it leaves abstract.

Now it is easy to create and use new stream filters. For example, the following code forces text to be lowercase:

```
package com.oozinoz.filter;
import java.io.*;

public class LowerCaseFilter extends OozinozFilter {
    public LowerCaseFilter(Writer out) {
        super(out);
    }
```

```
    public void write(int c) throws IOException {
        out.write(Character.toLowerCase((char) c));
    }
}
```

An example of a program that uses a lowercase filter is:

```
package app.decorator;

import java.io.IOException;
import java.io.Writer;

import com.oozinoz.filter.ConsoleWriter;
import com.oozinoz.filter.LowerCaseFilter;

public class ShowLowerCase {
    public static void main(String[] args)
            throws IOException {
        Writer out = new ConsoleWriter();
        out = new LowerCaseFilter(out);
        out.write("This Text, notably ALL in LoWeR casE!");
        out.close();
    }
}
```

This program writes "this text, notably all in lower case!" to the console.

The code for the UpperCaseFilter class is identical to the code for LowerCaseFilter, except for the write() method, which is:

```
public void write(int c) throws IOException {
        out.write(Character.toUpperCase((char) c));
}
```

The code for the TitleCaseFilter class is slightly more complex, as it has to keep track of whitespace:

```
package com.oozinoz.filter;
import java.io.*;

public class TitleCaseFilter extends OozinozFilter {
        boolean inWhite = true;
```

```
    public TitleCaseFilter(Writer out) {
            super(out);
    }

    public void write(int c) throws IOException {
            out.write(
                inWhite
                    ? Character.toUpperCase((char) c)
                    : Character.toLowerCase((char) c));
            inWhite = Character.isWhitespace((char) c)
            || c == '"';
    }
}
```

The CommaListFilter class puts a comma between elements:

```
package com.oozinoz.filter;

import java.io.IOException;
import java.io.Writer;

public class CommaListFilter extends OozinozFilter {
    protected boolean needComma = false;

    public CommaListFilter(Writer writer) {
        super(writer);
    }

    public void write(int c) throws IOException {
        if (needComma) {
            out.write(',');
            out.write(' ');
        }
        out.write(c);
        needComma = true;
    }


    public void write(String s) throws IOException {
        if (needComma)
            out.write(", ");

        out.write(s);
        needComma = true;
    }
}
```

The theme of these filters is the same: The development task consists of overriding the appropriate `write()` methods. The `write()` methods decorate the received stream of text and pass the modified text on to a subordinate stream.

CHALLENGE 27.1

Write the code for `RandomCaseFilter.java`.

A solution appears on page 419.

The code for the `WrapFilter` class is considerably more complex than the other filters. It offers to center its output and thus must buffer and count characters before passing them to its subordinate stream. You can inspect the code for `WrapFilter.java` by downloading it from www.oozinoz.com (see page 427 for details on downloading).

The constructor for the `WrapFilter` class accepts a `Writer` object as well as a `width` parameter that tells where to wrap lines. You can mix this filter and other filters together to create a variety of effects. For example, the following program wraps, centers, and **title cases** the text of an input file:

```
package app.decorator;
import java.io.*;
import com.oozinoz.filter.TitleCaseFilter;
import com.oozinoz.filter.WrapFilter;

public class ShowFilters {
    public static void main(String args[])
            throws IOException {
        BufferedReader in = new BufferedReader(
            new FileReader(args[0]));
        Writer out = new FileWriter(args[1]);
        out = new WrapFilter(new BufferedWriter(out), 40);
        out = new TitleCaseFilter(out);

        String line;
        while ((line = in.readLine()) != null)
            out.write(line + "\n");

        out.close();
```

```
        in.close();
    }
}
```

To see this program in action, suppose that a file adcopy.txt contains the text:

```
The "SPACESHOT" shell      hovers
         at 100 meters for 2 to 3
minutes,        erupting star bursts   every 10 seconds that
generate             ABUNDANT reading-level light for a
typical   stadium.
```

You can execute the ShowFilters program with the command line:

```
>ShowFilters adcopy.txt adout.txt
```

The contents of the adout.txt file will be something like:

```
  The "Spaceshot" Shell Hovers At 100
Meters For 2 To 3 Minutes, Erupting Star
 Bursts Every 10 Seconds That Generate
   Abundant Reading-level Light For A
          Typical Stadium.
```

Rather than writing to a file, it can be useful to direct output characters to the console. Figure 27.3 shows the design of a class that subclasses Writer and that will direct its characters to the console.

CHALLENGE 27.2

Write the code for ConsoleWriter.java.

A solution appears on page 420.

Input/output streams provide a classic example of how the DECORATOR pattern lets you assemble the behavior of an object at runtime. Another important application of DECORATOR occurs when you need to create mathematical functions at runtime.

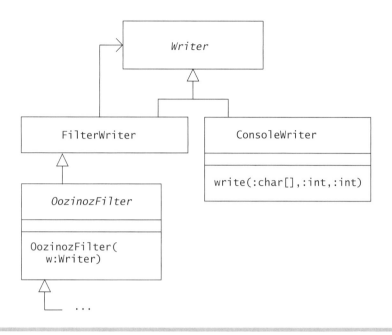

FIGURE 27.3 A `ConsoleWriter` object can serve as an argument to the constructor of any of the `OozinozFilter` subclasses.

Function Wrappers

The idea of composing new behaviors at runtime by using the Deco-RATOR pattern applies as nicely to mathematical functions as it does to I/O streams. The ability to create new functions at runtime is something you can pass along to your users, letting them specify new functions through a GUI or through a little language. You may also simply want to reduce the number of methods in your code and allow greater flexibility by creating mathematical functions as objects instead of new methods.

To create a library of function decorators, or function "wrappers," we can apply a structure similar to what we used for I/O streams. For the function wrapper superclass name, we'll use `Function`. For an initial design of the `Function` class, we could mimic the design for the `OozinozFilter` class, as Figure 27.4 shows.

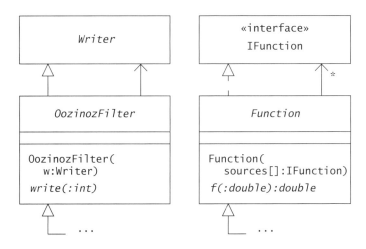

FIGURE 27.4 This initial design for the function wrapper hierarchy closely models the design for I/O filters.

The OozinozFilter class subclasses FilterWriter, and its constructor expects to receive another Writer object. The design for the Function class is similar. But instead of accepting a single IFunction object, the class accepts an array. Some functions, such as arithmetic functions, will require more than one subordinate function to work from.

In the case of function wrappers, no existing class like Writer already implements the operation that we need. As a result, there is no real need for an IFunction interface. We can more simply define the Function hierarchy without this interface, as Figure 27.5 shows.

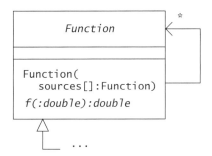

FIGURE 27.5 A simplified design for the Function class works without defining a separate interface.

As with the OozinozFilter class, the Function class defines a common operation that its subclasses must implement. A natural choice for the name of this operation is f. We can plan to implement parametric functions, basing all functions on a normalized "time" parameter that varies from 0 to 1. See the sidebar Parametric Equations, on page 39, for background on the power of using parametric equations.

We will create a subclass of Function for every function that we want to wrap around another function. Figure 27.6 shows an initial Function hierarchy.

The code for the Function superclass serves mainly to declare the sources array:

```
package com.oozinoz.function;

public abstract class Function {
    protected Function[] sources;

    public Function(Function f) {
        this(new Function[] { f });
    }

    public Function(Function[] sources) {
        this.sources = sources;
    }

    public abstract double f(double t);

    public String toString() {
        String name = this.getClass().toString();
        StringBuffer buf = new StringBuffer(name);
        if (sources.length > 0) {
            buf.append('(');
            for (int i = 0; i < sources.length; i++) {
                if (i > 0)
                    buf.append(", ");
                buf.append(sources[i]);
            }
            buf.append(')');
        }
        return buf.toString();
    }
}
```

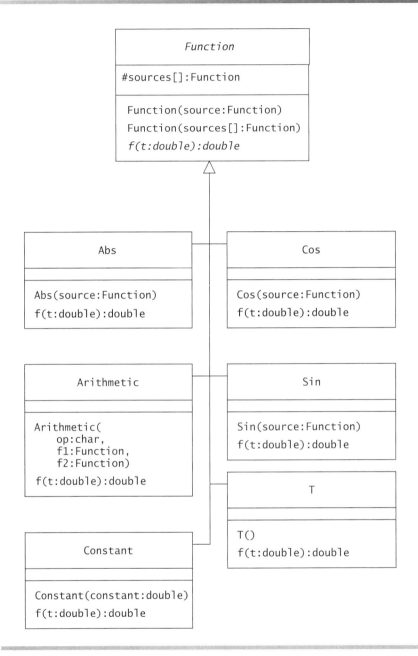

FIGURE 27.6 Each subclass of `Function` implements `f(t)` in a way that corresponds to the class's name.

The Function subclasses are generally simple. For example, here is code for the Cos class:

```
package com.oozinoz.function;
public class Cos extends Function {
    public Cos(Function f) {
        super(f);
    }

    public double f(double t) {
        return Math.cos(sources[0].f(t));
    }
}
```

The Cos class constructor expects a Function argument and passes this argument up to the superclass constructor, where the argument is stored in the sources array. The Cos.f() method evaluates the source function at time t, passes this value to Math.Cos(), and returns the result.

The Abs and Sin classes are nearly identical to the Cos class. The Constant class lets you create a Function object that holds a constant value to return in response to calls to the f() method. The Arithmetic class accepts an operator indicator that it applies in its f() method. The code for the Arithmetic class is:

```
package com.oozinoz.function;
public class Arithmetic extends Function {
    protected char op;

    public Arithmetic(char op, Function f1, Function f2) {
        super(new Function[] { f1, f2 });
        this.op = op;
    }

    public double f(double t) {
        switch (op) {
        case '+':
            return sources[0].f(t) + sources[1].f(t);
        case '-':
            return sources[0].f(t) - sources[1].f(t);
        case '*':
            return sources[0].f(t) * sources[1].f(t);
```

```
        case '/':
            return sources[0].f(t) / sources[1].f(t);
        default:
            return 0;
        }
    }
}
```

The T class returns the passed-in value of t. This behavior is useful if you want a variable to vary linearly with time. For example, the following expression creates a Function object whose f() value will vary from 0 to 2π as time varies from 0 to 1:

```
new Arithmetic('*', new T(), new Constant(2 * Math.PI))
```

You can use the Function classes to compose new mathematical functions without writing new methods. The FunPanel class accepts Function arguments for its *x* and *y* functions. This class also makes the functions fit within the plotting canvas. You can put this panel to work with a program such as the following:

```
package app.decorator;

import app.decorator.brightness.FunPanel;

import com.oozinoz.function.*;
import com.oozinoz.ui.SwingFacade;

public class ShowFun {
    public static void main(String[] args) {
        Function theta = new Arithmetic(
            '*', new T(), new Constant(2 * Math.PI));
        Function theta2 = new Arithmetic(
            '*', new T(), new Constant(2 * Math.PI * 5));
        Function x = new Arithmetic(
            '+', new Cos(theta), new Cos(theta2));
        Function y = new Arithmetic(
            '+', new Sin(theta), new Sin(theta2));

        FunPanel panel = new FunPanel(1000);
        panel.setPreferredSize(
            new java.awt.Dimension(200, 200));

        panel.setXY(x, y);
        SwingFacade.launch(panel, "Chrysanthemum");
    }
}
```

This program draws a function that lets one circle revolve around another multiple times. Running this program creates the display shown in Figure 27.7.

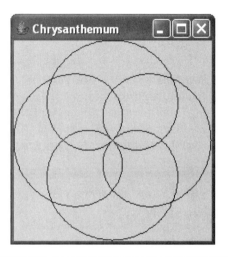

FIGURE 27.7 A complex mathematical function created without introducing any new methods.

If you want to extend your toolkit of function wrappers, it is often easy to add new mathematical functions into the `Function` hierarchy.

CHALLENGE 27.3

Write the code for an `Exp` function wrapper class. (Try to keep the book closed while you do this!)

A solution appears on page 420.

Suppose that the brightness of a star is a sine wave that decreases exponentially:

$$brightness = e^{-4t} \cdot \sin(\pi t)$$

As before, we can compose a function without writing new classes or methods for it:

```
package app.decorator.brightness;

import com.oozinoz.function.*;
import com.oozinoz.ui.SwingFacade;

public class ShowBrightness {
    public static void main(String args[]) {
        FunPanel panel = new FunPanel();
        panel.setPreferredSize(
            new java.awt.Dimension(200, 200));

        Function brightness = new Arithmetic(
            '*',
            new Exp(
                new Arithmetic(
                    '*',
                    new Constant(-4),
                    new T())),
            new Sin(
                new Arithmetic(
                    '*',
                    new Constant(Math.PI),
                    new T())));

        panel.setXY(new T(), brightness);

        SwingFacade.launch(panel, "Brightness");
    }
}
```

This code produces the plot in Figure 27.8.

CHALLENGE 27.4

Write the code to define a Brightness object that represents the brightness function.

A solution appears on page 421.

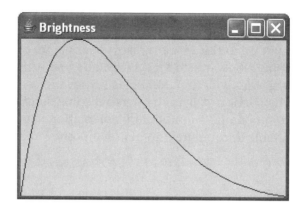

FIGURE 27.8 A star's brightness peaks quickly and then trails off.

You can add other functions to the Function hierarchy as needed. For example, you might add Random, Sqrt, and Tan classes. You can also create new hierarchies that work on different types, such as strings, or that have a different notion of how to define the f() operation. For example, you might define f() as a two- or three-dimensional function of time. Regardless of the hierarchy you create, you can apply DECORATOR to develop a rich set of functions that you can compose at runtime.

DECORATOR in Relation to Other Patterns

The mechanics of DECORATOR include a common operation implemented across a hierarchy. In this regard, DECORATOR is similar to STATE, STRATEGY, and INTERPRETER. In DECORATOR, classes also usually have a constructor that requires another, subordinate decorator object. DECORATOR resembles COMPOSITE in this regard. DECORATOR also resembles PROXY, in that decorator classes typically implement the common operation by forwarding the call to the subordinate decorator object.

Summary

The DECORATOR pattern lets you mix together variations of an operation. A classic example of this appears in input and output streams, whereby you can compose one stream from another. The Java class library supports DECORATOR in the implementation of I/O streams. You can extend this idea to create your own set of I/O filters. You can also apply DECORATOR to set up function wrappers that let you create a large family of function objects from a fixed set of function classes. The DECORATOR pattern offers a flexible design for cases in which a common operation has implementation variations that you want to be able to combine into new composite variations at runtime.

28

ITERATOR

WHEN YOU EXTEND a codebase by adding a new type of collection, you may find that you need to extend your extension by adding an iterator. This chapter examines the particular case of iterating over a composite. In addition to iterating over new types of collections, the topic of iterating in a multithreaded environment brings up a number of interesting problems that warrant review. Simple as it seems, iteration is not a completely solved problem.

The intent of the ITERATOR **pattern is to provide a way to access the elements of a collection sequentially.**

Ordinary Iteration

Java has several approaches to iteration:

- For, while, and repeat loops, typically using integer indexes

- The Enumeration class (in java.util)

- The Iterator class (also in java.util), added to support collections in JDK 1.2

- Extended for loops (foreach), added in JDK 1.5

We'll use the Iterator class for the bulk of this chapter; this section demonstrates an extended for loop.

An Iterator class has three methods: hasNext(), next(), and remove(). An iterator is allowed to throw UnsupportedOperation-Exception if it doesn't support the remove() operation.

An extended for loop has the form:

```
for (Type element : collection)
```

This creates a loop over the collection, pulling out one item at a time: called element here. There's no need to cast element to a particular type; that's handled implicitly. This construct can work with arrays as well. A class that wants to allow enhanced for loops over it must implement the Iterable interface and provide an iterator() method.

Here's a program that demonstrates the Iterator class and enhanced for loops:

```java
package app.iterator;

import java.util.ArrayList;
import java.util.Iterator;
import java.util.List;

public class ShowForeach {
    public static void main(String[] args) {
        ShowForeach example = new ShowForeach();
        example.showIterator();
        System.out.println();
        example.showForeach();
    }

    public void showIterator() {
        List names = new ArrayList();
        names.add("Fuser:1101");
        names.add("StarPress:991");
        names.add("Robot:1");

        System.out.println("JDK 1.2-style Iterator:");
        for (Iterator it = names.iterator(); it.hasNext();) {
            String name = (String) it.next();
            System.out.println(name);
        }
    }

    public void showForeach() {
        List<String> names = new ArrayList<String>();
        names.add("Fuser:1101");
        names.add("StarPress:991");
        names.add("Robot:1");

        System.out.println(
            "JDK 1.5-style Extended For Loop:");
        for (String name: names)
            System.out.println(name);
    }
}
```

When we run this program, we see these results:

```
JDK 1.2-style Iterator:
Fuser:1101
StarPress:991
Robot:1

JDK 1.5-style Extended For Loop:
Fuser:1101
StarPress:991
Robot:1
```

For now, Oozinoz has to continue to use the older-style `Iterator` classes; it can't upgrade until it's reasonably sure that its customers have the newer compilers. Nonetheless, you can start trying out generics and extended `for` loops today.

Thread-Safe Iteration

Rich applications often use threads to undertake tasks with the appearance of simultaneity. In particular, it is common to let time-consuming tasks happen in the background, without slowing down GUI responsiveness. Threading is useful, but it is also perilous. Many applications have crashed because of threaded tasks that did not cooperate effectively. Methods that iterate over collections can certainly be at fault when multithreaded applications fail.

The collection classes in the `java.util.Collections` offer a measure of thread safety by providing a `synchronized()` method. By returning, essentially, a version of the underlying collection, this method will prevent two threads from changing the collection at the same time.

A collection and its iterator cooperate to detect whether a list changes during iteration, that is, whether the list is synchronized. To see this behavior in action, suppose that the Oozinoz `Factory` single-ton can tell us which machines are up at a given moment and that we want to display a list of "up" machines. The sample code in the `app.iterator.concurrent` package hard-codes this list in method `upMachineNames()`.

The following program displays a list of the machines that are currently up, but simulates the condition that a new machines comes up while the program is displaying the list:

```
package app.iterator.concurrent;
import java.util.*;

public class ShowConcurrentIterator implements Runnable {
    private List list;

    protected static List upMachineNames() {
        return new ArrayList(Arrays.asList(new String[] {
            "Mixer1201", "ShellAssembler1301",
            "StarPress1401", "UnloadBuffer1501" }));
    }

    public static void main(String[] args) {
        new ShowConcurrentIterator().go();
    }

    protected void go() {
        list = Collections.synchronizedList(
            upMachineNames());
        Iterator iter = list.iterator();
        int i = 0;
        while (iter.hasNext()) {
            i++;
            if (i == 2) { // simulate wake-up
                new Thread(this).start();
                try { Thread.sleep(100); }
                catch (InterruptedException ignored) {}
            }
            System.out.println(iter.next());
        }
    }

    /**
     ** Insert an element in the list, in a separate thread.
     */
    public void run() {
        list.add(0, "Fuser1101");
    }
}
```

The main() method in this code constructs an instance of the class and calls the go() method. This method iterates over the list of up machines, taking care to construct a synchronized version of the list. This code simulates the condition that another machine comes up while this method iterates over the list. The run() method modifies the list, running in a separate thread.

The ShowConcurrentIterator program prints a machine or two and then crashes:

```
Mixer1201
java.util.ConcurrentModificationException
at java.util.AbstractList$Itr.checkForComodification(Unknown Source)
at java.util.AbstractList$Itr.next(Unknown Source)
at com.oozinoz.app.ShowConcurrent.ShowConcurrentIterator.go(Show-
ConcurrentIterator.java:49)
at com.oozinoz.app.ShowConcurrent.ShowConcurrentIterator.main(Show-
ConcurrentIterator.java:29)
Exception in thread "main" .
```

The program crashes because the list and iterator objects detect that the list has changed during the iteration. You don't need to create a new thread to show this behavior: You can create a program that crashes simply by altering a collection from within an iteration loop. In practice, a multithreaded application is much more likely to accidentally modify a list while an iterator is traversing it.

We *can* devise a thread-safe approach for iterating over a list; first, however, it is important to note that the ShowConcurrentIterator program crashes only because it uses an iterator. Iterating over even a synchronized list with a for loop will *not* trigger the exception that the previous program encounters but can still get into trouble. Consider the following variation of the program:

```
package app.iterator.concurrent;
import java.util.*;

public class ShowConcurrentFor implements Runnable {
    private List list;

    protected static List upMachineNames() {
        return new ArrayList(Arrays.asList(new String[] {
            "Mixer1201", "ShellAssembler1301",
            "StarPress1401", "UnloadBuffer1501" }));
    }
```

```java
    public static void main(String[] args) {
        new ShowConcurrentFor().go();
    }

    protected void go() {
        System.out.println(
            "This version lets new things "
            + "be added in concurrently:");

        list = Collections.synchronizedList(
            upMachineNames());
        display();
    }

    private void display() {
        for (int i - 0; i < list.size(); i++) {
            if (i == 1) {    // simulate wake-up
                new Thread(this).start();
                try { Thread.sleep(100); }
                catch (InterruptedException ignored) {}
            }
            System.out.println(list.get(i));
        }
    }

    /**
     ** Insert an element in the list, in a separate thread.
     */
    public void run() {
        list.add(0, "Fuser1101");
    }
}
```

Running this program prints out:

```
This version lets new things be added in concurrently:
Mixer1201
Mixer1201
ShellAssembler1301
StarPress1401
UnloadBuffer1501
```

CHALLENGE 28.1

Explain the output of the ShowConcurrentFor program.

A solution appears on page 421.

We have looked at two versions of the program: one that crashes and one that produces incorrect output. Neither of these results is acceptable, so we need some other way to protect a list while iterating over it.

There are two common approaches to providing safe iteration over a collection in a multithreaded application. Both approaches involve the use of an object, sometimes called a **mutex**, that is shared by threads that vie for control of the object's lock. In one approach, your design can require that all threads gain control of the mutex lock before accessing the collection. The following program shows this approach:

```
package app.iterator.concurrent;
import java.util.*;

public class ShowConcurrentMutex implements Runnable {
  private List list;

  protected static List upMachineNames() {
      return new ArrayList(Arrays.asList(new String[] {
          "Mixer1201", "ShellAssembler1301",
          "StarPress1401", "UnloadBuffer1501" }));
  }

  public static void main(String[] args) {
      new ShowConcurrentMutex().go();
  }

  protected void go() {
      System.out.println(
          "This version synchronizes properly:");
      list = Collections.synchronizedList(upMachineNames());
      synchronized (list) {
          display();
      }
  }
}
```

```
private void display() {
    for (int i = 0; i < list.size(); i++) {
        if (i == 1) {    // simulate wake-up
            new Thread(this).start();
            try { Thread.sleep(100);
            } catch (InterruptedException ignored) {}
        }
        System.out.println(list.get(i));
    }
}

/**
 ** Insert an element in the list, in a separate thread.
 */
public void run() {
    synchronized (list) {
        list.add(0, "Fuser1101");
    }
}
}
```

This program will print the original list:

```
This version synchronizes properly:
Mixer1201
ShellAssembler1301
StarPress1401
UnloadBuffer1501
```

The output shows the list as it exists before the run() method inserts a new object. The program outputs a consistent result, with no duplicates, because the program logic requires the run() method to wait for the iteration in the display() method to complete. Although the output is correct, the design may be impractical: You may not be able to afford to have other threads block while one thread iterates over a collection.

An alternative approach is to clone the collection in a mutex operation and then work on the clone. The advantage of cloning the list before traversing it is speed. Cloning a collection is often much faster than waiting for another method to finish operating on the collection's contents. However, cloning a collection and iterating over the clone may cause problems.

The clone() method for ArrayList produces a **shallow copy**: a new collection that refers to the same objects as the original. Relying on a clone will fail if other threads can change the underlying objects in a way that interferes with your method. But in some cases, this risk is small. For example, if you simply want to display a list of machine names, it may be unlikely or inconsequential if the names change while your method iterates over a clone of the list.

To summarize, we have discussed four approaches for iterating over a list in a multithreaded environment. Two of these approaches use a synchronized() method and fail, either crashing or producing an incorrect result. The latter two approaches, using locking and cloning, may produce correct results but have their consequences as well.

CHALLENGE 28.2

Provide an argument against using the synchronized() methods, or argue that a locking-based approach isn't always the answer, either.

A solution appears on page 422.

Java and its libraries provide substantial support for iteration in a multithreaded environment, but this support does not free you from the complexities of concurrent design. The Java class libraries build in good support for iterating over the many collections that they provide, but if you introduce your own collection type, you also may need to introduce an accompanying iterator.

Iterating over a Composite

It is usually easy to design algorithms that *traverse* a composite structure, visiting every node and performing some function. You may recall that Challenge 5.3 (from Chapter 5, COMPOSITE, page 50) asked you to design several algorithms that execute by recursively traversing a composite structure. Creating an iterator may be much more difficult than creating a recursive algorithm. The difficulty lies in returning control to another part of the program and saving some kind of bookmark that lets the iterator pick up where it left off.

Composites provide a good example of an iterator that is challenging to develop.

You might think that you will need a new iterator class for each domain-specific composite that you create. In fact, you can design a fairly reusable composite iterator, although you will have to modify your composite classes to return the right sort of iterator.

The design for a composite iterator is as naturally recursive as composites themselves are. To iterate over a composite, we iterate over its children, although this is a bit more complex than it may initially sound. First, we have a choice as to whether we return a node before or after its descendants (called **preorder** and **postorder traversal**). If we choose a preorder traversal, we must iterate over the children after returning the head, noting that each child may be a composite. A subtlety here is that we must maintain two iterators. One iterator (labeled 1 in Figure 28.1) keeps track of which is the current child. This iterator is a simple list iterator that iterates over the list of children. A second iterator (labeled 2) iterates over the current child as a composite. Figure 28.1 shows the three aspects of determining the current node in a composite iteration.

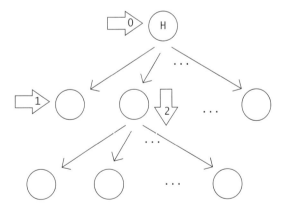

FIGURE 28.1 Iteration over a composite requires 0 noting a head node, 1 iterating sequentially across its children, and 2 iterating over each child as a composite.

To work out the design for a composite iterator, we might expect that iterating over a leaf will be trivial, whereas iterating over a node with children will be more difficult. We can anticipate a design for these iterators something like the one shown in Figure 28.2.

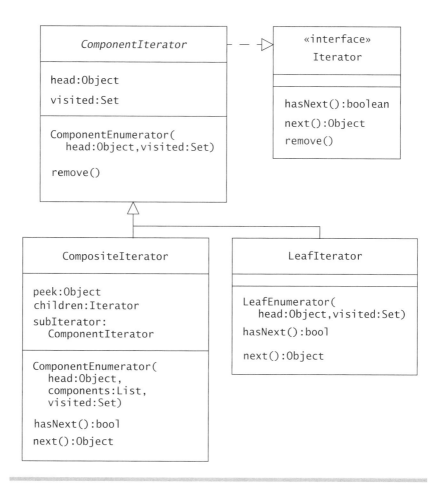

FIGURE 28.2 An initial design for a family of composite enumerators

The classes use the method names hasNext() and next(), so that the ComponentIterator class implements the Iterator interface from the java.util package.

The design shows that the enumerator class constructors will accept an object to enumerate. In practice, this object will be a composite, such as a machine composite or a process composite. The design also uses a visited variable to keep track of nodes that we have already

enumerated. This will keep us from stepping into an infinite loop
when a composite has cycles. The code for ComponentIterator at the
top of the hierarchy will initially look like the following:

```
package com.oozinoz.iterator;
import java.util.*;

public abstract class ComponentIterator
        implements Iterator {
    protected Object head;
    protected Set visited;
    protected boolean returnInterior = true;

    public ComponentIterator(Object head, Set visited) {
        this.head = head;
        this.visited = visited;
    }

    public void remove() {
        throw new UnsupportedOperationException(
            "ComponentIterator.Remove");
    }
}
```

This class leaves most of the difficult work to its subclasses.

In the CompositeIterator subclass, we can anticipate the need for a
list iterator to enumerate a composite node's children. This is the enumeration marked 1 in Figure 28.1, represented by the children variable in Figure 28.2. Composites also need an enumerator for the
enumeration marked 2 in Figure 28.1. The subiterator variable in
Figure 28.2 fills this need. The CompositeEnumerator class constructor
can initialize the child enumerator as follows:

```
public CompositeIterator(
        Object head, List components, Set visited) {
    super(head, visited);
    children = components.iterator();
}
```

When we begin an enumeration of a composite, we know that the
first node to return is the head node (marked H in Figure 28.1). Thus,
the code for the next() method of a CompositeIterator class looks
like this:

```
    public Object next() {
        if (peek != null) {
            Object result = peek;
            peek = null;
            return result;
        }

        if (!visited.contains(head)) {
            visited.add(head);
            return head;
        }

        return nextDescendant();
    }
```

The next() method uses the visited set to record whether the enumerator has already returned the head node. If the enumerator has already returned the head of a composite node, the nextDescendant() method must find the next node.

At any given time, the subiterator variable may be part-way through an enumeration of a child that is itself a composite node. If this enumerator is active, the next() method of the Composite-Iterator class can "move" the subiterator. If the subiterator cannot move, the code must move to the next element in the children list, get a new subenumerator for it, and move that enumerator. The code for the nextDescendant() method shows this logic:

```
protected Object nextDescendant() {
    while (true) {
        if (subiterator != null) {
            if (subiterator.hasNext())
                return subiterator.next();
        }

        if (!children.hasNext()) return null;

        ProcessComponent pc =
            (ProcessComponent) children.next();
        if (!visited.contains(pc)) {
            subiterator = pc.iterator(visited);
        }
    }
```

This method introduces the first constraint we have encountered regarding the kind of objects that we can enumerate: The code requires that children in a composite implement an iterator(:Set) method. Consider an example of a composite structure, such as the Process-Component hierarchy that Chapter 5 introduced. Figure 28.3 shows the process composite hierarchy that Oozinoz uses for modeling the manufacturing work flows that produce various types of fireworks.

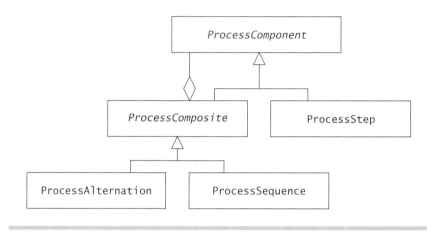

FIGURE 28.3 Manufacturing process flows at Oozinoz are composites.

The next() method of the CompositeIterator class needs to enumerate the nodes of each child that belongs to a composite object. We need the child's class to implement an iterator(:Set) method that the next() code can use. Figure 28.2 shows the relationship of these classes and interfaces.

To update the ProcessComponent hierarchy so that we can enumerate it, we need to provide an iterator() method:

```
public ComponentIterator iterator() {
    return iterator(new HashSet());
}

public abstract ComponentIterator iterator(Set visited);
```

The ProcessComponent class is abstract and leaves the iterator(:Set) method for subclasses to implement. For the ProcessComposite class, this code will look like:

```
public ComponentIterator iterator(Set visited) {
  return new CompositeIterator(this, subprocesses, visited);
}
```

The ProcessStep class implementation of iterator() will be:

```
public ComponentIterator iterator(Set visited) {
  return new LeafIterator(this, visited);
}
```

CHALLENGE 28.3

What pattern are you applying if you let classes in the ProcessComponent hierarchy implement iterator() to create instances of an appropriate iterator class?

A solution appears on page 422.

With these small additions to the ProcessComponent hierarchy in place, we can now write code that enumerates a process composite. The object model of a typical Oozinoz process is shown in Figure 28.4.

The ShellProcess class in the com.oozinoz.processes package has a static make() method that returns the object model shown in Figure 28.4. The following short program enumerates all the nodes in this model:

```
package app.iterator.process;

import com.oozinoz.iterator.ComponentIterator;
import com.oozinoz.process.ProcessComponent;
import com.oozinoz.process.ShellProcess;

public class ShowProcessIteration {
    public static void main(String[] args) {
        ProcessComponent pc = ShellProcess.make();
        ComponentIterator iter = pc.iterator();
        while (iter.hasNext())
            System.out.println(iter.next());
    }
}
```

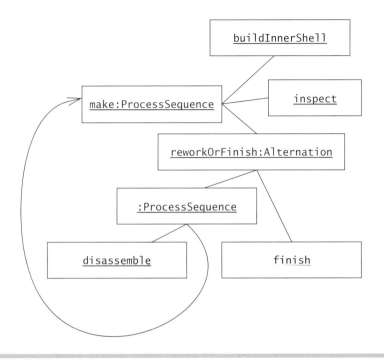

FIGURE 28.4 The process flow for making aerial shells is a cyclic composite. Each leaf node in this diagram is an instance of `ProcessStep`. The remaining nodes are instances of `ProcessComposite`.

Running this program prints out:

```
Make an aerial shell
Build inner shell
Inspect
Rework inner shell, or complete shell
Rework
Disassemble
Finish: Attach lift, insert fusing, wrap
```

The names shown are those that the `ShellProcess` class gives to the process steps. Note that in the object model, the step after `disassemble` is `make`. The printout omits this because the enumeration sees that it has already printed out that step once before, in the first line of output.

Adding Depth to a Composite Enumerator

The output of this program might be more clear if we indented each process step in accordance with its depth in the model. We can define the depth of a leaf enumerator to be 0 and note that the current depth of a composite enumerator is 1 plus the depth of its subiterator. We can make the getDepth() abstract in the ComponentIterator superclass as follows:

```
public abstract int getDepth();
```

The code for a getDepth() method for the LeafIterator class is:

```
public int getDepth() {
    return 0;
}
```

The code for CompositeIterator.getDepth() is:

```
public int getDepth() {
    if (subiterator != null)
        return subiterator.getDepth() + 1;
    return 0;
}
```

The following program produces more readable output:

```
package app.iterator.process;

import com.oozinoz.iterator.ComponentIterator;
import com.oozinoz.process.ProcessComponent;
import com.oozinoz.process.ShellProcess;

public class ShowProcessIteration2 {
    public static void main(String[] args) {
        ProcessComponent pc = ShellProcess.make();
        ComponentIterator iter = pc.iterator();
        while (iter.hasNext()) {
            for (int i = 0; i < 4 * iter.getDepth(); i++)
                System.out.print(' ');
            System.out.println(iter.next());
        }
    }
}
```

The output of this program is:

```
Make an aerial shell
    Build inner shell
    Inspect
    Rework inner shell, or complete shell
        Rework
            Disassemble
        Finish: Attach lift, insert fusing, wrap
```

Another improvement we can make to the ComponentIterator hierarchy is to allow for enumeration over only the leaves of a composite.

Enumerating Leaves

Suppose that we want to allow an enumeration to return only leaves. This can be useful if we are concerned with attributes that apply only to leaves, such as the time that a process step takes. We can add a returnInterior field to the ComponentIterator class to record whether interior (nonleaf) nodes should be returned from the enumeration:

```
protected boolean returnInterior = true;

public boolean shouldShowInterior() {
    return returnInterior;
}

public void setShowInterior(boolean value) {
    returnInterior = value;
}
```

In the nextDescendant() method of the CompositeIterator class, we'll need to pass this attribute down when we create a new enumeration for a composite node's child:

```
protected Object nextDescendant() {
    while (true) {
        if (subiterator != null) {
            if (subiterator.hasNext())
                    return subiterator.next();
        }
```

```
        if (!children.hasNext()) return null;

        ProcessComponent pc =
            (ProcessComponent) children.next();
        if (!visited.contains(pc)) {
            subiterator = pc.iterator(visited);
            subiterator.setShowInterior(
                        shouldShowInterior());
        }
    }
}
```

We will also need to update the next() method of the CompositeEnu-merator class. The existing code is:

```
public Object next() {
    if (peek != null) {
        Object result = peek;
        peek = null;
        return result;
    }

    if (!visited.contains(head)) {
        visited.add(head);
    }

    return nextDescendant();
}
```

CHALLENGE 28.4

Update the next() method of the CompositeIterator class to respect the value of the returnInterior field.

A solution appears on page 422.

Creating an iterator, or enumerator, for a new type of collection can be a significant design task. The resulting benefit is that your collection can become as easy to work with as any of the collection classes in Java's class libraries.

Summary

The intent of the Iterator pattern is to let a client access the elements of a collection sequentially. The collection classes in the Java libraries offer rich support for operating on collections, including support for iteration, or enumeration. If you create a new type of collection, you will often want to create an iterator to go with it. Domain-specific composites are a common example of a new collection type. Support for generics and enhanced for loops can make your code more readable than ever. You can design a fairly generic iterator that you can then apply against a variety of composite hierarchies.

When you instantiate an iterator, you should consider whether the collection can change while you are enumerating it. There is usually not much chance of this in a single-threaded application, but in a multithreaded application, you may want to ensure that access to a collection is synchronized. To safely iterate in a multithreaded application, you can synchronize access to a collection by locking on a mutex object. You can block out all access either while iterating or briefly while making a clone of the collection. With a proper design, you can provide thread safety to the clients of your iterator code.

29

VISITOR

To EXTEND AN existing class hierarchy, you normally just add methods that provide the behavior you need. It can happen, though, that the behavior you need is not consistent with the thrust of the existing object model. It can also happen that you don't have access to the existing code. In such a case, it may be impossible to extend the hierarchy's behavior without modifying the hierarchy's classes. The VISITOR pattern, however, lets a hierarchy developer build in support for the prospect that another developer may want to extend the behavior of the hierarchy.

As with INTERPRETER, VISITOR is most often layered over a COMPOSITE. You may want to review that pattern, as we'll use it throughout this chapter.

The intent of VISITOR is to let you define a new operation for a hierarchy without changing the hierarchy classes.

VISITOR Mechanics

The VISITOR pattern lets a small amount of forethought in developing a class hierarchy open a gateway to an unlimited variety of extensions that can be made by a developer who lacks access to the source code. The mechanics of the VISITOR pattern are as follows:

- Add an `accept()` operation to some or all of the classes in a class hierarchy. Every implementation of this method will accept an argument whose type is an interface that you will create.

- Create an interface with a set of operations that share a common name—usually, `visit`—but that have different argument types. Declare one such operation for each class in the hierarchy for which you will allow extensions.

Figure 29.1 shows a class diagram of the MachineComponent hierarchy modified to support VISITOR.

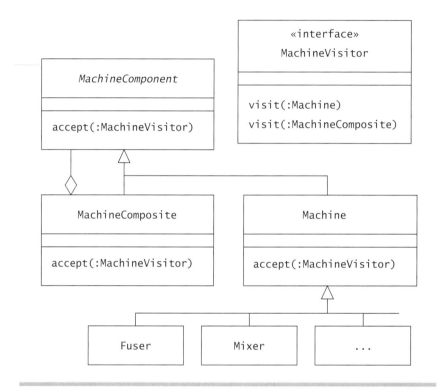

FIGURE 29.1 To prepare the MachineComponent hierarchy for VISITOR support, add the accept() methods and the MachineVisitor interface shown in this diagram.

The diagram in Figure 29.1 doesn't explain how VISITOR works; the next section does that. The figure simply shows some of the groundwork that lets you apply VISITOR.

Note that not all the classes in the MachineComponent diagram implement an accept() method. VISITOR does not require every class in the hierarchy to have its own implementation of the accepting method. As we shall see, though, it is important for each class that implements accept() to appear as an argument in a visit() method declared in the visitor interface.

The accept() method in the MachineComponent class is abstract. Both subclasses implement this method with exactly the same code:

```
public void accept(MachineVisitor v) {
    v.visit(this);
}
```

You might think that, because this method is identical in the Machine and MachineComposite classes, you could move the method up to the abstract MachineComponent class. However, a compiler will see a difference in these two "identical" methods.

CHALLENGE 29.1

What difference will a Java compiler see between the accept() methods in the Machine and MachineComposite classes?

(Don't peek on this one unless you have to; it's key to understanding VISITOR.)

A solution appears on page 423.

The MachineVisitor interface requires implementers to define methods for visiting machines and machine composites:

```
package com.oozinoz.machine;
public interface MachineVisitor {
    void visit(Machine m);
    void visit(MachineComposite mc);
}
```

The accept() methods in the MachineComponent, together with the MachineVisitor interface, invite developers to provide new operations to the hierarchy.

An Ordinary VISITOR

Suppose that you are working at the latest Oozinoz factory in Dublin, Ireland. The developers there have created an object model of

the new factory's machine composition and have made this model
accessible as the static dublin() method of the OozinozFactory
class. To display this composite, the developers created a Machine-
TreeModel class to adapt the model's information to a JTree object's
needs. (The code for MachineTreeModel is in the com.oozinoz.dublin
package.)

Displaying the factory's machines requires building an instance of
MachineTreeModel from the factory composite and wrapping this
model in Swing components:

```
package app.visitor;
import javax.swing.JScrollPane;
import javax.swing.JTree;
import com.oozinoz.machine.OozinozFactory;
import com.oozinoz.ui.SwingFacade;

public class ShowMachineTreeModel {
    public ShowMachineTreeModel() {
        MachineTreeModel model = new MachineTreeModel(
            OozinozFactory.dublin());
        JTree tree = new JTree(model);
        tree.setFont(SwingFacade.getStandardFont());
        SwingFacade.launch(
            new JScrollPane(tree),
            " A New Oozinoz Factory");
    }

    public static void main(String[] args) {
        new ShowMachineTreeModel();
    }
}
```

Running this program creates the display shown in Figure 29.2.

Many useful behaviors for a machine composite are possible. For
example, suppose that you need to find a particular machine within
the factory model. To add this ability without modifying the
MachineComponent hierarchy, you can create a FindVisitor class,
as Figure 29.3 shows.

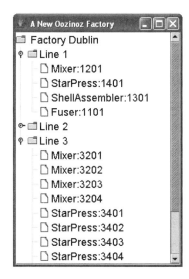

FIGURE 29.2 This GUI application presents the composition of machines at the new factory in Dublin.

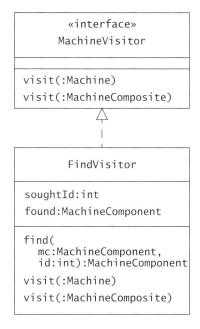

FIGURE 29.3 The FindVisitor class effectively adds a find() operation to the MachineComponent hierarchy.

The visit() methods do not return an object, so the FindVisitor class records the status of a search in its found instance variable:

```
package app.visitor;

import com.oozinoz.machine.*;
import java.util.*;

public class FindVisitor implements MachineVisitor {
    private int soughtId;
    private MachineComponent found;

    public MachineComponent find(
            MachineComponent mc, int id) {
        found = null;
        soughtId = id;
        mc.accept(this);
        return found;
    }

    public void visit(Machine m) {
        if (found == null && m.getId() == soughtId)
            found = m;
    }

    public void visit(MachineComposite mc) {
        if (found == null && mc.getId() == soughtId) {
            found = mc;
            return;
        }
        Iterator iter = mc.getComponents().iterator();
        while (found == null && iter.hasNext())
            ((MachineComponent) iter.next()).accept(this);
    }
}
```

The visit() methods check the found variable so that the tree traversal will end as soon as the desired component is found.

CHALLENGE 29.2

Write a program that finds and prints out the StarPress:3404
object within the instance of MachineComponent that
OozinozFactory.dublin() returns.

A solution appears on page 423.

The find() method does not worry about whether the MachineComponent it receives is an instance of Machine or of MachineComposite.
The method simply calls accept(), which in turn calls visit().

Note that the loop in the visit(:MachineComposite) method like-
wise does not worry about whether a child component is an instance
of Machine or of MachineComposite. The visit() method simply
invokes the accept() operation of each component. Which method
executes as a result of this invocation depends on the type of the
child. Figure 29.4 shows a typical sequence of method calls.

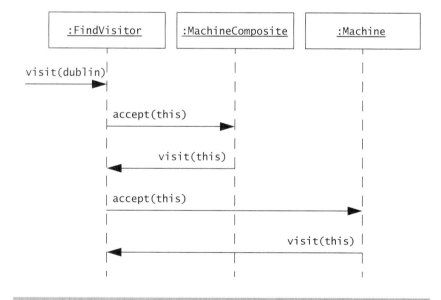

FIGURE 29.4 A FindVisitor object invokes an accept() operation to determine
which visit() method to execute.

When the visit(:MachineComposite) method executes, it invokes the accept() operation on each of the composite's children. A child responds by invoking a visit() operation on the Visitor object. As Figure 29.4 shows, the short trip from the Visitor object to the object that receives the accept() invocation and back again picks up the type of the receiving object. This technique, known as **double dispatch,** ensures that the right visit() method of the Visitor class executes.

The double dispatching in Visitor lets you create visitor classes with methods that are specific to the various types in the visited hierarchy.

You can add almost any behavior through Visitor as you might if you controlled the source code. As another example, consider a visitor that finds all the machines—the leaf nodes—in a machine component:

```
package app.visitor;
import com.oozinoz.machine.*;
import java.util.*;

public class RakeVisitor implements MachineVisitor {
    private Set leaves;

    public Set getLeaves(MachineComponent mc) {
        leaves = new HashSet();
        mc.accept(this);
        return leaves;
    }

    public void visit(Machine m) {
        // Challenge!
    }

    public void visit(MachineComposite mc) {
        // Challenge!
    }
}
```

CHALLENGE 29.3

Complete the code of the RakeVisitor class to collect the leaves of a machine component.

A solution appears on page 423.

A short program can find the leaves of a machine component and print them out:

```
package app.visitor;

import com.oozinoz.machine.*;
import java.io.*;
import com.oozinoz.filter.WrapFilter;

public class ShowRakeVisitor {
    public static void main(String[] args)
            throws IOException {
        MachineComponent f = OozinozFactory.dublin();
        Writer out = new PrintWriter(System.out);
        out = new WrapFilter(new BufferedWriter(out), 60);
        out.write(
            new RakeVisitor().getLeaves(f).toString());
        out.close();
    }
}
```

This program uses a comma-list filter and wrap filter to produce the output:

```
[StarPress:3401, Fuser:3102, StarPress:3402, Mixer:3202,
Fuser:3101, StarPress:3403, ShellAssembler:1301,
ShellAssembler:2301, Mixer:1201, StarPress:2401, Mixer:3204,
Mixer:3201, Fuser:1101, Fuser:2101, ShellAssembler:3301,
ShellAssembler:3302, StarPress:1401, Mixer:3203, Mixer:2202,
StarPress:3404, Mixer:2201, StarPress:2402]
```

The FindVisitor and RakeVisitor classes each effectively add a new behavior to the MachineComponent hierarchy. These classes appear to work correctly. However, a danger in writing visitors is that they require an understanding of the hierarchy that you are extending. A change in the hierarchy may break your visitor, and you may misunderstand the mechanics of the hierarchy initially. In particular, you may have to handle cycles if the composite you are visiting does not prevent them.

VISITOR Cycles

The ProcessComponent hierarchy that Oozinoz uses to model process flows is another composite structure that can benefit from building in support for VISITOR. Unlike machine composites, it is natural for process flows to contain cycles, and visitors must take care not to cause infinite loops while traversing process composites. Figure 29.5 shows the ProcessComponent hierarchy.

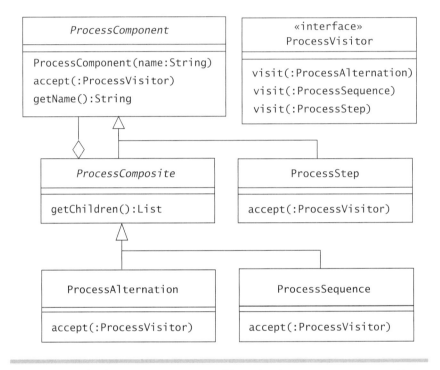

FIGURE 29.5 Like the MachineComponent hierarchy, the ProcessComponent hierarchy can build in support for VISITOR.

Suppose that you want to print out a process component in a "pretty," or indented, format. In Chapter 28, ITERATOR, you used an iterator to print out a process flow's steps. This printout looked like:

```
Make an aerial shell
    Build inner shell
    Inspect
    Rework inner shell, or complete shell
        Rework
            Disassemble
        Finish: Attach lift, insert fusing, wrap
```

Reworking a shell involves disassembling it and then making it again; the step after "Disassemble" is "Make an aerial shell." The printout doesn't show this step, because the iterator sees that the step has already appeared once. However, it would be more informative to show the step name and to indicate that the process enters a cycle at this point. It would also be helpful to indicate which composites are alternations as opposed to sequences.

To create a pretty-printer for processes, you can create a visitor class that initializes a StringBuilder object and that adds to this buffer as the visitor visits the nodes in a process component. To indicate that a composite step is an alternation, the visitor can prepend a question mark (?) to an alternation step's name. To indicate that a step has occurred before, the visitor can attach an ellipsis (...) to the end of the step's name. With these changes, the aerial shell process will print out as:

```
Make an aerial shell
    Build inner shell
    Inspect
    ?Rework inner shell, or complete shell
        Rework
            Disassemble
            Make an aerial shell...
        Finish: Attach lift, insert fusing, wrap
```

A process component visitor has to watch for cycles, but this is easily achieved by using a Set object to keep track of the nodes the visitor has already seen. The code for this class starts out as:

```
package app.visitor;
import java.util.List;
import java.util.HashSet;
import java.util.Set;
import com.oozinoz.process.*;

public class PrettyVisitor implements ProcessVisitor {
    public static final String INDENT_STRING = "    ";
    private StringBuffer buf;
    private int depth;
    private Set visited;
```

```
    public StringBuffer getPretty(ProcessComponent pc) {
        buf = new StringBuffer();
        visited = new HashSet();
        depth = 0;
        pc.accept(this);
        return buf;
    }

    protected void printIndentedString(String s) {
        for (int i = 0; i < depth; i++)
            buf.append(INDENT_STRING);
        buf.append(s);
        buf.append("\n");
    }
    // ... visit() methods ...
}
```

This class uses a `getPretty()` method to initialize an instance's variables and to kick off the visitor algorithm. The `printIndentedString()` method handles the indentation of steps as the algorithm goes deeper and deeper into a composite. When visiting a Process-Step object, the code simply prints the step's name:

```
public void visit(ProcessStep s) {
    printIndentedString(s.getName());
}
```

You might note from Figure 29.5 that the `ProcessComposite` class does not implement an `accept()` method but that its subclasses do. Visiting a process alternation or process sequence requires nearly identical logic, as follows:

```
public void visit(ProcessAlternation a) {
    visitComposite("?", a);
}

public void visit(ProcessSequence s) {
    visitComposite("", s);
}
```

```
protected void visitComposite(
        String prefix, ProcessComposite c) {
    if (visited.contains(c)) {
        printIndentedString(prefix + c.getName() + "...");
    } else {
        visited.add(c);
        printIndentedString(prefix + c.getName());
        depth++;

        List children = c.getChildren();
        for (int i = 0; i < children.size(); i++) {
            ProcessComponent child =
                (ProcessComponent) children.get(i);
            child.accept(this);
        }

        depth--;
    }
}
```

The difference between visiting an alternation and a sequence is that
an alternation prints a question mark as a prefix. For either type of
composite, if the algorithm has visited the node before, we print its
name and an ellipsis. Otherwise, we add this node to a collection of visited nodes, print its prefix—a question mark or nothing—and "accept"
the node's children. As is typical of the VISITOR pattern, the code uses
polymorphism to decide whether child nodes are instances of the
ProcessStep, ProcessAlternation, or ProcessSequence classes.

A short program can now pretty-print a process flow:

```
package app.visitor;

import com.oozinoz.process.ProcessComponent;
import com.oozinoz.process.ShellProcess;

public class ShowPrettyVisitor {
    public static void main(String[] args) {
        ProcessComponent p = ShellProcess.make();
        PrettyVisitor v = new PrettyVisitor();
        System.out.println(v.getPretty(p));
    }
}
```

Running this program prints out:

```
Make an aerial shell
    Build inner shell
    Inspect
    ?Rework inner shell, or complete shell
        Rework
            Disassemble
            Make an aerial shell...
        Finish: Attach lift, insert fusing, wrap
```

This output is more informative that the printout we achieved by simply iterating over the process model. The one question mark that appears signals that this composite's steps are alternatives. Also, showing the Make step a second time, followed by an ellipsis, is more clear than simply omitting a repeated step.

The developers of the ProcessComponent hierarchy built in support for VISITOR by including accept() methods in the hierarchy and by defining the ProcessVisitor interface. These developers are well aware of the need to avoid infinite loops while traversing process flows. As the PrettyVisitor class shows, the developers of the visitor also have to be aware of the potential for cycles in process components. It might help prevent errors if the ProcessComponent developers could provide some degree of cycle-management support as part of their support of VISITOR.

CHALLENGE 29.4

How can the ProcessComponent developers include cycle-management support in the hierarchy's support for VISITOR?

A solution appears on page 424.

VISITOR Risks

VISITOR is a controversial pattern. Some developers consistently avoid applying it, whereas others defend its use and suggest ways to strengthen it, although these suggestions usually add complexity. The fact is that many design problems can accompany the VISITOR pattern.

The fragility of VISITOR shows up in the examples in this chapter. For instance, in the MachineComponent hierarchy, the hierarchy developers decided to differentiate between Machine nodes and Machine-Composite nodes but not to differentiate between Machine subclasses. If you need to distinguish between types of machines in your visitor, you will have to resort to using type checks or some other technique to tell which type of machine a visit() method has received. You might argue that the hierarchy developers should have included all machine types as well as a catchall visit(:Machine) method in the visitor interface. But new machine types come along all the time, so this does not appear to be any sturdier.

Whether VISITOR is a good choice depends on the characteristics of change: If the hierarchy is stable and the attached behaviors change, the choice may be good. If the behaviors are stable and the hierarchy changes, the choice will be less good, as you'll have to go back and update existing visitors to support the new node types.

Another example of fragility showed up in the ProcessComponent hierarchy. The developers of the hierarchy are aware that cycles are a danger that lurks within process-flow models. How can they convey their concerns to a visitor developer?

These problems may expose the fundamental problem with VISITOR: Extending a hierarchy's behavior usually requires some expert knowledge of the hierarchy's design. If you lack that expertise, you may step in a trap, such as not avoiding cycles in a process flow. If you do have expert knowledge of the hierarchy's mechanics, you may build in dangerous dependencies that will break if the hierarchy changes. The division of expertise and code control can make VISITOR a dangerous pattern to apply.

The classic case in which VISITOR seems to work well without creating downstream problems is in computer language parsers. Parser developers often arrange for the parser to create an **abstract syntax tree**, a structure that organizes the input text according to the language's grammar. You may want to develop a variety of behaviors to accompany these trees, and the VISITOR pattern is an effective approach for allowing this. In this classic case, there is usually little or no behavior in the visited hierarchy. All the responsibility for behavior design lies with visitors, avoiding the split of responsibility that this chapter's examples must endure.

Like any pattern, Visitor is never necessary; if it were, it would automatically appear everywhere it was needed. For Visitor, though, there are often alternatives that provide a sturdier design.

CHALLENGE 29.5

List two alternatives to building Visitor into the Oozinoz machine and process hierarchies.

A solution appears on page 425.

So should you use Visitor or not? It works best when

- The set of node types is stable

- A common change is adding new functions that apply to the various nodes

- The new functions would have to "smear" across all node types.

Summary

The Visitor pattern lets you define a new operation for a hierarchy without changing the hierarchy classes. The mechanics for Visitor include defining an interface for visitors and adding `accept()` methods in the hierarchy that a visitor will call. The `accept()` methods dispatch their calls back to the visitor in a double-dispatching scheme. This scheme arranges for the execution of a `visit()` method that applies to the specific type of object from the hierarchy.

A visitor developer must be aware of some, if not all, of the subtleties in the design of the visited hierarchy. In particular, visitors need to beware of cycles that may occur in the visited object model. This type of difficulty leads some developers to eschew Visitor, regularly applying alternatives instead. Whether you use Visitor should probably be a decision that depends on your design philosophy, your team, and the specifics of your application.

PART VI

APPENDIXES

A

DIRECTIONS

IF YOU HAVE read the book up to this point, allow us to say, "Congratulations!" If you have worked through all the challenges, we salute you! If you have read this book and worked all the challenges, you have developed a strong, working knowledge of design patterns. Now where can you go from here?

Get the Most from This Book

If you have *not* worked through the challenges in this book, you are not alone! We are all busy, and it is quite tempting to think about a challenge momentarily and then glance at the solution. That is certainly an ordinary experience, but you have the potential to become an extraordinary developer. Go back and rework the challenges, turning to the solutions only when you think you've got a correct answer or when you're completely stumped. Work through the challenges *now*; don't kid yourself that you'll somehow have more time later. By exercising your patterns knowledge on these challenges, you'll build the confidence you need to start applying patterns in your work.

In addition to working through the challenges in this book, we suggest that you download the code from www.oozinoz.com and ensure that you can repeat the results of this book's examples on your own system. Knowing that you can get the code to run will give you more confidence than simply working examples on paper. You may also want to set up new challenges for yourself. Perhaps you will want to combine decorator filters in a new way or implement a data adapter that shows data from a familiar domain.

As you build fluency with design patterns, you should start to see that you understand classic examples of design patterns. You will also begin to see places where it is appropriate to use design patterns in your own code.

Understand the Classics

Design patterns often make a design stronger. This is not a new idea, so it is no surprise that many design patterns are built into the Java class libraries. If you can spot the design pattern in a body of code, you can grasp the design yourself and communicate it to others who understand design patterns. For example, if a developer understands how DECORATOR works, it is meaningful to explain that Java streams are decorators.

Here is a test of your understanding of some of the classic examples of design patterns that appear in Java and its libraries.

- How do GUI controls use the OBSERVER pattern?

- Why do menus often use the COMMAND pattern?

- Why do drivers provide a good example of the BRIDGE pattern? Is each particular driver an instance of the ADAPTER pattern?

- What does it mean to say that Java streams use the DECORATOR pattern?

- Why is the PROXY pattern fundamental to the design of RMI?

- If sorting provides a good example of the TEMPLATE METHOD pattern, which step of the algorithm is left unspecified?

A good goal is to be able to answer these questions without referring to this book. It is also good exercise to write down your answers and to share your answers with a colleague.

Weave Patterns into Your Code

A primary purpose for learning design patterns is to become a better developer. Think about how to use patterns in the codebase that you work with most often. Here you have two choices: Apply design patterns as you add new code, or apply design patterns through refactoring. If part of your code is complex and difficult to maintain, you may be able to improve it by refactoring the code and using a design pattern. Before diving into such a project, make sure that you have a customer for the result. Also, before you change the code, be sure to create an automated test suite for the code that you are refactoring.

Now, suppose that you understand the patterns you have studied and are determined to use them carefully and appropriately. How do you find an opportunity? Some opportunities arise fairly frequently. If you're looking for a chance to apply design patterns, consider the following.

- Does your codebase have any complex code that deals with the state of a system or the state of the application user? If so, you may be able to improve the code by applying the STATE pattern.

- Does your code combine the selection of a strategy with the execution of that strategy? If it does, you may be able to make the code better by using the STRATEGY pattern.

- Does your customer or analyst supply you with flowcharts that translate into code that is difficult to comprehend? If so, you can apply the INTERPRETER pattern, letting each node of the flowchart become an instance of a class in the interpreter hierarchy. You can thus provide a direct translation from the flowchart to the code.

- Does your code contain a weak composite that doesn't allow children to be composites themselves? You may be able to strengthen such code with the COMPOSITE pattern.

- Have you encountered relational-integrity errors in your object model? You may be able to prevent them by applying the MEDIATOR pattern to centralize the modeling of object relations.

- Are there places in your code where clients are using information from a service to decide which class to instantiate? You may be able to improve and simplify such code by applying the FACTORY METHOD pattern.

By learning design patterns, you have developed a rich vocabulary of design ideas. If you are on the lookout for opportunities, it probably won't be long before you find a design that you can improve by applying a pattern. But don't overdo it.

Keep Learning

Somehow, you had the opportunity, drive, and ambition to acquire and read this book. All we can say is, "Keep it up!" Decide how many hours a week you want to spend on your career. Take 5 hours off the top and pay yourself first. Spend that time away from the office, reading books and magazines or writing software related to any topic that interests you. Make this practice as regular as your office hours. Treat this aspect of your career seriously, and you'll become a much better developer, and you'll probably find that you enjoy your job more.

Now, suppose that you have given yourself plenty of time and that you simply need to set your direction. Before learning more about patterns, you may want to make sure that you understand the basics. If you haven't read *The Java™ Programming Language* [Arnold and Gosling 1998] or *The Unified Modeling Language User Guide* [Booch, Rumbaugh, and Jacobsen 1999], we recommend that you do so. If you want to learn more about patterns, you have a lot of choices. For a walkthrough of realistic examples of applying design patterns, try *Pattern Hatching: Design Patterns Applied* [Vlissides 1998]. Most shops would benefit from having a local expert on concurrency patterns. To learn about this important and often neglected aspect of development, look at *Concurrent Programming in Java™* [Lea 2000].

For a basic introduction to refactoring and a catalog of refactorings, see *Refactoring* [Fowler et al. 1999]. For practice refactoring in a format similar to that of this book, see the *Refactoring Workbook* [Wake 2004]. Once you understand refactoring and want to see how to systematically use it to move to various design patterns, see *Refactoring to Patterns* [Kerievsky 2005].

You can go in many directions, but the most important practice is to keep going. Make learning a part of your career, and pursue the topics that interest you most. Think of how strong you can become as a developer, and become that strong. Keep up the good work!

Steve.Metsker@acm.org
William.Wake@acm.org

B

SOLUTIONS

Introducing Interfaces

Solution 2.1 (from page 12)

An abstract class with no nonabstract methods is similar to an interface in terms of its utility. However, note the following.

- A class can implement any number of interfaces but can subclass at most one abstract class.

- An abstract class can have nonabstract methods; all the methods of an interface are effectively abstract.

- An abstract class can declare and use fields; an interface cannot, although it can create `static final` constants.

- An abstract class can have methods whose access is `public`, `protected`, `private`, or none (package). An interface's methods are implicitly `public`.

- An abstract class can define constructors; an interface cannot.

Solution 2.2 (from page 13)

A. *True.* Interface methods are always abstract, whether or not they declare it.

B. *True.* Interface methods are public, whether or not they declare it.

C. *False!* An interface's visibility may be limited to the package in which it resides. In this case, it is marked `public`, so classes outside `com.oozinoz.simulation` *can* access it.

D. *True.* For example, the `List` and `Set` interfaces both extend the `Collection` interface in `java.util`.

E. *False.* An interface with no methods is known as a **marker interface.** Sometimes, a method high in a class hierarchy, such as `Object.clone()`, is not appropriate for every subclass. You can create a marker interface that requires subclasses to opt in or opt out of participation in such a scheme. The `clone()` method on `Object` requires subclasses to opt in, by declaring that they implement the `Cloneable` marker interface.

F. *False.* An interface cannot declare instance fields, although it can create constants by declaring fields that are `static` and `final`.

G. *False.* It might be a good idea, but there is no way for a Java interface to require that implementing classes provide a particular constructor.

Solution 2.3   (from page 14)

One example occurs when classes may be registered as listeners for events; the classes receive notification for their own benefit, not the caller's. For example, we may want to take action on `Mouse-Listener.mouseDragged()` but have an empty body for `Mouse-Listener.mouseMoved()` for the same listener.

ADAPTER

Solution 3.1   (from page 20)

Your solution should look something like the diagram in Figure B.1.

Instances of the `OozinozRocket` class can function as either `PhysicalRocket` objects or `RocketSim` objects. The ADAPTER pattern lets you adapt the methods you have to the ones that a client needs.

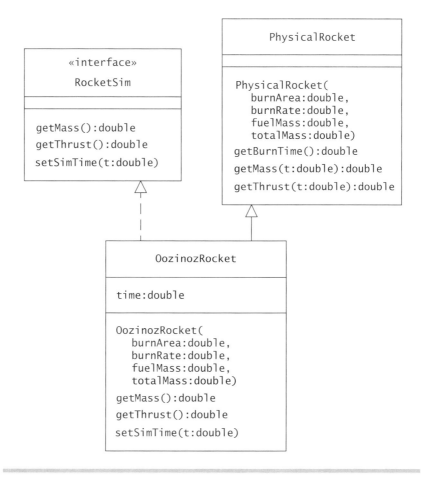

FIGURE B.1 The OozinozRocket class adapts the PhysicalRocket class to meet the needs declared in the RocketSim interface.

Solution 3.2   (from page 21)

The code for the completed class should be:

```
package com.oozinoz.firework;

import com.oozinoz.simulation.*;

public class OozinozRocket
             extends PhysicalRocket implements RocketSim {
    private double time;
```

```
public OozinozRocket(
        double burnArea,
        double burnRate,
        double fuelMass,
        double totalMass) {
    super(burnArea, burnRate, fuelMass, totalMass);
}

public double getMass() {
    return getMass(time);
}

public double getThrust() {
    return getThrust(time);
}

public void setSimTime(double time) {
    this.time = time;
}
}
```

You can find this code in the com.oozinoz.firework package in the source code for this book.

Solution 3.3   (from page 23)

Figure B.2 shows a solution.

The OozinozSkyrocket class is an object adapter. The class subclasses Skyrocket so that an OozinozSkyrocket object can function where a Skyrocket object is needed.

Solution 3.4   (from page 25)

The object adapter design that the OozinozSkyrocket class uses may be more fragile than a class adapter approach for the following reasons.

- There is no specification of the interface that the Oozinoz-Skyrocket class provides. As a result, the Skyrocket might change in ways that would create problems at runtime but go undetected at compile time.

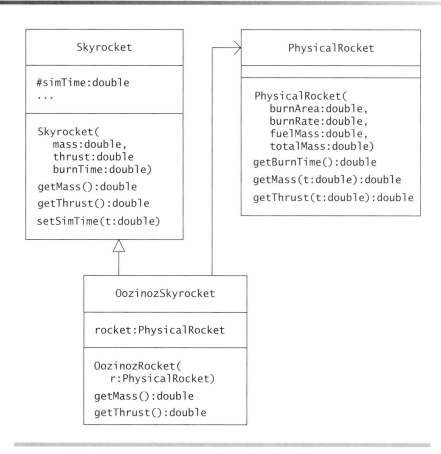

FIGURE B.2 An OozinozSkyrocket object is a Skyrocket object but gets its work done by forwarding calls to a PhysicalRocket object.

- The OozinozSkyrocket counts on being able to access the sim-Time variable of its parent class, although there is no guarantee that this variable will always be declared as protected and no guarantee about the meaning of this field in the Skyrocket class. (We don't expect the providers to go out of their way to change the Skyrocket code we rely on, but on the other hand, we have limited control over what they do.)

Solution 3.5   (from page 29)

Your code might look something like this:

```
package app.adapter;
import javax.swing.table.*;
import com.oozinoz.firework.Rocket;

public class RocketTable extends AbstractTableModel {
    protected Rocket[] rockets;
    protected String[] columnNames = new String[] {
                "Name", "Price", "Apogee" };

    public RocketTable(Rocket[] rockets) {
        this.rockets = rockets;
    }

    public int getColumnCount() {
        return columnNames.length;
    }

    public String getColumnName(int i) {
        return columnNames[i];
    }

    public int getRowCount() {
        return rockets.length;
    }

    public Object getValueAt(int row, int col) {
        switch (col) {
        case 0:
            return rockets[row].getName();
        case 1:
            return rockets[row].getPrice();
        case 2:
            return new Double(rockets[row].getApogee());
        default:
            return null;
        }
    }
}
```

The TableModel interface provides a good example of the power of planning ahead for adaptation. This interface, along with its partial implementation `AbstractTableModel`, reduces the work of showing domain objects in a standard GUI table. Your solution should show how easy it is to adapt when adaptation is supported with an interface.

Solution 3.6 (from page 31)

- *One argument:* When the user clicks the mouse, I need to translate, or adapt, the resulting Swing call into an appropriate action. In other words, when I need to adapt GUI events to my application's interface, I use Swing adapter classes. I am translating from one interface to another, fulfilling the intent of the ADAPTER pattern.

- *A counterargument:* The "adapter" classes in Swing are stubs: They don't translate or adapt anything. You subclass these classes, overriding the methods you need to do something. If anything, it is your methods and your class that form an example of ADAPTER. Had the Swing "adapter" been named something like `DefaultMouseListener`, this argument never would have arisen.

FACADE

Solution 4.1 (from page 34)

Some differences to note between demos and facades are as follows.

- A demo is usually a stand-alone application; a facade is usually not.

- A demo usually includes sample data; a facade does not.

- A facade is usually configurable; a demo is not.

- A facade is intended for reuse; a demo is not.

- A facade is intended for use in production; a demo is not.

Solution 4.2 (from page 35)

The `JOptionPane` class is one of the few examples of a FACADE in the Java class libraries. It is production worthy, configurable, and designed for reuse. Above all else, the `JOptionPane` class fulfills the intent of the

FACADE pattern by providing a simple interface that makes it easy to use the JDialog class. You might argue that a facade simplifies a "subsystem" and that the solitary JDialog class does not qualify as a subsystem. But it is exactly the richness of this class's features that make a facade valuable.

Sun Microsystems bundles many demos in with the JDK. However, these classes are never part of the Java class libraries. That is, these classes do not appear in packages with a java prefix. A facade may belong in the Java class libraries, but demos do not.

JOptionPane has dozens of static methods that effectively make it a utility as well as a FACADE. Strictly speaking, though, it does not meet the UML definition of a utility, which requires it to possess solely static methods.

Solution 4.3   (from page 35)

Here are a few reasonable but opposing views regarding the paucity of facades in the Java class libraries.

- As a Java developer, you are well advised to develop a thorough knowledge of the tools in the library. Facades necessarily limit the way you might apply any system. They would be a distracting and potentially misleading element of the class libraries in which they might appear.

- A facade lies somewhere between the richness of a toolkit and the specificity of a particular application. To create a facade requires some notion of the type of applications it will support. This predictability is impossible given the huge and diverse audience of the Java class libraries.

- The scarcity of facades in the class libraries is a weakness. Adding more facades would be a big help.

Solution 4.4   (from page 42)

Your result should look something like Figure B.3.

Note that createTitledPanel() is not a static method. Does your solution make these methods static? Why or why not?

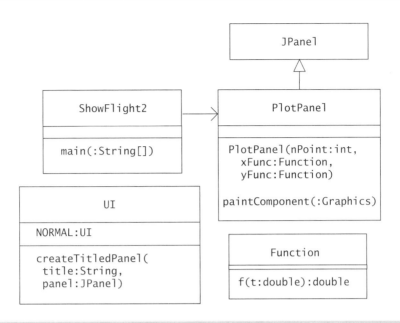

FIGURE B.3 This diagram shows the flight path application refactored into classes that each have one job.

The code for this book makes the UI methods nonstatic so that a UI subclass can override them, creating a different kit for building user interfaces. To make a standard user interface available, this design refers to the singleton NORMAL object.

Here is the relevant code from UI:

```
public class UI {
    public static final UI NORMAL = new UI();
    protected Font font =
        new Font("Book Antiqua", Font.PLAIN, 18);

    // lots omitted

    public Font getFont() {
        return font;
    }
}
```

```
public TitledBorder createTitledBorder(String title) {
    TitledBorder border =
        BorderFactory.createTitledBorder(
            BorderFactory.createBevelBorder(
                BevelBorder.RAISED),
            title,
            TitledBorder.LEFT,
            TitledBorder.TOP);
    border.setTitleColor(Color.black);
    border.setTitleFont(getFont());
    return border;
}

public JPanel createTitledPanel(
        String title, JPanel in) {
    JPanel out = new JPanel();
    out.add(in);
    out.setBorder(createTitledBorder(title));
    return out;
}
}
```

See Chapter 17, ABSTRACT FACTORY, for more information on building GUI kits, and Chapter 8, SINGLETON, for more information on singletons.

COMPOSITE

Solution 5.1   (from page 47)

Designing the Composite class to maintain a collection of Component objects lets a Composite object hold either Leaf objects or other Composite objects.

In other words, this design lets us model groups as collections of other groups. For example, we might want to define a user's system privileges as a collection of either specific privileges or other groups of privileges. As another example, we might want to be able to define a work process as a collection of process steps and other processes. Such definitions are much more flexible than defining a composite to be a collection of leaves.

If we allowed only collections of leaves, our "composites" could be only one layer deep.

Solution 5.2 (from page 48)

For the Machine class, getMachineCount() should be something like:

```
public int getMachineCount() {
    return 1;
}
```

The class diagram shows that MachineComposite uses a List object to track its components. To count the machines in a composite, you might write:

```
public int getMachineCount() {
    int count = 0;
    Iterator i = components.iterator();
    while (i.hasNext()) {
        MachineComponent mc = (MachineComponent) i.next();
        count += mc.getMachineCount();
    }
    return count;
}
```

If you're using JDK 1.5, you may have used an extended for loop.

Solution 5.3   (from page 50)

Method	Class	Definition
getMachineCount()	MachineComposite	Return the sum of the counts for each component in components.
	Machine	Return 1.
isCompletelyUp()	MachineComposite	Return true if all components are "completely up."
	Machine	Return true if this machine is up.
stopAll()	MachineComposite	Tell all components to "stop all."
	Machine	Stop this machine.
getOwners()	MachineComposite	Create a set, not a list; add the owners of all components; and return the set.
	Machine	Return this machine's owners.
getMaterial()	MachineComposite	Return a collection of all the material on components.
	Machine	Return the material that is on this machine.

Solution 5.4   (from page 54)

The program prints out

```
Number of machines: 4
```

There are, in fact, only three machines in the plant factory, but the mixer is counted by both plant and bay. Both of these objects contain lists of machine components that refer to the mixer.

The results could be worse. If, say, an engineer adds the plant object as a component of the bay composite, a call to getMachineCount() will enter an infinite loop.

Solution 5.5 (from page 55)

A reasonable implementation of MachineComposite.isTree() is:

```
protected boolean isTree(Set visited) {
    visited.add(this);
    Iterator i = components.iterator();
    while (i.hasNext()) {
        MachineComponent c = (MachineComponent) i.next();
        if (visited.contains(c) || !c.isTree(visited))
            return false;
    }
    return true;
}
```

Solution 5.6 (from page 58)

Your solution should show the links in Figure B.4.

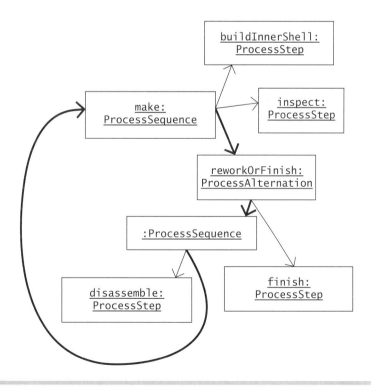

FIGURE B.4 The thick lines in this object diagram cycle show the cycle inherent in manufacturing aerial shells.

BRIDGE

Solution 6.1   (from page 64)

To control various machines with a common interface, you can apply the ADAPTER pattern, creating an adapter class for each controller. Each adapter class can translate the standard interface calls into calls that existing controllers support.

Solution 6.2   (from page 65)

Your code should look something like the following:

```
public void shutdown() {
    stopProcess();
    conveyOut();
    stopMachine();
}
```

Solution 6.3   (from page 67)

Figure B.5 shows a solution.

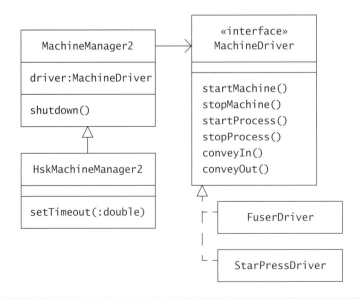

FIGURE B.5 This diagram shows an abstraction—a hierarchy of types of machine managers—separated from implementations of the abstract `driver` object the abstraction uses.

Solution 6.4   (from page 70)

Figure B.6 suggests a solution.

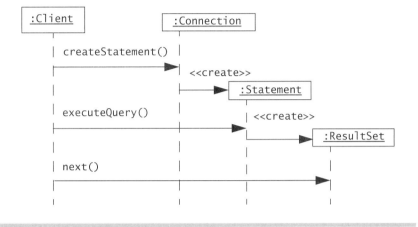

FIGURE B.6 This diagram shows most of the typical message flow in a JDBC application.

Solution 6.5   (from page 71)

Two arguments in favor of writing code specific to SQL Server are as follows.

1. We can't predict the future, so spending money now to prepare for eventualities that may never occur is a classic mistake. We have SQL Server now, and more speed means better response times, which is money in the bank today.

2. By committing to SQL Server, we can use every feature available in the database, without worrying whether other database drivers support it.

Two arguments in favor of using the generic SQL drivers are as follows.

1. If we use generic SQL objects to write our code, it will be easier to modify it if we ever change database providers and start using, say, Oracle. By locking the code into SQL Server, we diminish our ability to benefit from the competitive database market.

2. Using generic drivers will let us write experimental code that runs against inexpensive databases, such as MySql, without relying on a test SQL Server database.

Introducing Responsibility

Solution 7.1   (from page 75)

Following are some problems with the given diagram.

- The Rocket.thrust() method returns a Rocket instead of some type of number or physical quantity.

- The LiquidRocket class has a getLocation() method, although nothing in the diagram or in the problem domain suggests that we model rockets as having a location. Even if we did, there is no reason for liquid-fueled rockets, but not other Rocket objects, to have a location.

- The isLiquid() method may be an acceptable alternative to using the instanceof operator, but then we'd expect the superclass to also have an isLiquid() method that would return false.

- CheapRockets is plural, although class names are conventionally singular.

- The CheapRockets class implements Runnable, although this interface has nothing to do with cheap rocket objects from the problem domain.

- We could model cheapness with attributes alone, so there is no justification for creating a class just for cheap rockets.

- The CheapRockets class introduces a factoring that conflicts with factoring the rocket model as liquid or solid. For example, it is not clear how to model a cheap liquid rocket.

- The model shows that Firework is a subclass of LiquidRocket, implying that all fireworks are liquid rockets, which is false.

- The model shows a direct relation between reservations and types of firework, although no such relation exists in the problem domain.

- The Reservation class has its own copy of city, which it should get by delegation to a Location object.

- CheapRockets is composed of Runnable objects, which is simply bizarre.

Solution 7.2   (from page 76)

The value of this challenge is not to get the right answer but rather to exercise your thinking about what makes up a good class. Consider whether your definition addresses the following points.

- A nuts-and-bolts description of a class is: "A named collection of fields that hold data values and methods that operate on those values" [Flanagan 2005, p. 71].

- A class establishes a collection of fields; that is, it defines the attributes of an object. The attribute types are other classes, primitive data types, such as boolean and int, or interfaces.

- A class designer should be able to justify how a class's attributes are related.

- A class should have a cohesive purpose.

- The name of a class should reflect the meaning of the class both as a collection of attributes and with respect to the class's behavior.

- A class must support all the behaviors it defines, as well as all those in superclasses and all methods in interfaces that the class implements. (A decision to *not* support a superclass or an interface method is occasionally justifiable.)

- A class should have a justifiable relationship to its superclass.

- The name of each of a class's methods should be a good commentary on what the method does.

Solution 7.3   (from page 77)

Two good observations are that the effects of invoking an operation may depend on the state of the receiving object or on the class of the receiving object. Other times, you're using a name dictated by somebody else.

An example of a method whose effect depends on an object's state appeared in Chapter 6, BRIDGE, where the MachineManager2 class has a stopMachine() method. The effects of calling this method depend on which driver is in place for the MachineManager2 object.

When polymorphism is part of a design, the effect of invoking an operation can depend partly or entirely on the class of the receiving object. This principle appears in many patterns, especially FACTORY METHOD, STATE, STRATEGY, COMMAND, and INTERPRETER. For example, a hierarchy of strategy classes may all implement a getRecommended() method, using different strategies to recommend a firework. It is easy to predict that getRecommended() will recommend a firework, but without knowing the class of the object that receives the getRecommended() call, it is impossible to know which strategy will be used.

A third situation occurs when somebody else defines the name. Suppose that your method is acting as a callback; you've overridden the mouseDown() method of the MouseListener class. You have to use mouseDown() as your method name, even though that says nothing about the intended effect of your method.

Solution 7.4   (from page 78)

The code compiles with no problems. Access is defined at a class level, not an object level. So, for example, one Firework object can access another Firework object's private variables and methods.

SINGLETON

Solution 8.1   (from page 82)

To prevent other developers from instantiating your class, create a single constructor with private access. Note that if you create other, nonprivate constructors or no constructors at all, other objects will be able to instantiate your class.

Solution 8.2   (from page 82)

Two reasons for lazy-initializing singletons are as follows.

1. You might not have enough information to instantiate a singleton at static initialization time. For example, a Factory singleton
   might have to wait for the real factory's machines to establish
   communication channels.

2. You might choose to lazy-initialize a singleton that requires
   resources, such as a database connection, especially if there is a
   chance that the containing application will not need the singleton in a particular session.

Solution 8.3   (from page 84)

Your solution should eliminate the possibility of confusion that can
occur when two threads call the recordWipMove() method at approximately the same time:

```
public void recordWipMove() {
    synchronized (classLock) {
        wipMoves++;
    }
}
```

Is it possible that a thread might activate in the middle of an increment operation? Absolutely: Not all machines have a single instruc-
tion that can increment a variable, and even those that do cannot
guarantee that the compiler will use them in every situation. It's a
good policy to carefully restrict access to a singleton's data in a multithreaded application. See *Concurrent Programming in Java™* [Lea 2000]
for more information on such applications.

Solution 8.4   (from page 85)

OurBiggestRocket: This class has an inappropriate name. You would
                  normally model attributes, such as "biggest," with
                  attributes, not with class names. If a developer
                  must sustain this class, perhaps it is a singleton.

TopSalesAssociate: This class has the same problem as
                   OurBiggestRocket.

Math:	This class is a **utility**, with all static methods and *no* instances. It is not a singleton. Note that it does, however, have a private constructor.
System:	This also is a utility.
PrintStream:	Although the System.out object is a Print-Stream object with unique responsibilities, it is not a unique instance of PrintStream, which is not a singleton class.
PrintSpooler:	PrintSpoolers are associated with one or a few printers; it's unlikely that this is a singleton.
PrinterManager:	At Oozinoz, you have many printers, and you can look up their addresses through the PrinterManager singleton.

OBSERVER

Solution 9.1   (from page 90)

One solution is:

```
public JSlider slider() {
    if (slider == null) {
        slider = new JSlider();
        sliderMax = slider.getMaximum();
        sliderMin = slider.getMinimum();
        slider.addChangeListener(this);
        slider.setValue(slider.getMinimum());
    }
    return slider;
}


public void stateChanged(ChangeEvent e) {
    double val = slider.getValue();
    double tp = (val - sliderMin) / (sliderMax - sliderMin);
    burnPanel().setTPeak(tp);
    thrustPanel().setTPeak(tp);
    valueLabel().setText(Format.formatToNPlaces(tp, 2));
}
```

This assumes that a helper class Format exists to format the value label. You might have used an expression such as ""+tp or Double.toString(tp) instead. (Using a fixed number of digits gives a smoother animation.)

Solution 9.2   (from page 91)

One solution is shown in Figure B.7. To allow a label to register for slider events, the design in Figure B.7 creates a JLabel subclass that implements ChangeListener. The new design lets the components that depend on the slider register their interest and update themselves. This is arguably an improvement, but we will refactor the design again, to a Model-View-Controller architecture.

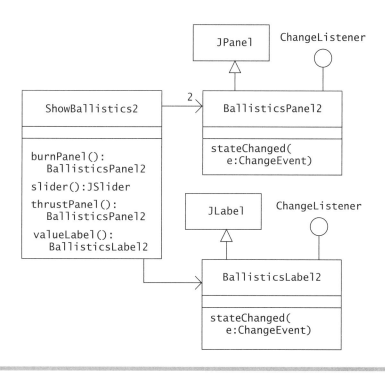

FIGURE B.7 In this design, components that depend on the slider implement ChangeListener so that they can register for slider events.

Solution 9.3   (from page 93)

Figure B.8 shows a solution.

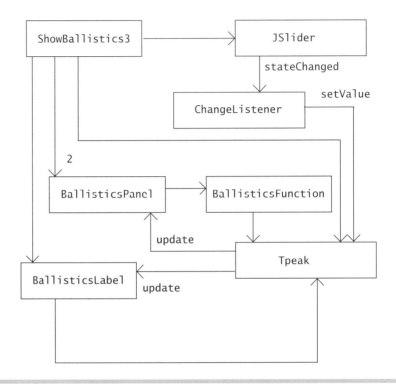

FIGURE B.8 This design has the application watch the slider; the text box and the plotting panels watch an object that holds the **tPeak** value.

A Tpeak object that holds a peak-time value plays a central role in this design. The ShowBallistics3 application creates the Tpeak object, and the slider updates it whenever it moves. The display components (the text box and the plotting panels) "listen to" the Tpeak object by registering as observers of the Tpeak object.

Solution 9.4   (from page 96)

One solution is:

```
package app.observer.ballistics3;
import javax.swing.*;
import java.util.*;

public class BallisticsLabel extends JLabel
               implements Observer {
    public BallisticsLabel(Tpeak tPeak) {
        tPeak.addObserver(this);
    }

    public void update(Observable o, Object arg) {
        setText("" + ((Tpeak) o).getValue());
        repaint();
    }
}
```

Solution 9.5   (from page 97)

One solution is:

```
protected JSlider slider() {
    if (slider == null) {
        slider = new JSlider();
        sliderMax = slider.getMaximum();
        sliderMin = slider.getMinimum();
        slider.addChangeListener(new ChangeListener() {
            public void stateChanged(ChangeEvent e) {
                if (sliderMax == sliderMin) return;
                tPeak.setValue(
                    (slider.getValue() - sliderMin)
                  / (sliderMax - sliderMin));
            }
        });
        slider.setValue(slider.getMinimum());
    }
    return slider;
}
```

Solution 9.6   (from page 97)

Figure B.9 shows the calls that flow when a user moves the slider in the ballistics application.

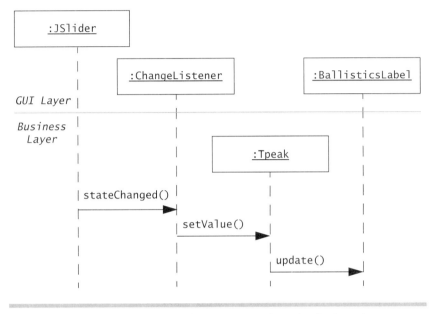

FIGURE B.9 MVC causes the path of change to go through a business layer.

Solution 9.7   (from page 100)

Your diagram should look something like Figure B.10. Note that you can apply the same design with Observer and Observable. The key to the design is that the interesting Tpeak class makes itself observable by maintaining an object with good listening skills.

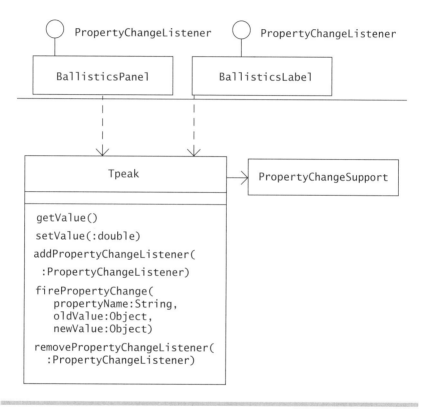

FIGURE B.10 The Tpeak class can add in listening behavior by delegating listening-oriented calls to a PropertyChangeSupport object.

MEDIATOR

Solution 10.1   (from page 106)

Figure B.11 shows a solution.

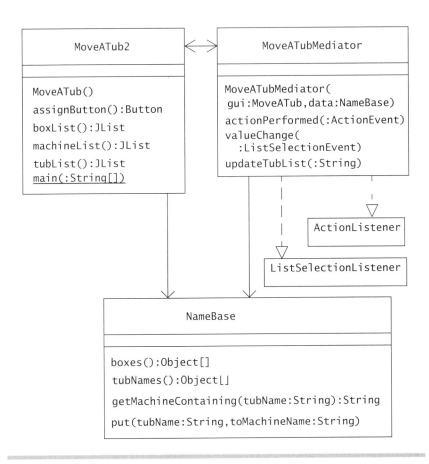

FIGURE B.11 The MoveATub class handles component building, and the MoveATub-Mediator class handles events.

In this design, the mediator class has what Fowler et al. [1999] call "feature envy." The class seems more interested in the GUI class than in itself, as the valueChanged() method shows:

```
public void valueChanged(ListSelectionEvent e) {
    // ...
    gui.assignButton().setEnabled(
            ! gui.tubList().isSelectionEmpty()
        && ! gui.machineList().isSelectionEmpty());
}
```

Some developers' distaste for feature envy will keep them from this type of design. You may find, though, that you like having one class for GUI component construction and layout and a separate class for component interaction and the flow of use cases.

Solution 10.2   (from page 107)

Figure B.12 shows one solution.

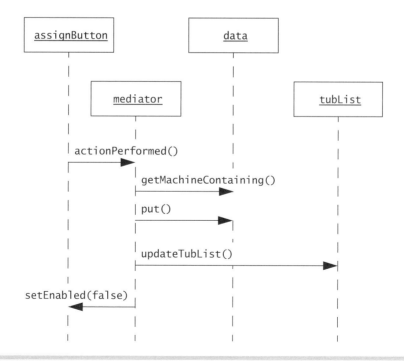

FIGURE B.12 This diagram highlights the central role of the mediator.

The provided solution shows the role of the mediator as a dispatcher, receiving an event and taking responsibility for updating all objects affected by it.

Solution 10.3   (from page 111)

Figure B.13 shows an updated object diagram.

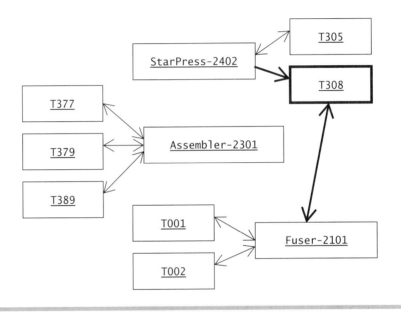

FIGURE B.13 Two machines think that they contain tub T308. The object model accepts a situation that neither a relational table nor reality will allow. (Thick lines highlight the problematic situation.)

The problem that the developer's code introduces is that StarPress-2402 still thinks that it has tub T308. In a relational table, changing the machine attribute of a row automatically removes the tub from the prior machine. This automated removal does not occur when the relation is dispersed across a distributed object model. The proper modeling of the tub/machine relation requires special logic that you can remove to a separate mediator object.

Solution 10.4   (from page 114)

The complete code for the `TubMediator` class should look something like:

```
package com.oozinoz.machine;
import java.util.*;

public class TubMediator {
    protected Map tubToMachine = new HashMap();

    public Machine getMachine(Tub t) {
        return (Machine) tubToMachine.get(t);
    }

    public Set getTubs(Machine m) {
        Set set = new HashSet();
        Iterator i = tubToMachine.entrySet().iterator();
        while (i.hasNext()) {
            Map.Entry e = (Map.Entry) i.next();
            if (e.getValue().equals(m))
                set.add(e.getKey());
        }
        return set;
    }

    public void set(Tub t, Machine m) {
        tubToMachine.put(t, m);
    }
}
```

Solution 10.5   (from page 115)

- The FACADE pattern may help to refactor a large application.

- The BRIDGE pattern moves abstract operations to an interface.

- The OBSERVER pattern may appear as you refactor code to support an MVC architecture.

- The FLYWEIGHT pattern extricates the immutable part of an object so that this part can be shared.

- The BUILDER pattern moves the construction logic for an object outside of the class to instantiate.

- The FACTORY METHOD pattern lets you reduce the amount of responsibility in a class hierarchy by moving an aspect of behavior to a parallel hierarchy.

- The STATE and STRATEGY patterns let you move state-specific and strategy-specific behavior into separate classes.

PROXY

Solution 11.1   (from page 122)

One solution is:

```
public int getIconHeight() {
    return current.getIconHeight();
}

public int getIconWidth() {
    return current.getIconWidth();
}

public synchronized void paintIcon(
        Component c, Graphics g, int x, int y) {
    current.paintIcon(c, g, x, y);
}
```

Solution 11.2   (from page 122)

Problems with the design include the following.

- Forwarding only a subset of calls to an underlying ImageIcon object is dangerous. The ImageIconProxy class inherits a dozen fields and at least 25 methods from the ImageIcon class. To be a true proxy, the ImageIconProxy object needs to forward most or all of these calls. Thorough forwarding would require many potentially erroneous methods, and this code would require maintenance as the ImageIcon class and its superclasses change over time.

- You might question whether the "Absent" image and the desired image are in the right places in the design. It might make more sense to have the images passed in rather than making the class responsible for finding them.

Solution 11.3   (from page 124)

The `load()` method sets the image to Loading..., whereas the `run()` method, executing in a separate thread, loads the desired image:

```
public void load(JFrame callbackFrame) {
    this.callbackFrame = callbackFrame;
    setImage(LOADING.getImage());
    callbackFrame.repaint();
    new Thread(this).start();
}

public void run() {
    setImage(new ImageIcon(
        ClassLoader.getSystemResource(filename))
            .getImage());
    callbackFrame.pack();
}
```

Solution 11.4   (from page 129)

As the class diagram shows, a `RocketImpl` constructor accepts a price and an apogee:

```
Rocket biggie = new RocketImpl(29.95, 820);
```

You could declare `biggie` to be of type `RocketImpl`. However, what is important about `biggie` is that it fulfills the `Rocket` interface that a client will look for.

Solution 11.5   (from page 130)

The completed diagram should appear as in Figure B.14. A legitimate but less informative labeling would name both receivers of `get-Apogee()` as being of type `Rocket`. In fact, both the server and the client programs refer to these objects as instances of the `Rocket` interface.

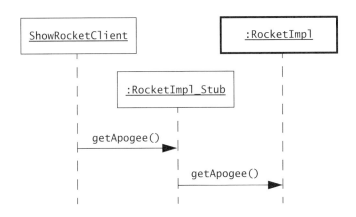

FIGURE B.14 A proxy forwards a client's calls so that, to the client, the remote object appears as if it were local.

CHAIN OF RESPONSIBILITY

Solution 12.1   (from page 139)

Some potential disadvantages of the CHAIN OF RESPONSIBILITY design that Oozinoz uses for finding a machine's responsible engineer include the following.

- We haven't specified how the chain will be set up so that machines know their parent. In practice, it may be difficult to ensure that parents are never null.

- It is conceivable that the search for a parent could enter an infinite loop, depending how the parents are set up.

- Not all objects have all the behaviors implied by these new methods. (For example, the top-level item has no parent.)

- The present design is light on details regarding how the system knows which engineers are currently in the factory and available. It's not clear how "real time" this responsibility needs to be.

Solution 12.2   (from page 141)

Your diagram should look similar to Figure B.15.

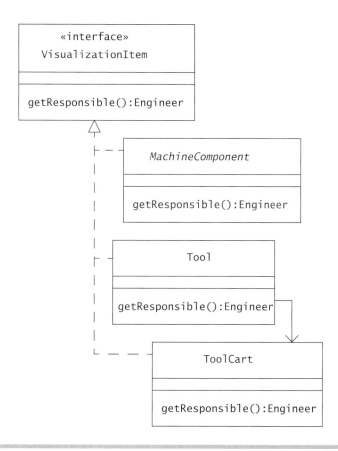

FIGURE B.15 Every VisualizationItem object can tell its responsible engineer. Internally, a VisualizationItem object may forward the request to another object parent.

With this design, any client of any simulated item can simply ask the item for the responsible engineer. This approach relieves clients from the task of determining which objects understand responsibility and puts the onus on objects that implement VisualizationItem interface.

Solution 12.3   (from page 142)

A. A MachineComponent object may have an explicitly assigned responsible person. If it doesn't, it passes the request to its parent:

```
public Engineer getResponsible() {

    if (responsible != null)
        return responsible;
    if (parent != null)
        return parent.getResponsible();
    return null;
}
```

B. The code for Tool.Responsible reflects the statement that "tools are always assigned to tool carts":

```
public Engineer getResponsible() {
    return toolCart.getResponsible();
}
```

C. The ToolCart code reflects the statement that "tool carts have a responsible engineer":

```
public Engineer getResponsible() {
    return responsible;
}
```

Solution 12.4   (from page 143)

Your solution should look something like Figure B.16.

Your constructors should allow Machine and MachineComposite objects to be instantiated with or without an assigned engineer. Whenever a MachineComponent object does not have an assigned engineer, it can get a responsible engineer from its parent.

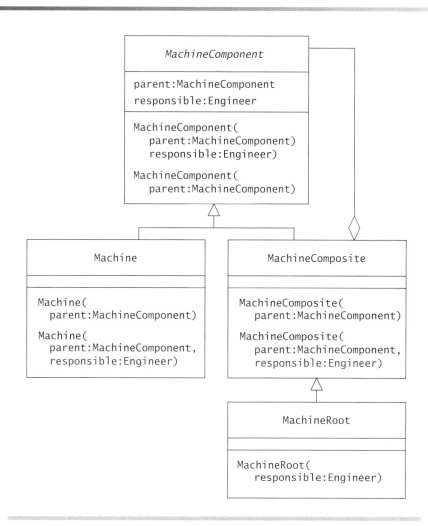

FIGURE B.16 The constructors in the MachineComponent hierarchy support the rules that a MachineRoot object must have a responsible engineer and that every MachineComponent object except a root must have a parent.

Solution 12.5   (from page 144)

CHAIN OF RESPONSIBILITY might apply to objects that do not form a composite when

- A chain of on-call engineers follows a standard rotation. If the primary on-call engineer does not answer a production support page in a specific amount of time, the notification system pages the next engineer in the chain.

- Users enter information, such as the date of an event; a chain of parsers can take turns trying to decode the user's text.

FLYWEIGHT

Solution 13.1   (from page 146)

An argument *for* the immutability of strings: In practice, strings are frequently shared between clients, which is frequently the crux of defects that emerge when one client inadvertently affects another. For example, a method that returns a customer's name as a string will typically retain its reference to the name. If the client, say, uppercases the string to use it in a hash table, the `Customer` object's name would change as well, if not for the immutability of strings. In Java, you can produce an uppercase version of a string, but this must be a new object, not an altered version of the initial string. The immutability of strings makes them safe to share among multiple clients. Furthermore, immutable strings help the system avoid certain security risks.

An argument *against* the immutability of strings: The immutability of strings protects us from certain errors but at a heavy price. First, developers are cut off from any ability to change a string, regardless of how we might justify this need. Second, adding special rules to a language makes it more difficult to learn and use. Java is far more difficult to learn than the equally powerful Smalltalk language. Finally, no computer language can keep me from making errors. I'd be much better off if you let me learn the language quickly, so that I have time to also learn how to set up and use a testing framework.

Solution 13.2 (from page 148)

You can move the immutable aspects of Substance—including its name, symbol, and atomic weight—into the Chemical class, as Figure B.17 shows.

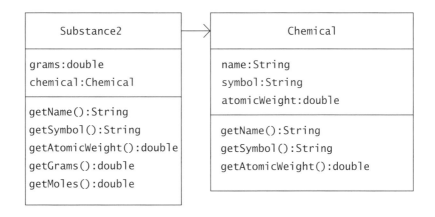

FIGURE B.17 This diagram shows the immutable part of the original Substance class extracted into a separate class: Chemical.

The Substance2 class now maintains a reference to a Chemical object. As a result, the Substance2 class can still offer the same accessors as the earlier Substance class. Internally, these accessors rely on the Chemical class, as the following Substance2 methods demonstrate:

```
public double getAtomicWeight() {
    return chemical.getAtomicWeight();
}

public double getGrams() {
    return grams;
}

public double getMoles() {
    return grams / getAtomicWeight();
}
```

Solution 13.3   (from page 150)

One way that won't work is to make the Chemical constructor private. That would prevent the ChemicalFactory class from instantiating the Chemical class.

To help prevent developers from instantiating the Chemical class themselves, you could place Chemical and ChemicalFactory classes in the same package and give the Chemical class's constructor default ("package") access.

Solution 13.4   (from page 150)

Using a nested class is a more complex but more thorough approach to ensuring that only the ChemicalFactory2 class can instantiate new flyweights. The resulting code will look something like this:

```java
package com.oozinoz.chemical2;
import java.util.*;

public class ChemicalFactory2 {
    private static Map chemicals = new HashMap();

    class ChemicalImpl implements Chemical {
        private String name;
        private String symbol;
        private double atomicWeight;

        ChemicalImpl(
                String name,
                String symbol,
                double atomicWeight) {
            this.name = name;
            this.symbol = symbol;
            this.atomicWeight = atomicWeight;
        }

        public String getName() {
            return name;
        }

        public String getSymbol() {
            return symbol;
        }
```

```
        public double getAtomicWeight() {
            return atomicWeight;
        }


    public String toString() {
        return name + "(" + symbol + ")[" +
            atomicWeight + "]";
        }
    }
    static {
        ChemicalFactory2 factory = new ChemicalFactory2();
        chemicals.put("carbon",
            factory.new ChemicalImpl("Carbon", "C", 12));
        chemicals.put("sulfur",
            factory.new ChemicalImpl("Sulfur", "S", 32));
        chemicals.put("saltpeter",
            factory.new ChemicalImpl(
                "Saltpeter", "KNO3", 101));
        //...
    }

    public static Chemical getChemical(String name) {
        return (Chemical) chemicals.get(
            name.toLowerCase());
    }
}
```

This code addresses the three challenges as follows.

1. The ChemicalImpl nested class should be private so that only
   the ChemicalFactory2 class can use the class. Note that the
   nested class's access must be package or public so that the containing class can instantiate the nested class. Even if you make
   the constructor public, no other class can use the constructor if
   the nested class itself is marked private.

2. The ChemicalFactory2 constructor uses a static initializer to
   ensure that the class will build the list of chemicals exactly once.

3. The getChemical() method should look up chemicals by name
   in the class's hash table. The example code stores and looks up
   chemicals, using the lowercase version of the chemical name.

Introducing Construction

Solution 14.1   (from page 155)

Special rules regarding constructors include the following.

- If you do not supply a constructor for a class, Java will provide a default.

- Constructor names must match the class name. (Thus, constructor names typically start with a capital letter, unlike most method names.)

- Constructors can invoke other constructors with this() and super(), so long as this invocation is the first statement in the constructor.

- The "result" of a constructor is an instance of the class, whereas the return type of an ordinary method can be anything.

- You use new, or reflection, to invoke a constructor.

Solution 14.2   (from page 156)

The following code will fail to compile when put into Fuse.java and QuickFuse.java:

```
package app.construction;
public class Fuse {
    private String name;
    public Fuse(String name) { this.name = name; }
}
```

and

```
package app.construction;
public class QuickFuse extends Fuse { }
```

The compiler will issue an error something like:

```
Implicit super constructor Fuse() is undefined for default
constructor. Must define an explicit constructor.
```

This error occurs when the compiler encounters the QuickFuse class and provides a default constructor for it. The default constructor has no arguments and, again by default, invokes its superclass's constructor with no arguments. However, the presence of a `Fuse()` constructor that accepts a `String` parameter means that the compiler will no longer supply a default constructor for `Fuse`. The default constructor for `QuickFuse` cannot invoke a superclass constructor with no arguments, because this constructor no longer exists.

Solution 14.3 (from page 157)

The program prints:

```
java.awt.Point[x=3,y=4]
```

(It has successfully found a constructor that takes two arguments and created a new point with the arguments given.)

BUILDER

Solution 15.1 (from page 162)

One way to make the parser more flexible is to let it accept multiple blanks after a comma. To do so, change the construction of the `split()` call as follows:

```
s.split(", *");
```

Or, instead of accepting blanks after a comma, you can allow any kind of whitespace by initializing the `Regex` object as follows:

```
s.split(",\\s*")
```

The \s characters indicate the whitespace "character class" in regular expressions. Note that all these solutions assume that there will be no commas embedded inside the fields.

Rather than making the regular expression more flexible, you might question the entire approach. In particular, you might want to press the travel agencies to begin sending reservations in an XML format. You might establish a set of tags to use and read them in with an XML parser.

Solution 15.2   (from page 164)

The build() method of UnforgivingBuilder throws an exception if
any attribute is invalid and otherwise returns a valid Reservation
object. Here is one implementation:

```
public Reservation build() throws BuilderException {
    if (date == null)
        throw new BuilderException("Valid date not found");

    if (city == null)
        throw new BuilderException("Valid city not found");

    if (headcount < MINHEAD)
        throw new BuilderException(
            "Minimum headcount is " + MINHEAD);

    if (dollarsPerHead.times(headcount)
            .isLessThan(MINTOTAL))
        throw new BuilderException(
            "Minimum total cost is " + MINTOTAL);

    return new Reservation(
        date,
        headcount,
        city,
        dollarsPerHead,
        hasSite);
}
```

The code checks that date and city values are set and checks that
headcount and dollars/head values are acceptable. The Reservation-
Builder superclass defines the constants MINHEAD and MINTOTAL.

If the builder encounters no problems, it returns a valid Reservation
object.

Solution 15.3   (from page 165)

As before, the code must throw an exception if the reservation fails to specify a city or a date, as there is no way to guess these values. Regarding missing values for headcount or dollars/head, note the following.

- If the reservation request specifies no headcount and no dollars/head, set the headcount to the minimum, and set dollars/head to the minimum total, divided by the headcount.

- If there is no headcount but there is a dollars/head value, set the headcount to be at least the minimum attendance and at least enough to generate enough money for the event.

- If there is a headcount but no dollars/head value, set the dollars/head value to be high enough to generate the minimum take.

Solution 15.4   (from page 165)

One solution is as follows:

```
public Reservation build() throws BuilderException {
    boolean noHeadcount = (headcount == 0);
    boolean noDollarsPerHead = (dollarsPerHead.isZero());

    if (noHeadcount && noDollarsPerHead) {
        headcount = MINHEAD;
        dollarsPerHead = sufficientDollars(headcount);
    } else if (noHeadcount) {
        headcount = (int) Math.ceil(
            MINTOTAL.dividedBy(dollarsPerHead));
        headcount = Math.max(headcount, MINHEAD);
    } else if (noDollarsPerHead) {
        dollarsPerHead = sufficientDollars(headcount);
    }

    check();

    return new Reservation(
        date,
        headcount,
        city,
        dollarsPerHead,
        hasSite);
}
```

This code relies on a check() method that is similar to the build() method of the UnforgivingBuilder class:

```
protected void check() throws BuilderException {
    if (date == null)
        throw new BuilderException("Valid date not found");

    if (city == null)
        throw new BuilderException("Valid city not found");

    if (headcount < MINHEAD)
        throw new BuilderException(
            "Minimum headcount is " + MINHEAD);

    if (dollarsPerHead.times(headcount)
            .isLessThan(MINTOTAL))
        throw new BuilderException(
            "Minimum total cost is " + MINTOTAL);
}
```

FACTORY METHOD

Solution 16.1   (from page 168)

A good answer, perhaps, is that you do not need to know what class of object an iterator() method returns. What is important is that you know the interface that the iterator supports, which lets you walk through the elements of a collection. However, if you *must* know the class, you can print out its name with a line like:

```
System.out.println(iter.getClass().getName());
```

This statement prints out:

```
java.util.AbstractList$Itr
```

The class Itr is an inner class of AbstractList. You should probably never see this class in your work with Java.

Solution 16.2 (from page 168)

There are many possible answers, but `toString()` is probably the most commonly used method that creates a new object. For example, the following code creates a new `String` object:

```
String s = new Date().toString();
```

The creation of strings often happens behind the scenes. Consider:

```
System.out.println(new Date());
```

This code creates a `String` object from the `Date` object, ultimately by calling the `toString()` method of the `Date` object.

Another frequently used method that creates a new object is `clone()`, a method that usually returns a copy of the receiving object.

Solution 16.3 (from page 169)

The intent of the FACTORY METHOD pattern is to let an object provider determine which class to instantiate when creating an object. By comparison, clients of `BorderFactory` know exactly what object types they're getting. The pattern at play in `BorderFactory` is FLYWEIGHT, in that `BorderFactory` uses sharing to efficiently support large numbers of borders. The `BorderFactory` class isolates clients from managing the reuse of objects, whereas FACTORY METHOD isolates clients from knowing which class to instantiate.

Solution 16.4 (from page 171)

Figure B.18 shows that the two credit check classes implement the `CreditCheck` interface. The factory class provides a method that returns a `CreditCheck` object. The client that calls `createCred-itCheck()` does not know the precise class of the object it receives.

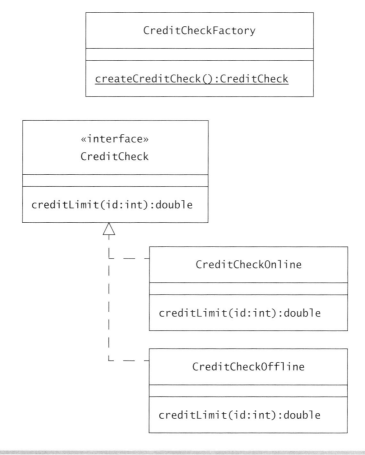

FIGURE B.18 Two classes implement the CreditCheck interface. The decision of which class to instantiate lies with the service provider rather than with the client that needs a credit check.

The createCreditCheck() method is a static method, so clients need not instantiate the CreditCheckFactory class in order to get a CreditCheck object. You can make this class abstract or give it a private constructor if you want to actively prevent other developers from instantiating it.

Solution 16.5 $\qquad$ (from page 171)

If you take the leap of faith that the static method isAgencyUp()
accurately reflects reality, the code for createCreditCheck() is
simple:

```
public static CreditCheck createCreditCheck() {
    if (isAgencyUp()) return new CreditCheckOnline();
    return new CreditCheckOffline();
}
```

Solution 16.6 $\qquad$ (from page 172)

Figure B.19 shows a reasonable diagram for the Machine/Machine-
Planner parallel hierarchy.

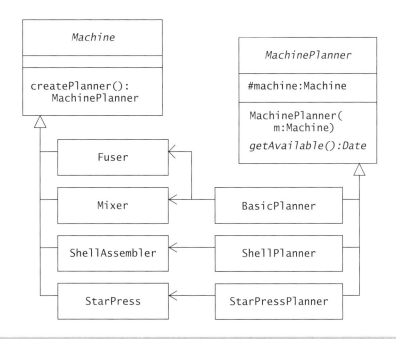

FIGURE B.19 Planning logic is now in a separate hierarchy. Each subclass of
Machine knows which planner to instantiate in response to a createPlanner() call.

This diagram indicates that subclasses of MachinePlanner must implement the getAvailable() method. The diagram also indicates that classes in the MachinePlanner hierarchy accept a Machine object in their constructors. This allows the planner to interrogate the object it is planning for, regarding such criteria as the machine's location and the amount of material it is currently processing.

Solution 16.7   (from page 173)

A createPlanner() method for the Machine class might look like:

```
public MachinePlanner createPlanner() {
    return new BasicPlanner(this);
}
```

The Fuser and Mixer classes can rely on inheriting this method, whereas the ShellAssembler and StarPress class will need to override it. For the StarPress class, the createPlanner() method might be:

```
public MachinePlanner createPlanner() {
    return new StarPressPlanner(this);
}
```

These methods show the FACTORY METHOD pattern at work. When we need a planner object, we call the createPlanner() method of the machine we want to plan for. The specific planner that we receive depends on the machine.

ABSTRACT FACTORY

Solution 17.1   (from page 179)

One solution is as follows:

```
public class BetaUI extends UI {
    public BetaUI () {
        Font oldFont = getFont();
        font = new Font(
            oldFont.getName(),
            oldFont.getStyle() | Font.ITALIC,
            oldFont.getSize());
    }
```

```
public JButton createButtonOk() {
    JButton b = super.createButtonOk();
    b.setIcon(getIcon("images/cherry-large.gif"));
    return b;
}

public JButton createButtonCancel() {
    JButton b = super.createButtonCancel();
    b.setIcon(getIcon("images/cherry-large-down.gif"));
    return b;
}
}
```

This code takes the approach of using the base class methods as much as possible.

Solution 17.2   (from page 180)

One solution for producing a more resilient design would be to specify the expected creation methods and standard GUI properties in an interface, as Figure B.20 shows.

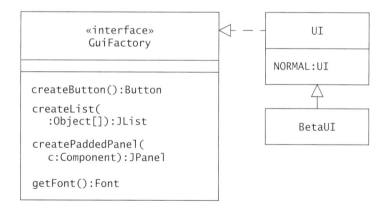

FIGURE B.20 This design of abstract factories for GUI controls reduces the dependency of subclasses on method modifiers in the UI class.

Solution 17.3   (from page 182)

Figure B.21 shows a solution to providing in Credit.Canada concrete classes that implement the interfaces and abstract class in Credit.

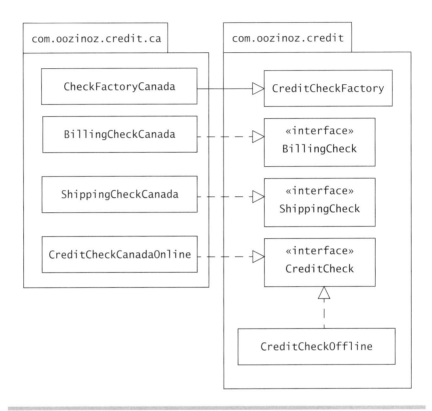

FIGURE B.21 The com.oozinoz.credit.ca package provides a family of concrete classes that conduct a variety of checks for Canadian calls.

One subtlety is that you need only one concrete class for offline credit checking, because at Oozinoz, offline checking is the same for calls from the United States and Canada.

Solution 17.4 (from page 183)

Here is one solution:

```
package com.oozinoz.credit.ca;
import com.oozinoz.check.*;

public class CheckFactoryCanada extends CheckFactory {
    public BillingCheck createBillingCheck() {
        return new BillingCheckCanada();
    }

    public CreditCheck createCreditCheck() {
        if (isAgencyUp())
            return new CreditCheckCanadaOnline();
        return new CreditCheckOffline();
    }

    public ShippingCheck createShippingCheck() {
        return new ShippingCheckCanada();
    }
}
```

Your solution should

- Implement create- methods for methods inherited from the abstract CreditCheckFactory class

- Have the proper interface for the return type of each create- method

- Return a CreditCheckOffline object if the agency is down

Solution 17.5 (from page 185)

An example *justification* is: Placing country-specific classes in separate packages helps our Oozinoz developers to organize our software and our development efforts. By placing the classes for each country in a separate package, we keep country-specific packages independent of one another. We can be confident, for example, that U.S.-specific classes have no impact on Canada-specific classes. We can also easily add support for new countries. For example, when we start doing business with Mexico, we can create a new package that provides the check services we need in a way that makes sense in that country.

This has the further advantage of letting us assign the credit.mx package to a developer who has expertise in working with services and data from Mexico.

An argument *against*: Although this separation is nice in theory, it's overwrought in practice. I'd rather have one package with all the classes in it, at least until we expand to nine or ten countries. Spreading these classes over multiple packages winds up causing me three or more times the configuration-managements work when I need to implement a change that cuts across all these packages.

PROTOTYPE

Solution 18.1   (from page 188)

Advantages of this design include the following.

- We can create new factories without creating a new class; we could even create a new GUI kit at runtime.

- We can produce a new factory by copying one and making slight adjustments. For example, we can make the GUI kit for a beta release identical to the normal kit except for font differences. The PROTOTYPE approach lets a new factory's buttons and other controls "inherit" values, such as colors, from a predecessor factory.

Disadvantages include the following.

- The PROTOTYPE approach lets us change values, such as colors and fonts, for each factory but does not allow us to produce new kits that have different behavior.

- The motivation for stopping the proliferation of UI kit classes is not clear; why is this proliferation a problem? We have to put the kit-initialization software somewhere, presumably on static methods on the proposed UIKit class. This approach doesn't really cut down on the amount of code we have to manage.

What's the right answer? In a situation like this, it may help to experiment: Write code that follows both designs, and evaluate how the design looks in practice. There will be times, though, when team members fundamentally disagree about which direction to take. This is a good thing: It shows that you are surfacing issues and discussing design. If you never disagree, you are probably not hammering out the best design. (For those times when you do disagree, even after thoughtful discussion, you might use an architect, a lead designer, or a neutral third party to break ties.)

Solution 18.2 (from page 189)

One way to summarize the function of clone() is "new object, same fields." The clone() method creates a new object with the same class and attribute types as the original. The new object also receives all the same field values as the original. If these fields are base types, such as integers, the values are copied. But if the fields are references, the *references* are copied.

The object that the clone() method creates is a *shallow copy*; it shares any subordinate objects with the original. A *deep copy* would include complete copies of all the parent object's attributes. For example, if you clone an object A that points to an object B, a shallow copy will create a new A' that points to the original B; a deep copy will create a new A' pointing to a new B'. If you want a deep copy, you'll have to implement your own method that does what you want.

Note that to use clone(), you must declare that your class implements Cloneable. This **marker interface** has no methods but serves as a flag to indicate that you're intentionally supporting clone().

Solution 18.3 (from page 189)

The suggested code will leave only three objects, as Figure B.22 shows.

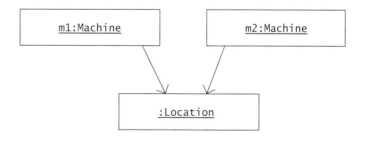

FIGURE B.22 An insufficient design for cloning can create an incomplete copy that shares some objects with its prototype.

The current version of the clone() method for MachineSimulator calls super.clone(), which class Object implements. This method creates a new object with the same fields. Primitive types, such as the int instance fields in a MachineSimulator, are copied. In addition, object references, such as the Location field in MachineSimulator, are copied. Note that the *reference* is copied, not the object. This means that Object.clone() produces the situation that Figure B.22 shows.

Suppose that you changed the bay and coordinates of the second machine's location. Because there is really only one Location object, this modification changes the location of both simulated machines!

Solution 18.4   (from page 190)

A reasonable solution is as follows:

```
public OzPanel copy2() {
    OzPanel result = new OzPanel();
    result.setBackground(this.getBackground());
    result.setForeground(this.getForeground());
    result.setFont(this.getFont());
    return result;
}
```

Both the copy() method and the copy2() method relieve clients of OzPanel from invoking a constructor and thus support the PROTOTYPE idea. However, the manual approach of copy2() may be much safer. This approach relies on knowing which attributes are important to copy, but it avoids copying attributes that you may know nothing about.

MEMENTO

Solution 19.1   (from page 198)

Here is one implementation of undo() for FactoryModel:

```
public boolean canUndo() {
    return mementos.size() > 1;
}
```

```
public void undo() {
    if (!canUndo()) return;
    mementos.pop();
    notifyListeners();
}
```

This code is careful to ignore undo() requests if the stack is down to its initial state with a single memento. The top of the stack is always the current state, so the undo() code has only to pop the stack to expose the previous memento.

When you write a createMemento() method, you should convince yourself or your colleagues that the method returns all the information necessary to reconstruct the receiving object. In this example, a machine simulator can reconstruct itself from a clone, and a factory simulator can reconstruct itself from a list of machine simulator clones.

Solution 19.2   (from page 201)

One solution is:

```
public void stateChanged(ChangeEvent e) {
    machinePanel().removeAll();

    List locations = factoryModel.getLocations();

    for (int i = 0; i < locations.size(); i++) {
        Point p = (Point) locations.get(i);
        machinePanel().add(createPictureBox(p));
    }

    undoButton().setEnabled(factoryModel.canUndo());
    repaint();
}
```

Each time the state changes, this code rebuilds from scratch the machine list in machinePanel().

Solution 19.3   (from page 201)

Storing a memento as an object assumes that the application will still
be running when the user wants to restore the original object. Reasons that will force you to save a memento to persistent storage
include the following.

- The ability to restore an object's state has to survive a system
  crash.

- You anticipate that the user will exit the system and will want to
  resume work later.

- You need to reconstruct an object on another computer.

Solution 19.4   (from page 204)

One solution is:

```
public void restore(Component source) throws Exception {
    JFileChooser dialog = new JFileChooser();
    dialog.showOpenDialog(source);

    if (dialog.getSelectedFile() == null)
        return;

    FileInputStream out = null;
    ObjectInputStream s = null;
    try {
        out = new FileInputStream(dialog.getSelectedFile());
        s = new ObjectInputStream(out);
        ArrayList list = (ArrayList) s.readObject();
        factoryModel.setLocations(list);
    } finally {
        if (s != null)
            s.close();
    }
}
```

This code is almost a mirror of the save() method, although the
restore() method must ask the factory model to push the recovered
location list.

Solution 19.5   (from page 205)

To *encapsulate* is to limit access to an object's state and operations. Saving an object, such as a collection of factory location points, in textual form exposes the object's data and allows anyone with a text editor to change the object's state. Thus, saving an object in XML form violates encapsulation, at least to some degree.

Violation of encapsulation through persistent storage may be a concern in practice, depending on your application. To address this threat, you might limit access to the data, as is common in a relational database. In other cases, you might encrypt the data, as is common when transmitting sensitive HTML text. The point here is not whether the words *encapsulation* and *memento* apply to a design but rather the real importance of ensuring data integrity while supporting the data's storage and transmission.

Introducing Operations

Solution 20.1   (from page 210)

CHAIN OF RESPONSIBILITY distributes an operation across a chain of objects. Each method implements the operation's service directly or forwards calls to the next object in the chain.

Solution 20.2   (from page 210)

A complete list of Java method modifiers, with informal definitions of their meanings, follows:

- `public`: access permitted to all clients

- `protected`: access permitted within the declaring package and to subclasses of the class

- `private`: access permitted only within the class

- `abstract`: no implementation provided

- `static`: associated with the class as a whole, not with individual objects

- `final`: not allowed to be overridden

- `synchronized`: method acquires access to the object monitor or to the class's, if the method is `static`

- `native`: implemented somewhere else in platform-dependent code

- `strictfp`: `double` and `float` expressions evaluated according to FP-strict rules, thus requiring intermediate results to be valid according to the IEEE standards

Although some developers might be tempted to explore using all these modifiers in a single method definition, several rules limit the ability to use them in combination. Section 8.4.3 of the *Java™ Language Specification* [Gosling et al. 2005] lists these limitations.

Solution 20.3   (from page 211)

It depends.

For pre–Java 5 versions: If you were to somehow change the return value of `Bitmap.clone()`, the code wouldn't compile. The `clone()` signature matches the signature of `Object.clone()`, so the return type must match as well.

In Java 5: The language definition has changed to allow **covariant return types**, whereby a subclass *can* declare a more specific return type.

Solution 20.4   (from page 212)

One argument *for* leaving exception declarations out of method headers: We should first note that even Java does not require methods to declare all the exceptions that might be thrown. Any method might, for example, encounter a null pointer and throw an undeclared exception. It's impractical, as Java admits, to force programmers to declare all possible exceptions. Applications need a strategy for handling all exceptions. Requiring developers to declare certain types of exceptions is no substitute for architecting in an exception-handling policy.

On the other hand: Programmers need all the help they can get. It's true that an application architecture needs to have a solid exception-handling strategy. It's also clearly impractical to force developers to declare in every method the possibility of pervasive problems, such as null pointers. But for some errors, such as problems in opening a file, requiring the caller of a method to handle possible exceptions is a useful reminder. C# throws out the baby with the bathwater by removing any declaration of possible exceptions from method headers.

Solution 20.5   (from page 214)

The figure shows one algorithm—the procedure to determine whether an object model is a tree—two operations—appearing as two signatures in the MachineComponent class—and four methods.

TEMPLATE METHOD

Solution 21.1   (from page 221)

Your completed program should look something like:

```
package app.templateMethod;
import java.util.Comparator;
import com.oozinoz.firework.Rocket;

public class ApogeeComparator implements Comparator {
   public int compare(Object o1, Object o2) {
      Rocket r1 = (Rocket) o1;
      Rocket r2 = (Rocket) o2;
      return Double.compare(r1.getApogee(), r2.getApogee());
   }
}
```

and

```
package app.templateMethod;
import java.util.Comparator;
import com.oozinoz.firework.Rocket;

public class NameComparator implements Comparator {
    public int compare(Object o1, Object o2) {
        Rocket r1 = (Rocket) o1;
        Rocket r2 = (Rocket) o2;
        return r1.toString().compareTo(r2.toString());
    }
}
```

Solution 21.2   (from page 223)

The code for markMoldIncomplete() passes the information about an incomplete mold to the material manager. One solution is:

```
package com.oozinoz.ozAster;
import aster.*;
import com.oozinoz.businessCore.*;

public class OzAsterStarPress extends AsterStarPress {
    public MaterialManager getManager() {
        return MaterialManager.getManager();
    }

    public void markMoldIncomplete(int id) {
        getManager().setMoldIncomplete(id);
    }
}
```

Solution 21.3   (from page 225)

What you want is a hook. You might phrase your request something like: I wonder whether you could be so kind as to add a call in your shutDown() method, after discharging the paste and before flushing. If you call it something like collectPaste(), I can use it to save the paste that we reuse here at Oozinoz.

The developers are likely to negotiate with you about the name of the method. The point is that by requesting a hook in a TEMPLATE METHOD, you can make your code more resilient than you can by working around an inadequacy in the existing code.

Solution 21.4   (from page 227)

The getPlanner() method in the Machine class should take advantage of the abstract createPlanner() method:

```
public MachinePlanner getPlanner() {
    if (planner == null)
        planner = createPlanner();
    return planner;
}
```

This code requires that you add a `planner` field to the `Machine` class. After adding this attribute and the `getPlanner()` method in `Machine`, you can delete this attribute and method in the subclasses.

This refactoring creates a TEMPLATE METHOD. The `getPlanner()` method lazy-initializes the planner variable, relying on the `createPlanner()` step that subclasses supply.

STATE

Solution 22.1   (from page 231)

As the state machine shows, when the door is open, touching the one-touch button will take the door to the `StayOpen` state, and a second touch will start the door closing.

Solution 22.2   (from page 233)

Your code should look something like:

```
public void complete() {
    if (state == OPENING)
        setState(OPEN);
    else if (state == CLOSING)
        setState(CLOSED);
}

public void timeout() {
    setState(CLOSING);
}
```

Solution 22.3   (from page 237)

Your code should look something like:

```
package com.oozinoz.carousel;

public class DoorClosing extends DoorState {
    public DoorClosing(Door2 door) {
        super(door);
    }
```

```
        public void touch() {
            door.setState(door.OPENING);
        }

        public void complete() {
            door.setState(door.CLOSED);
        }
}
```

Solution 22.4   (from page 239)

Figure B.23 shows a reasonable diagram.

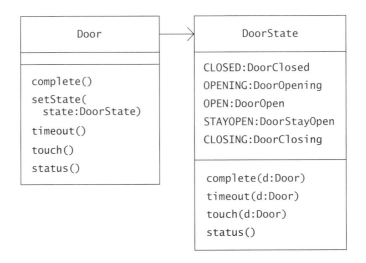

FIGURE B.23 This design lets DoorState objects be constants. The DoorState state transition methods update the state of a Door object that they receive as a parameter.

STRATEGY

Solution 23.1   (from page 245)

Figure B.24 shows one solution.

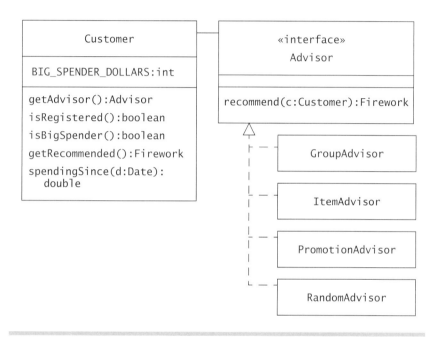

FIGURE B.24 The advertising policy at Oozinoz includes four strategies that appear as four implementations of the Advisor interface.

Solution 23.2   (from page 247)

The GroupAdvisor and ItemAdvisor classes are instances of ADAPTER, providing the interface a client expects, using the services of a class with a different interface.

Solution 23.3   (from page 248)

Your code should look something like:

```
public Firework getRecommended() {
    return getAdvisor().recommend(this);
}
```

Once the advisor is known, polymorphism does all the work.

Solution 23.4   (from page 249)

Is a reusable sort routine an example of TEMPLATE METHOD or of STRATEGY?

For STRATEGY: TEMPLATE METHOD, according to the original *Design Patterns* book, lets "subclasses" redefine certain steps of an algorithm. But the Collections.sort() method doesn't work with subclasses; it uses a Comparator instance. Each instance of Comparator provides a new method and thus a new algorithm and a new strategy. The sort() method is a good example of STRATEGY.

For TEMPLATE METHOD: There are many sorting algorithms, but Collections.sort() uses only one (QuickSort). Changing the algorithm would mean changing to, say, a heap sort or a bubble sort. The intent of STRATEGY is to let you plug in different algorithms. That doesn't happen here. The intent of TEMPLATE METHOD is to let you plug a step into an algorithm. That is precisely how the sort() method works.

COMMAND

Solution 24.1   (from page 252)

Many Java Swing applications apply the MEDIATOR pattern, registering a single object to receive all GUI events. This object mediates the interaction of the components and translates user input into commands for business domain objects.

Solution 24.2   (from page 253)

Your code should look something like this:

```java
package com.oozinoz.visualization;
import java.awt.event.*;
import javax.swing.*;
import com.oozinoz.ui.*;

public class Visualization2 extends Visualization {
    public static void main(String[] args) {
        Visualization2 panel = new Visualization2(UI.NORMAL);
        JFrame frame = SwingFacade.launch(
            panel,
            "Operational Model");
        frame.setJMenuBar(panel.menus());
        frame.setVisible(true);
    }
    public Visualization2(UI ui) {
        super(ui);
    }
    public JMenuBar menus() {
        JMenuBar menuBar = new JMenuBar();

        JMenu menu = new JMenu("File");
        menuBar.add(menu);

        JMenuItem menuItem = new JMenuItem("Save As...");
        menuItem.addActionListener(new ActionListener() {
            public void actionPerformed(ActionEvent e) {
                save();
            }
        });
        menu.add(menuItem);

        menuItem = new JMenuItem("Restore From...");
        menuItem.addActionListener(new ActionListener() {
            public void actionPerformed(ActionEvent e) {
                restore();
            }
        });
        menu.add(menuItem);
        return menuBar;
    }
```

```
public void save() {
    try {
        mediator.save(this);
    } catch (Exception ex) {
        System.out.println("Failed save: " +
            ex.getMessage());
    }
}

public void restore() {
    try {
        mediator.restore(this);
    } catch (Exception ex) {
        System.out.println("Failed restore: " +
            ex.getMessage());
    }
}
}
```

Although the actionPerformed() method requires an ActionEvent argument, you can safely ignore it. The menus() method registers a single instance of an anonymous class with the Save menu item and a single instance of another anonymous class with the Load menu item. When these methods are called, there is no doubt about the source of the event.

Solution 24.3   (from page 255)

The testSleep() method passes the doze command to the time() utility method:

```
package app.command;

import com.oozinoz.robotInterpreter.Command;
import com.oozinoz.utility.CommandTimer;

import junit.framework.TestCase;
```

```
public class TestCommandTimer extends TestCase {
    public void testSleep() {
        Command doze = new Command() {
            public void execute() {
                try {
                    Thread.sleep(
                        2000 + Math.round(10 * Math.random()));
                } catch (InterruptedException ignored) {
                }
            }
        };

        long actual = CommandTimer.time(doze);

        long expected = 2000;
        long delta = 5;
        assertTrue(
            "Should be " + expected + " +/- " + delta + " ms",
                expected - delta <= actual
            && actual <= expected + delta);
    }
}
```

Solution 24.4   (from page 257)

You code should look something like:

```
public void shutDown() {
    if (inProcess()) {
        stopProcessing();
        moldIncompleteHook.execute(this);
    }
    usherInputMolds();
    dischargePaste();
    flush();
}
```

Note that the code doesn't bother checking whether moldIncom-pleteHook is null, as it is always set to a real Hook object. (Initially, it is set to a do-nothing NullHook object, but a user can install a different hook.)

You might use it like this:

```
package app.templateMethod;

import com.oozinoz.businessCore.*;
import aster2.*;

public class ShowHook {
   public static void main(String[] args) {
      AsterStarPress p = new AsterStarPress();
      Hook h = new Hook() {
        public void execute(AsterStarPress p) {
            MaterialManager m = MaterialManager.getManager();
            m.setMoldIncomplete(p.getCurrentMoldID());
        }
      };

      p.setMoldIncompleteHook(h);
   }
}
```

Solution 24.5   (from page 258)

In FACTORY METHOD, a client knows *when* to create a new object but not *what kind* of object to create. FACTORY METHOD moves object creation to a method that isolates a client from knowing which class to instantiate. This principle also occurs in ABSTRACT FACTORY.

Solution 24.6   (from page 258)

The intent of the MEMENTO pattern is to provide storage and restoration of an object's state. Typically, you can add a new memento to a stack with each execution of a command, popping and reapplying these mementos when a user needs to undo commands.

INTERPRETER

Solution 25.1   (from page 269)

The execute() method of the ForCommand class should look some-thing like the following code:

```
private void execute(MachineComponent mc) {
    if (mc instanceof Machine) {
        Machine m = (Machine) mc;
        variable.assign(new Constant(m));
        body.execute();
        return;
    }

    MachineComposite comp = (MachineComposite) mc;
    List children = comp.getComponents();
    for (int i = 0; i < children.size(); i++) {
        MachineComponent child =
            (MachineComponent) children.get(i);
        execute(child);
    }
}
```

The execute() code walks through a machine composite. When it encounters a leaf node—a machine—the code assigns the variable to the machine and executes the ForMachine object's body command.

Solution 25.2   (from page 273)

One solution is:

```
public void execute() {
    if (term.eval() != null)
        body.execute();
    else
        elseBody.execute();
}
```

Solution 25.3   (from page 273)

One way to write `WhileCommand.java` is:

```
package com.oozinoz.robotInterpreter2;

public class WhileCommand extends Command {
    protected Term term;

    protected Command body;

    public WhileCommand(Term term, Command body) {
        this.term = term;
        this.body = body;
    }

    public void execute() {
        while (term.eval() != null)
            body.execute();
    }
}
```

Solution 25.4   (from page 274)

One answer is: The intent of the INTERPRETER pattern is to let you compose executable objects from a hierarchy of classes that provide various interpretations of a common operation. The intent of COMMAND is merely to encapsulate a request in an object.

Can an interpreter object function as a command? Sure! The question of which pattern applies depends on your intent. Are you creating a toolkit for composing executable objects, or are you encapsulating a request in an object?

Introducing Extensions

Solution 26.1   (from page 281)

In mathematics, a circle is certainly a special case of an ellipse. However, in OO programming, an ellipse has certain behaviors that a circle does not. For example, an ellipse may be twice as wide as it is tall;

a circle can't do that. If that behavior is important to your program, a Circle object won't function as an Ellipse object and will represent a violation of LSP.

Note that if you're considering **immutable** objects, this may not apply. This is simply an area in which naive mathematics is not a smooth fit for the semantics of standard type hierarchies.

Solution 26.2   (from page 282)

The expression tub.getLocation().isUp() might lead to programming errors if there are any subtleties around the value of a tub object's Location property. For example, the location might be null or might be a Robot object if the tub is in transit. If location is null, evaluating tub.getLocation().isUp() will throw an exception. If location is a Robot object, the problem may be even worse, as we try to use a robot to collect a tub from itself. These potential problems are manageable, but do we want the ensuing code to be in the method that uses the tub.getLocation().isUp() expression? No. The necessary code may already be in the Tub class! If not, it belongs there, to prevent us from having to recode around the same subtleties in other methods that interact with tubs.

Solution 26.3   (from page 283)

One example is:

```
public static String getZip(String address) {
    return address.substring(address.length() - 5);
}
```

There are a few smells here, including *primitive obsession* (using a string to contain several attributes).

Solution 26.4   (from page 284)

One set of solutions is:

Example	Pattern at Play
A fireworks simulation designer establishes an interface that defines the behaviors your object must possess in order to participate in the simulation.	ADAPTER
A toolkit lets you compose executable objects at runtime.	INTERPRETER
A superclass has a method that requires subclasses to fill in a missing step.	TEMPLATE METHOD
An object lets you extend its behavior by accepting a method encapsulated in an object and invoking that method at an appropriate moment.	COMMAND
A code generator inserts behavior that provides the illusion that an object executing on another machine is local.	PROXY
A design lets you register for callbacks that will be issued when an object changes.	OBSERVER
A design lets you define abstract operations that depend on a well-defined interface and lets you add new drivers that fulfill the interface.	BRIDGE

DECORATOR

Solution 27.1   (from page 293)

One solution is:

```
package com.oozinoz.filter;
import java.io.*;

public class RandomCaseFilter extends OozinozFilter {
    public RandomCaseFilter(Writer out) {
        super(out);
    }

    public void write(int c) throws IOException {
        out.write(Math.random() < .5
            ? Character.toLowerCase((char) c)
            : Character.toUpperCase((char) c));
    }
}
```

Random case can be eye-catching. Consider the following program:

```
package app.decorator;
import java.io.BufferedWriter;
import java.io.IOException;

import com.oozinoz.filter.ConsoleWriter;
import com.oozinoz.filter.RandomCaseFilter;

public class ShowRandom {
    public static void main(String[] args)
                throws IOException {
        BufferedWriter w =
            new BufferedWriter(
                new RandomCaseFilter(new ConsoleWriter()));
        w.write("buy two packs now and get a "
                + "zippie pocket rocket -- free!");
        w.newLine();
        w.close();
    }
}
```

This program uses the `ConsoleWriter` class developed later in Chapter 27, DECORATOR. Running the program prints out something like:

```
bUy tWO pAcks NOw ANd geT A ZiPpIE PoCkEt RocKeT -- frEe!
```

Solution 27.2   (from page 294)

One solution is:

```java
package com.oozinoz.filter;
import java.io.Writer;

public class ConsoleWriter extends Writer {
    public void close() {}
    public void flush() {}

    public void write(
            char[] buffer, int offset, int length) {
        for (int i = 0; i < length; i++)
            System.out.print(buffer[offset + i]);
    }
}
```

Solution 27.3   (from page 301)

One solution is:

```java
package com.oozinoz.function;

public class Exp extends Function {
    public Exp(Function f) {
        super(f);
    }

    public double f(double t) {
        return Math.exp(sources[0].f(t));
    }
}
```

Solution 27.4   (from page 302)

One solution is:

```
package app.decorator.brightness;

import com.oozinoz.function.Function;

public class Brightness extends Function {
    public Brightness(Function f) {
        super(f);
    }

    public double f(double t) {
        return Math.exp(-4 * sources[0].f(t))
            * Math.sin(Math.PI * sources[0].f(t));
    }
}
```

ITERATOR

Solution 28.1   (from page 311)

The display() routine launches a new thread that can wake up at any time, although the sleep() call helps to ensure that run() executes while display() is sleeping. The output indicates that in the given run, the display() method retains control through one iteration, printing the list at index 0:

```
Mixer1201
```

At this point, the second thread wakes up and places Fuser1101 at the beginning of the list, bumping all the other machine names down one slot. In particular, Mixer1201 moves from index 0 to index 1.

When the primary thread regains control, the display() method prints the remainder of the list, from index 1 to the end:

```
Mixer1201
ShellAssembler1301
StarPress1401
UnloadBuffer1501
```

Solution 28.2   (from page 313)

An argument *against the use of* synchronized() *methods* is: The synchronized() methods either misfire completely—if you iterate with a for loop—or crash the program, unless you build in the logic to catch the exception InvalidOperationException that gets thrown.

An argument *against a locking-based approach* is: Designs that provide thread-safe iteration rely on cooperation between threads that may access the collection. The whole point of the synchronized() methods is to catch the case in which threads aren't cooperating.

Neither the synchronized() methods nor the locking support built into Java can make multithreaded development easy and foolproof. For an excellent source on concurrent programming, see *Concurrent Programming in Java™* [Lea 2000].

Solution 28.3   (from page 319)

As Chapter 16, FACTORY METHOD, describes, iterators provide a classic example of the FACTORY METHOD pattern. A client that wants an enumerator for an instance of a ProcessComponent knows when to create the iterator, but the receiving class knows which class to instantiate.

Solution 28.4   (from page 323)

One solution is:

```
public Object next() {
    if (peek != null) {
        Object result = peek;
        peek = null;
        return result;
    }

    if (!visited.contains(head)) {
        visited.add(head);
        if (shouldShowInterior()) return head;
    }

    return nextDescendant();
}
```

VISITOR

Solution 29.1   (from page 327)

The difference is in the type of the this object. The accept() method calls the visit() method of a MachineVisitor object. The accept() method in the Machine class will look up a visit() method with the signature visit(:Machine), whereas the accept() method in the MachineComposite class will look up a method with the signature visit(:MachineComposite).

Solution 29.2   (from page 331)

One solution is:

```
package app.visitor;

import com.oozinoz.machine.MachineComponent;
import com.oozinoz.machine.OozinozFactory;

public class ShowFindVisitor {
    public static void main(String[] args) {
        MachineComponent factory = OozinozFactory.dublin();
        MachineComponent machine = new FindVisitor().find(
            factory, 3404);
        System.out.println(machine != null ?
            machine.toString() : "Not found");
    }
}
```

Solution 29.3   (from page 332)

A solution is:

```
package app.visitor;
import com.oozinoz.machine.*;
import java.util.*;

public class RakeVisitor implements MachineVisitor {
    private Set leaves;
```

```
public Set getLeaves(MachineComponent mc) {
    leaves = new HashSet();
    mc.accept(this);
    return leaves;
}

public void visit(Machine m) {
    leaves.add(m);
}

public void visit(MachineComposite mc) {
    Iterator iter = mc.getComponents().iterator();
    while (iter.hasNext())
        ((MachineComponent) iter.next()).accept(this);
}
}
```

Solution 29.4   (from page 338)

One solution is to add a Set argument to all the accept() and
visit() methods, so that the set of visited nodes gets passed around.
The ProcessComponent class should then have a concrete accept()
method that calls its abstract accept() method, passing it a new Set
object:

```
public void accept(ProcessVisitor v) {
    accept(v, new HashSet());
}
```

The accept() method for the ProcessAlternation, ProcessSequence, and ProcessStep subclasses would be:

```
public void accept(ProcessVisitor v, Set visited) {
    v.visit(this, visited);
}
```

Now visitor developers must create classes with visit() methods that
accept the visited set. This is a significant hint that using the set is a
good idea, although the visitor developer retains the responsibility for
populating the set.

Solution 29.5   (from page 340)

Alternatives to applying VISITOR include the following.

- Add the behavior you need to the original hierarchy. You can achieve this if you are in good communication with the hierarchy developers or if your shop uses collective code ownership.

- You can let a class that must operate on a machine or process structure simply traverse the structure. If you need to know the type of, say, a composite's child, you can use the `instanceof` operator, or you might build in Boolean functions, such as `isLeaf()` and `isComposite()`.

- If the behavior you want to add is of a significantly different thrust than the existing behavior, you can create a parallel hierarchy. For example, the `MachinePlanner` class in Chapter 16, FACTORY METHOD, places a machine's planning behavior in a separate hierarchy.

C

OOZINOZ SOURCE

THE PRIMARY BENEFIT of learning about design patterns is that understanding them will help you improve your code. Design patterns can
make your code smaller, simpler, more elegant, easier to maintain,
and more powerful. For design patterns to pay off, you need to see
them manifest in working code, and you must become comfortable
building and rebuilding design patterns into a codebase. Because it
can be helpful to start with working examples, this book includes
many examples that show the use of design patterns in Java code.
Building the Oozinoz source and walking through the code examples
that support this book's text will help you to begin using design patterns in your own code.

Acquiring and Using the Source

To get the source code that goes with this book, go to www.oozi-
noz.com, download the source code zip file, and unzip its contents,
placing the code anywhere you like. The Oozinoz source code is free.
You may use it as you wish, with the sole restriction that you may not
claim that you wrote it. On the other hand, neither we nor the publisher of this book warrant the code to be useful for any particular
purpose.

Building the Oozinoz Code

If you do not have a development environment for developing Java
programs, you need to acquire one and gain some expertise in using
it, so that you are able to write, compile, and execute your own programs. You can purchase a development tool, such as Intellij's Idea, or
you can work with open source tools, such as Eclipse.

Testing the Code with JUnit

The Oozinoz libraries include a `com.oozinoz.testing` package that is designed for use with JUnit, a free, automated testing framework. You can download JUnit from http://junit.org. If you're not familiar with it, the best way to learn how to use this tool is to learn from a friend or a peer. Barring that, you can work through the online documentation for this tool or find a book on the topic. There is more of a learning curve than with, say, Ant, but learning to use an automated test framework will equip you with a skill that you will use for years to come.

Finding Files Yourself

It can be difficult to find a particular file that corresponds to code that you see in the book. Often, the easiest way to find, say, a particular application is to search the source tree for the application's name. The code is organized, though, so that you should be able to find files by browsing the `oozinoz` directory tree. Table C.1 shows the subdirectories of `oozinoz` and explains their contents.

TABLE C.1 Names and Contents of Subdirectories of the `oozinoz` Directory

Directory Name	Directory Contents
app	Subdirectories for "applications": Java files that build into executable programs. Generally, these are organized by chapter, so `app.decorator` contains sample code related to Chapter 27, Decorator.
aster	Source code from Aster, an imaginary company.
com	Source code for Oozinoz applications.
images	Images that various Oozinoz applications use.

Summary

Your investment in learning design patterns will begin to bear fruit as you change the way you write and refactor code. You may be able to apply design patterns in your own code immediately, but it sometimes helps to peruse another developer's working code. Getting the Oozinoz code working on your machine is a useful exercise, as is learning to use open source tools, such as Ant and JUnit. Learning these tools and getting the Oozinoz code or anyone else's code to run can be hard work, but that hard work will pay off for years to come by increasing skills that you can use as new technologies come along. Good luck! If you have problems or get stuck, please feel free to send one of us a note.

Steve Metsker (Steve.Metsker@acm.org)
William Wake (William.Wake@acm.org)

D

UML AT A GLANCE

THIS APPENDIX BRIEFLY explains the Unified Modeling Language (UML) features that this book uses. UML provides conventional notation that this book applies to illustrate the design of object-oriented systems. Although UML is not overly complex, you can easily underestimate the richness of its features. For a rapid introduction to most of the features of the UML, read *UML Distilled* [Fowler with Scott 2003]. For a more thorough review, see *The Unified Modeling Language User Guide* [Booch, Rumbaugh, and Jacobsen 1999]. By learning to use standard nomenclatures and notations, we learn to communicate at a design level, making us all more productive.

Classes

Figure D.1 applies some of the UML features for illustrating classes.

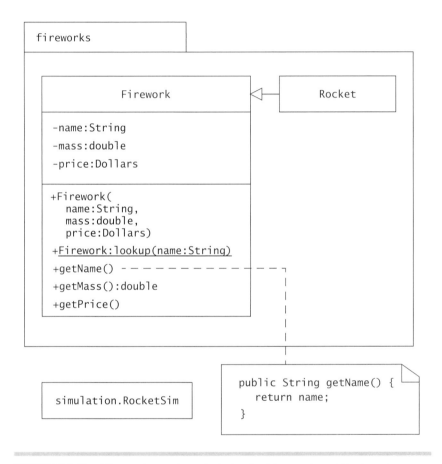

FIGURE D.1 The `Fireworks` package includes the `Firework` and `Rocket` classes.

Following are notes on class diagrams.

- Draw a class by centering its name in a rectangle. Figure D.1 shows three classes: `Firework`, `Rocket`, and `simulation.RocketSim`.

- There is no requirement in UML that a diagram show everything about a portrayed element, such as all the methods of a class or the complete contents of a package.

- Indicate a package by left-aligning its name in a rectangle, within a larger box that may show classes and other types. For example, the classes in Figure D.1 are in the `Fireworks` package.

- When showing a class outside a package diagram, you may prepend the class's namespace and a dot to the class's name. For example, Figure D.1 shows that the `RocketSim` class is in the `simulation` package.

- You can show a class's instance variables in a rectangle beneath the class name. The `Firework` class has instance variables `name`, `mass`, and `price`. Follow the variable's name by a colon and the variable's type.

- You may indicate that an instance variable or a method is private by preceding it with a minus sign (-). A plus sign (+) indicates that a variable or a method is public, and a pound sign (#) indicates that a variable or a method is protected.

- You can show a class's methods in a second rectangle beneath the class name.

- When a method accepts parameters, you may show them, as the `lookup()` method does.

- Variables in method signatures usually appear as the name of the variable, a colon, and the type of the variable. You may omit or abbreviate the variable name if its type implies the variable's role.

- Indicate that a method is static by underlining it, as the `lookup()` method shows.

- Make notes by drawing a dog-eared rectangle. The text in notes may contain comments, constraints, or code. Use a dashed line to attach notes to other diagram elements. Notes can appear in any UML diagram.

Class Relationships

Figure D.2 shows a few of the UML's features for modeling class relationships.

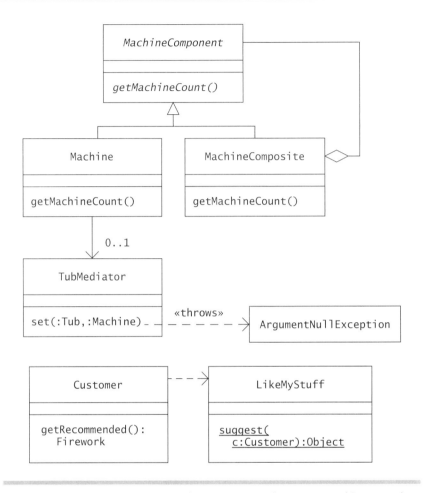

FIGURE D.2 A MachineComposite object contains either Machine objects or other composites. The Customer class depends on the LikeMyStuff class without instantiating it.

Following are notes on class relationship notation.

- Show a class name or a method name in italics to indicate that it is abstract. Underline a method name to indicate that it is static.

- Use a closed, hollow arrowhead to point to a class's superclass.

- Use a line between classes to indicate that instances of the classes are connected in some way. Most commonly, a line on a class diagram means that one class has an instance variable that refers to the other class. The Machine class, for example, uses an instance variable to retain a reference to a TubMediator object.

- Use a diamond to show that instances of a class contain a collection of instances of another class.

- An open arrowhead indicates navigability. Use it to emphasize that one class has a reference to another and that the pointed-to class does not have a back reference.

- A multiplicity indicator, such as 0..1, indicates how many connections may appear between objects. Use an asterisk (*) to indicate that zero or more instances of an object of a class may be connected to objects of an associated class.

- When a method may throw an exception, you can show this with a dashed arrow pointing from the method to the exception class. Label the arrow with a «throws» stereotype.

- Use a dashed arrow between classes to show a dependency that does not use an object reference. For example, the Customer class relies on a static method from the LikeMyStuff recommendation engine.

Interfaces

Figure D.3 shows the basic features for illustrating interfaces.

Following are notes on interfaces.

- You can draw an interface by placing in a rectangle the text «interface» and the name of the interface, as Figure D.3 shows. You can use a dashed line and a closed, hollow arrowhead to show that a class implements the interface.

- You can also show that a class implements an interface by using a line and a circle (a "lollipop") and the name of the interface.

- Interfaces and their methods are always abstract in Java. Oddly enough, interfaces and their methods do *not* appear in italics, unlike abstract classes and abstract methods in classes.

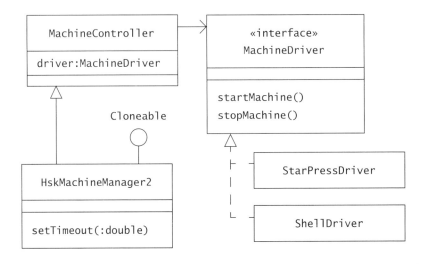

FIGURE D.3 You can indicate an interface with either an «interface» stereotype or a lollipop.

Objects

An object diagram illustrates specific instances of classes, as Figure D.4 shows.

Following are notes on object diagrams.

- You can show an object by giving its name and type, separated by a colon. You may optionally show only the name or only a colon and the type. In any case, underline the name and/or type of the object.

- Use a line between objects to indicate that one object has a reference to another. You can use an open arrowhead to emphasize the direction of the reference.

- You can show a sequence of objects sending messages to other objects, as the lower part of Figure D.4 shows. The order of messages is top to bottom, and the dashed lines indicate the existence of the object over time.

- Use the «create» stereotype to show that one object creates another. Figure D.4 shows the ShowClient class creating a local Rocket object.

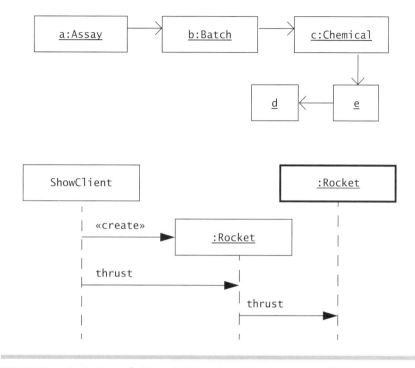

FIGURE D.4 Depictions of objects indicate the objects' names and/or types. A sequence diagram shows a succession of method calls.

- Draw a thick boxed line around an object to indicate that it is active in another thread, process, or computer. Figure D.4 shows a local `Rocket` object forwarding a request for its `thrust()` method to a `Rocket` object running on a server.

States

Figure D.5 shows a UML statechart diagram.

Following are notes on illustrating states.

- Show a state in a rectangle with rounded corners.

- Show state transitions with open arrows.

- A statechart need not map directly to a class or object diagram, though you may arrange for a direct translation, as Figure 22.3 in Chapter 22, STATE, shows.

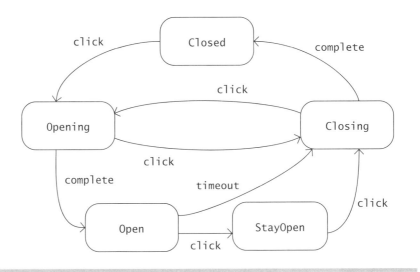

FIGURE D.5 A statechart diagram shows transitions from state to state.

GLOSSARY

ABSTRACT SYNTAX TREE	A structure, created by a *parser*, that organizes input text according to a *language's grammar*.
ABSTRACTION	A class that depends on abstract methods implemented in subclasses or in implementations of an *interface*.
AERIAL SHELL	A firework that is fired from a *mortar* and that explodes midflight, ejecting and igniting *stars*.
ALGORITHM	A well-defined computational procedure that takes a set of values as input and produces a value as output.
APOGEE	The greatest height that a fired, or flying, firework achieves.
APPLICATION PROGRAMMING INTERACE (API)	The interface, or set of calls, that a system makes publicly available.
ASSAY	An analysis, usually of a chemical mixture.
BUSINESS OBJECT	An object that models an entity or a process in a business.
CAROUSEL	A large, smart rack that accepts material through a door-way and stores it.
CLASS ADAPTER	An ADAPTER that works by subclassing the class to be adapted and meeting a required interface. Compare *object adapter*.
CLIENT	An object that uses or needs to use another object's methods.
COMPOSITE	A group of objects in which some objects may contain others, so that some objects represent groups and others represent individual items, or *leaves*.

CONSOLIDATION LANGUAGE	A computer language, such as Java or C#, that attempts to absorb the strengths and to discard the weaknesses of its predecessors.
CONSTRUCTOR	In Java, a special method whose name matches the class name, used to instantiate the class.
CONTEXT-FREE LANGUAGE	A *language* that can be described with a particular type of *grammar.*
CORBA	Common Object Request Broker Architecture; a standard design (common architecture) for facilitating (brokering) object requests that pass between systems.
COVARIANT RETURN TYPE	When a subclass overrides a method and declares its return type to be a subclass of the parent's return type.
CYCLE	A *path* in which a node, or object, appears twice.
DEEP COPY	A complete copy of an object in which the new object's attributes are complete copies of the original object's attributes.
DESIGN PATTERN	A *pattern*—a way to pursue an intent—that operates at about a class level.
DIRECTED GRAPH	A *graph* in which edges have a direction: They point.
DOUBLE DISPATCH	A design in which a class B object dispatches a request to a class A object, which immediately dispatches a request back to the class B object, with additional information about the class A object's type.
DRIVER	An object that operates a computer system, such as a database, or an external device, such as a line plotter, according to a well-specified interface.
DUD	A firework that does not work correctly, particularly a firework that is designed to explode but doesn't.
ENCAPSULATION	A design that limits, through a specified interface, access to an object's data and operations.
ENTERPRISE JAVABEANS (EJB)	A specification of an *n*-tier, component-based architecture.

EXTENSIBLE MARKUP LANGUAGE (XML)	A particular textual language that relies on tags, or *markup*, to contain information about the text and that specifically separates classes or types of documents from their instances.
GRAMMAR	A set of composition rules.
GRAPH	A collection of nodes and edges.
GRAPH THEORY	A mathematical conception of nodes and edges. When applied to an object model, a graph's nodes are usually objects, and a graph's edges are usually object references.
GRAPHICAL USER INTERFACE (GUI)	A layer of software in an application that lets a human interact with graphical depictions of buttons, menus, sliders, text areas, and other components.
GUI	See *graphical user interface*.
HOOK	A provision that a developer places in code to give other developers a chance to insert code at a specific spot in a procedure.
HOPPER	A container that dispenses chemicals, usually into a machine.
IDE	See *integrated development environment*.
IMMUTABLE	Unchangeable; specifically, an object with values that cannot change.
IMPLEMENTATION	The code statements that make up the bodies of a class's methods.
INTEGRATED DEVELOPMENT ENVIRONMENT (IDE)	A software tool collection that combines support for code editing and debugging with other tools for creating new software.
INTERFACE	The collection of methods and fields that a class permits objects of other classes to access. Also, a Java interface that defines the methods that an implementing class must provide.
INTERPRETER	An object composed from a composition hierarchy in which each class represents a composition rule that determines how the class implements, or "interprets," an operation that occurs throughout the hierarchy.

JAVA DEVELOPMENT KIT (JDK)	A collection of software that includes the Java class libraries, a compiler, and other supporting tools; usually refers specifically to kits at java.sun.com.
JDBC	An application programming interface for executing SQL statements. JDBC is a trademarked name, not an acronym.
JDK	See *Java Development Kit.*
JUNIT	A testing framework, written by Erich Gamma and Kent Beck, that lets you implement automated regression tests in Java. Available at www.junit.org.
KIT	A class with creation methods that return instances of a family of objects. See Chapter 17, ABSTRACT FACTORY.
LAW OF DEMETER	An object-oriented design principle that maintains that an object's method should send messages only to argument objects, the object itself, or the object's attributes.
LAYER	A group of classes with similar responsibilities, often collected in a single class library, and usually with well-defined dependencies on other layers.
LAZY-INITIALIZE	To instantiate an object when it is first needed.
LEAF	An individual item within a *composite*.
LISKOV SUBSTITUTION PRINCIPLE (LSP)	An object-oriented design principle that maintains that an instance of a class should function as an instance of its superclass.
LOCK	An exclusive resource that represents possession of the object by a thread.
LOOSE COUPLING	A comparatively small and well-defined amount of responsibility that interacting objects bear to each other.
MARKER INTERFACE	An interface that declares no fields or methods, whose mere presence indicates something. For example, `Cloneable` is a marker interface that promises that its implementers will support the `clone()` method defined in `Object`.
METHOD	An *implementation* of an *operation*.

MODEL/VIEW/ CONTROLLER (MVC)	A design that separates an interesting object, the model, from user interface elements that portray it: the view and the controller.
MOLE	A number—Avogadro's number—defined as the number of atoms in 12 grams of carbon 12. The beauty of this number is that it lets you apply chemical equations while working with measurable quantities of chemical batches. If you know that the molecular weight of a chemical is mw, mw grams of the chemical will contain one mole of the chemical.
MORTAR	A tube from which an aerial shell is fired.
MUTEX	An object shared by threads that contend for control of the object's *lock*. The word *mutex* is a contraction of the words *mutual exclusion*.
N-TIER	A type of system that assigns layers of responsibility to objects running on different computers.
OBJECT ADAPTER	An ADAPTER that works by subclassing the required class and delegating to an existing class. Compare *class adapter*.
OOZINOZ	A fictional fireworks company that takes its name from the audience's sounds at an exhibition.
OPERATION	A specification of a service that can be requested from an instance of a class.
PARALLEL HIERARCHY	A pair of class hierarchies in which each class in one hierarchy has a corresponding class in the other hierarchy.
PARAMETRIC EQUATIONS	Equations that define a group of variables, such as x and y, in terms of a standard parameter, such as t.
PARSER	An object that can recognize elements of a *language* and decompose their structure according to a set of rules into a form suitable for further processing.
PATH	In an object model, a series of objects such that each object in the series has a reference to the next object in the series.
PATTERN	A way of doing something; a way of pursuing an intent.

PERSISTENT STORAGE	Storage of information on a device, such as a disk, that retains the information even when powered down.
POLYMORPHISM	The principle that method invocation depends on both the operation invoked and the class of the invocation receiver.
POSTORDER TRAVERSAL	An iteration over a tree or other composite object in which a node is returned after its descendants.
PREORDER TRAVERSAL	An iteration over a tree or other composite object in which a node is returned before its descendants.
RANDOM CASE	A STRiNG like thIS, wHOSE ChARActErs MAY bE uPPeR- OR LOwERcaSe, AT RANdom.
REFACTOR	Change code to improve its internal structure without changing its external behavior.
REFLECTION	The ability to work with types and type members as objects.
RELATION	The way in which objects stand with regard to each other. In an object model, the subset of all possible references from objects of one type to objects of a second type.
REMOTE METHOD INVOCATION (RMI)	A Java facility that lets objects on different computers communicate.
ROMAN CANDLE	A stationary tube that contains a mixture of explosive charges, sparks, and stars.
ROOT	In a *tree,* a distinguished node or object that has no parent.
SESSION	The event of a user running a program, conducting transactions within the program, and exiting.
SHALLOW COPY	As opposed to *deep copy.* A shallow copy limits the depth to which it copies an object's attributes, letting the new object share subordinate objects with the original.
SHELL	See *aerial shell.*
SIGNATURE	A combination of the name of a method and the number and types of formal parameters to the method.

SQL	See *Structured Query Language*.
STAR	A compressed pellet of an explosive mixture, usually part of an *aerial shell* or *Roman candle*.
STAR PRESS	A machine that molds chemical paste into fireworks stars.
STATE	A combination of the current values of an object's attributes.
STRATEGY	A plan, or approach, for achieving an aim given certain input conditions.
STREAM	A serial collection of bytes or characters, such as those that appear in a document.
STRUCTURED QUERY LANGUAGE (SQL)	A computer language for querying relational databases.
TIER	A layer that executes on a computer.
TITLE CASE	A String Like This Whose Characters Are Uppercase If They Follow Whitespace.
TREE	An object model that contains no *cycles*.
UML	See *Unified Modeling Language*.
UNIFIED MODELING LANGUAGE (UML)	A notation for illustrating design ideas.
UNIFORM RESOURCE LOCATOR (URL)	A pointer to a resource on the World Wide Web.
URL	See *Uniform Resource Locator*.
WIP	See *work in process*.
WORK IN PROCESS (WIP)	Partially manufactured goods in a factory.
XML	See *Extensible Markup Language*.

BIBLIOGRAPHY

Alexander, Christopher. 1979. *The Timeless Way of Building*. Oxford, England: Oxford University Press.

Alexander, Christopher, Sara Ishikawa, and Murray Silverstein. 1977. *A Pattern Language: Towns, Buildings, Construction*. Oxford, England: Oxford University Press.

Arnold, Ken, and James Gosling. 1998. *The Java™ Programming Language, Second Edition*. Reading, MA: Addison-Wesley.

Booch, Grady, James Rumbaugh, and Ivar Jacobsen. 1999. *The Unified Modeling Language User Guide*. Reading, MA: Addison-Wesley.

Buschmann, Frank, et al. 1996. *Pattern-Oriented Software Architecture: A System of Patterns*. Chichester, West Sussex, England: John Wiley & Sons.

Cormen, Thomas H., Charles E. Leiserson, and Ronald L. Rivest. 1990. *Introduction to Algorithms*. Cambridge, MA: MIT Press.

Cunningham, Ward, ed. The Portland Patterns Repository. www.c2.com.

Flanagan, David. 2005. *Java™ in a Nutshell*, 5th ed. Sebastopol, CA: O'Reilly & Associates.

Flanagan, David, Jim Farley, William Crawford, and Kris Magnusson. 2002. *Java™ Enterprise in a Nutshell*, 2d ed. Sebastopol, CA: O'Reilly & Associates.

Fowler, Martin, Kent Beck, John Brant, William Opdyke, and Don Roberts. 1999. *Refactoring: Improving the Design of Existing Code*. Reading, MA: Addison-Wesley.

Fowler, Martin, with Kendall Scott. 2003. *UML Distilled, Third Edition*. Boston, MA: Addison-Wesley.

Gamma, Erich, Richard Helm, Ralph Johnson, and John Vlissides. *Design Patterns*. 1995. Boston, MA: Addison-Wesley.

Gosling, James, Bill Joy, Guy Steele, and Gilad Bracha. 2005. *The Java™ Language Specification, Third Edition*. Boston, MA: Addison-Wesley.

Kerievsky, Joshua. 2005. *Refactoring to Patterns*. Boston, MA: Addison-Wesley.

Lea, Doug. 2000. *Concurrent Programming in Java™, Second Edition*. Boston, MA: Addison-Wesley.

Lieberherr, Karl J., and Ian Holland. 1989. "Assuring Good Style for Object-Oriented Programs." Washington, DC. IEEE Software.

Liskov, Barbara. May 1987. "Data Abstraction and Hierarchy." *SIGPLAN Notices*, volume 23, number 5.

Metsker, Steven J. 2001. *Building Parsers with Java™*. Boston, MA: Addison-Wesley.

Russell, Michael S. 2000. *The Chemistry of Fireworks*. Cambridge, UK: Royal Society of Chemistry.

Vlissides, John. 1998. *Pattern Hatching: Design Patterns Applied*. Reading, MA: Addison-Wesley.

Wake, William C. 2004. *Refactoring Workbook*. Boston, MA: Addison-Wesley.

Weast, Robert C., ed. 1983. *CRC Handbook of Chemistry and Physics*, 63rd ed. Boca Raton, FL: CRC Press.

White, Seth, Mayderne Fisher, Rick Cattell, Graham Hamilton, and Mark Hapner. 1999. *JDBC™ API Tutorial and Reference, Second Edition*. Boston, MA: Addison-Wesley.

Wolf, Bobby. 1998. "Null Object," in *Pattern Languages of Program Design 3*, ed. Robert Martin, Dirk Riehle, and Frank Buschmann. Reading, MA: Addison-Wesley.

INDEX

Addison-Wesley Professional
Is the Ultimate Resource for Patterns!

In 1994, Addison-Wesley published *Design Patterns,* the first and definitive book on patterns for software development. Addison-Wesley continues to publish the thought leaders in the patterns community and remains the most comprehensive and authoritative resource on software patterns for developers of all levels and experience.

0-201-63361-2

0-321-12697-1

0-321-12742-0

0-321-33302-0

0-321-24714-0

0-321-20068-3

0-321-21335-1

0-321-32194-4

For sample material and more information on these titles and others, please visit www.awprofessional.com

Interface Patterns

ADAPTER (17) Provide the interface that a client expects, using the services of a class with a different interface.

FACADE (33) Provide an interface that makes a subsystem easy to use.

COMPOSITE (47) Allow clients to treat individual objects and compositions of objects uniformly.

BRIDGE (63) Decouple a class that relies on abstract operations from the implementation of those abstract operations so that the class and the implementation can vary independently.

Responsibility Patterns

SINGLETON (81) Ensure that a class has only one instance, and provide a global point of access to it.

OBSERVER (87) Define a one-to-many dependency between objects so that when one object changes state, all its dependents are notified and updated automatically.

MEDIATOR (103) Define an object that encapsulates the way that a set of objects interact. This keeps the objects from referring to each other explicitly and lets you vary their interaction independently.

PROXY (117) Provide a placeholder for another object to control access to it.

CHAIN OF RESPONSIBILITY (137) Avoid coupling the sender of a request to its receiver, by giving more than one object a chance to handle the request.

FLYWEIGHT (145) Use sharing to support large numbers of fine-grained objects efficiently.